Pluralism and Freedom

Pluralism and Freedom

Faith-Based Organizations in a Democratic Society

Stephen V. Monsma

ROWMAN & LITTLEFIELD PUBLISHERS, INC.
Lanham • Boulder • New York • Toronto • Plymouth, UK

Published by Rowman & Littlefield Publishers, Inc.
A wholly owned subsidiary of The Rowman & Littlefield Publishing Group, Inc.
4501 Forbes Boulevard, Suite 200, Lanham, Maryland 20706
www.rowmanlittlefield.com

Estover Road, Plymouth PL6 7PY, United Kingdom

British Library Cataloguing in Publication Information Available

Library of Congress Cataloging-in-Publication Data

The hardback edition of this book was previously cataloged by the Library of Congress
as follows:

Monsma, Stephen V., 1936–
  Pluralism and freedom : faith-based organizations in a democratic society /
Stephen V. Monsma.
    p. cm.
  Includes bibliographical references and index.
  1. Faith-based human services—United States. 2. Democracy—Religious aspects.
3. United States—Social policy. I. Title.
  HV530.M66 2012
  361.7'50973—dc23   2011037530

ISBN: 978-1-4422-1430-9 (cloth : alk. paper)
ISBN: 978-1-4422-1431-6 (pbk. : alk. paper)
ISBN: 978-1-4422-1432-3 (electronic)

∞™ The paper used in this publication meets the minimum requirements of American
National Standard for Information Sciences—Permanence of Paper for Printed Library
Materials, ANSI/NISO Z39.48-1992.

Printed in the United States of America

To Henry Martin Monsma

Contents

Preface

There is a legitimate place for faith-based organizations and their religiously rooted beliefs and religiously inspired actions in the public life of the nation . . . and the same holds true for secular organizations and their beliefs and actions. Pluralism, diversity, and tolerance demand no less. We as a society, however, find it easier to affirm these principles in theory than to follow them in practice. Too often the secularly minded see the religiously minded and their organizational expressions as posing dangers to be resisted. Religion must be kept enclosed behind the prison walls of private belief and action. And too often those of a religious bent see attempts to limit faith-based organizations and some of their actions as efforts to rip away the religious heritage of our nation and force a secular mindset onto us and our children. Meanwhile, pluralism, diversity, and tolerance insist that all have the right to be wrong.[1] These principles insist that those we believe to be wrong—whether their beliefs are religiously or secularly grounded—are still citizens and that their organizations are free to play active roles in the public square.

This book describes the challenge religious freedom for all is facing today when faith-based organizations enter the public realm by offering health care, education, and other human services to the public—and when government helps fund these efforts. In it I contend that the ideal of safeguarding the freedom of persons and organizations of all religions and of none can be met. But to do so we need to abandon many of the familiar categories and concepts both the left and the right have brought to the table and seek some new ways of viewing and understanding faith-based organizations and their rightful role in the public square. There are traditions within Christianity itself that can be called upon to define and defend a pluralism that defends the rights and freedoms of the religious and the nonreligious alike. But they need to be explained, understood, and applied. That is what I seek to do in this book.

In writing a book such as this, one acquires more debts than one can properly acknowledge and thank. But I surely must thank the many persons associated with faith-based organizations and their associations whose time spent in meeting with me and whose willingness to share information and perspectives made chapter 2 possible. They are too numerous to mention by name, but my appreciation for their willingness to help is nonetheless great. Also, a special thanks is due to Lew Daly and Stanley Carlson-Thies, who read the entire manuscript and followed with enthusiasm my injunction to be tough on me and what I had written. Kenneth Grasso read an early version of chapter 5, and his suggestions did much to improve it. My son, Martin Monsma, read the manuscript and suggested many changes that improved its readability and the flow of ideas. I also wish to thank Calvin College's Paul Henry Institute for the Study of Christianity and Politics, its director, Corwin Smidt, and its administrative assistant, Ellen Hekman, for providing me with the support and help needed to carry this project forward to completion. Thanks are also due Jonathan Sisk of Rowman and Littlefield Publishers and an anonymous reviewer, as well as the other professionals at Rowman and Littlefield, for their confidence in me and their help in improving and bringing to publication what I have written. This is the fourth of my books published by Rowman and Littlefield, and each time I found their editors and the others involved in the publication process models of professionalism. I must also add the traditional but sincerely meant disclaimer that all errors of fact and interpretation are mine alone.

Finally, I dedicate this book to my youngest grandchild, Henry Martin Monsma, whose birth and the delightful distraction he gave his grandfather probably delayed the completion of this book by several months.

Stephen V. Monsma

Chapter 1

The Issue That Will Not Go Away

In 2007, World Vision, a large international relief and development agency in the evangelical Protestant tradition, fired three of its employees because they no longer agreed with its statement of religious faith. The fired employees brought suit, charging religious discrimination in employment, a practice barred by federal law.[1] World Vision countered that it is a religious organization and therefore exempt from legal bars to hiring and firing decisions based on religion. In 2010, the Ninth Circuit Court of Appeals decided in a split 2-to-1 decision that World Vision is indeed a religious organization and therefore could legally dismiss the three employees. Some commentators applauded the decision; others condemned it.

In 2006, Catholic Charities of Boston announced it would end all adoption work, work it had been active in for over one hundred years.[2] Why? Because Massachusetts law required it to place children with same-sex couples on the same basis as with traditional husband-wife families, a practice that runs counter to Catholic moral doctrine. Is it appropriate—is it good public policy—for state nondiscrimination laws to force religious organizations such as Catholic Charities to choose between violating their religiously shaped consciences or giving up a program that had been part of its mission for one hundred years?

In 2010, the U.S. Supreme Court decided a case that arose out of the Hastings College of Law in San Francisco.[3] A student chapter of the Christian Legal Society had insisted that its leaders had to support historic, traditional Christian beliefs and disavow "unrepentant participation in or advocacy of a sexually immoral lifestyle."[4] The law school labeled this stance "discrimination" and refused to grant the club official school recognition that it had granted to sixty other student groups, resulting in it losing various campus

1

privileges and the use of campus facilities on the same terms as other student groups. The Christian Legal Society group claimed the school was interfering in its internal affairs to the point of violating its right of freedom of expression. The Supreme Court by a 5-to-4 vote ruled Hastings could exclude the Christian group from official recognition. In the Supreme Court's majority opinion, Justice Ruth Bader Ginsberg declared that the school's policy was "reasonable and viewpoint neutral,"[5] while Justice Samuel Alito, writing for the four dissenting justices, declared that "today's decision is a serious setback for freedom of expression in this country."[6] The controversy continues.

All three of these examples raise the question of how much autonomy, or independence, the legal system ought to allow faith-based organizations when their beliefs, values, and practices—whether in the minority or the majority—clash with those held by others.

Two terms require definition at the outset. Throughout this book I use the term "faith-based organizations" to refer to religiously based or religiously oriented organizations that provide health, educational, or social services to the public. I do not use the term to refer to religious congregations in their core religious celebrations and rituals. Instead, the term includes an enormous variety of religiously based organizations, from health clinics and hospitals to colleges and universities to such social service programs as homeless shelters, drug treatment centers, immigration resettlement efforts, prisoner reentry programs, welfare-to-work programs, disaster relief efforts, international aid and relief agencies, and more. Chapter 2 documents the number and variety of such efforts. Included are both programs run directly by churches or other religious congregations or groups of congregations and programs run by organizations that, while not formally affiliated with any religious congregation or group of congregations, nevertheless have a religious orientation and are rooted in a commitment to certain religious beliefs and values. The latter type of organization is often called a parachurch organization.[7]

"Autonomy" is a second term in need of definition. It refers to the ability of an organization to be independent, self-defining, self-directing, and even in a sense sovereign in its field of operation, in distinction from being subject to conditions and requirements that restrict what it is and what it may and may not do. In the case of faith-based organizations, autonomy includes the ability to define one's religiously rooted beliefs and to act on the basis of those beliefs.

All nonprofit human service and educational organizations face the issue of autonomy in light of government rules and regulations—rules and regulations that increase dramatically when, as is often the case, government funding is present. But faith-based organizations face potential challenges to their autonomy that are unique to them because of their faith-based nature.

As in the three examples just cited, faith-based organizations often hold to or abstain from certain practices or insist on certain standards of belief or conduct because of their religiously rooted convictions and a desire to maintain their distinctive religious character. The exact nature of these practices and standards vary from one faith-based organization to another; what unites them is their being rooted in their distinctive religious traditions. Thus the attorney Mark Chapko has defined religious autonomy as "the right of religious communities . . . to decide upon and administer their own internal religious affairs without interference by the institutions of government."[8] And he goes on to make the important additional observation that his definition of religious autonomy applies not only to "the core religious worship institution and its ministers," but also "include[s] auxiliary institutions: primary and secondary schools, religious charitable entities, religious colleges and universities, and hospitals."[9] And the German legal scholar, Gerhard Robbers, defines religious autonomy as "the right of self-determination of religious bodies."[10] In other words, the religious autonomy of faith-based organizations consists of their ability to define a religiously based self-identity—which includes the ability to determine that they indeed are a religious or faith-based entity—and to pursue practices and to refrain from practices in keeping with that self-identity free from legal constraints and limitations. Faith-based organizations' autonomy of this nature is the topic of this book. Legal rules and regulations that more broadly hedge about nonprofit human service organizations, and under which they often chafe, constitute a different issue and one on which this book is not focused.

At the outset, it is important to recognize that the religious autonomy of faith-based organizations must be a limited or constrained autonomy, not an absolute autonomy. The religious autonomy of faith-based organizations is real and should be protected by our system of laws. Simultaneously, there are limitations on their religious autonomy that are also real and should be enforced by our system of laws. To sort out the reality of that autonomy and its limitations will take the remainder of this book.

In this chapter I first consider the nature of diversity and pluralism, as well as the basic fact that autonomy is a precondition for diversity and pluralism. Next, I will describe two distinct questions concerning the religious freedom and autonomy of faith-based organizations. Both questions continue to be the source of seemingly endless court cases and bitter controversy and debate in the political arena and the media. I will then argue that the reason for our disagreements lies largely in the underlying assumptions and theoretical concepts individuals bring to the debates. Therefore, this book focuses on those underlying assumptions and concepts. Until we get them right, it will be impossible to reach agreement on more concrete issues, and the religious freedom and diversity to value in theory will be at risk in practice. The final section of the chapter briefly outlines the topics I will consider in the remaining chapters.

DIVERSITY, PLURALISM, AND AUTONOMY

We are a pluralistic society marked by a diversity of peoples, ethnicities, regions, opinions . . . and religions. Usually this is seen as a source of pride. "E Pluribus Unum"—out of many, one—as our coins proudly proclaim. Go to almost any college or university website and one finds self-congratulatory claims of racial and ethnic diversity among their faculties and students. It is a point of pride if in casual conversations we can let drop that we live in a racially and economically diverse neighborhood. If one attends a church that contradicts the oft repeated claim that eleven o'clock Sunday morning is the most segregated hour in American society, one is sure to mention this when asked where one worships. And this is good. The fact that we are a pluralistic society where persons of different backgrounds, ethnicities, racial identities, and religions can live and work together is appropriately a source of pride. It is an achievement not many societies down through human history have managed.

But underlying this achievement and the resulting sense of pride remain questions concerning the nature and extent of the oneness that is to emerge out of the many. Robert Bellah relates how in the 1920s Henry Ford once sponsored a pageant celebrating the American melting pot.[11] He had a line of people, in their native dress and singing traditional folk songs from their native lands, enter from one side of the stage and march into a giant pot. Then from the other side of the pot emerged a line of people, all dressed alike in clothes typical for the United States of the 1920s and singing in unison the national anthem. Today we cringe at the imposed uniformity this pageant and the melting pot analogy suggest. To think of men and women as being melted down like so much scrap iron and then stamped out as uniform copies indistinguishable from each other sounds more like a totalitarian than a democratic ideal. But if this is not the ideal, how much and what types of diversity ought we to accept and even celebrate? We are both one and many, but we are uncertain when to insist on our oneness and when to celebrate our "manyness."

In addition, one needs to be clear that societal pluralism, on the one hand, and autonomy for ethnic, religious, racial, regional, and other societal groupings, on the other hand, are inescapably linked. If we as a society are to have a rich pluralism, we must allow ethnic, religious, racial, regional, and even belief and philosophical groups in society a certain freedom—or autonomy—to be who they wish to be, even when who they are, what they believe, and what they do run counter to majority desires or beliefs. A true pluralism moves far beyond talking about and extolling diversity to genuinely respecting and tolerating those whose beliefs and practices run counter to one's own deeply held beliefs and practices. Americans as a people are more comfortable talking about and celebrating pluralism and diversity than we are with the autonomy on which that pluralism and diversity depend. We are quickly back to the question of when to insist on our oneness and when to celebrate our "manyness."

This question becomes especially urgent when it comes to religious diversity, since religious beliefs and practices deal with some of the deepest felt of human beliefs and are rooted in faith communities that in many instances have endured for thousands of years. The freedom of religion is often referred to as the first freedom for more reasons than its being mentioned first in the Bill of Rights. But how far are we willing to go in our toleration of religious diversity? Does World Vision have the right to fire employees on religious grounds, does Catholic Charities have the right to refuse to place children for adoption with same-sex couples, and do Christian on-campus student clubs have the right to refuse non-Christian and gay students for leadership positions? We as a people are not agreed on the answer to these and a host of similar questions.

Americans are generally supportive of religious autonomy and the resulting diversity as long as religion is a purely private affair, limited to the realm of religious congregations, personal beliefs, and private practices. The construction of mosques has at times resulted in local controversies, but a diversity of Christian churches, Jewish synagogues, and Hindu temples is usually seen as a basis for community pride, not distrust and fear. We generally respect the Amish, with what to most of us appear to be their quaint ways and a strong sense of community. Schools teach our children to respect Native American religion as beliefs deeply embedded in traditional cultures that the majority culture has grievously wronged. Few question the legality of Mormons limiting its clergy to males, even though this would be viewed as blatant, illegal gender discrimination in other contexts. Even after 9/11 it is hard to conceive of Americans supporting a ban on Muslim women wearing traditional Muslim dress in public, as France has done. In the United States, several cases of whether or not Muslim women could wear head scarves or other distinctive Muslim dress have been quickly resolved in favor of the women, with hardly a ripple of public comment.[12]

However, differences of opinion arise when religion is no longer a matter of private belief or practices or is not limited to religious congregations as they engage in private worship, prayers, and religious rituals, but instead intersects with the public life of the nation. When the Amish drive their horse-drawn buggies on public roads and refuse to place a triangular warning symbol on the back, or when Native American religion involves the use of peyote, a mildly hallucinogenic drug that violates some states' drug laws, we suddenly are not so sure that diversity is a good thing.[13] If the Christian student group at the Hastings College of Law had not sought official recognition, had met off-campus, and had been content not to post notices of its meetings on official campus bulletin boards or to have a table at new student orientation, it is unlikely anyone would have complained, no matter what standards of belief or behavior it insisted on for its officers. It only ran into challenges when it entered the public realm of official campus organizations at a state-sponsored school of law. Similarly, if World Vision had not been active in the world of international relief and development and had not accepted government funding, but had acted like a traditional missionary society sending persons abroad to evangelize and teach, it almost certainly would not have been challenged over its employment practices. In the case of Catholic Charities of Boston, if it had been a purely private agency running an adoption program for only members of the Catholic Church, it might have escaped the clutches of Massachusetts' nondiscrimination law.

However, because in all three cases these faith-based organizations had in one way or another entered the realm of public services and government subsidies, they were confronted with challenges to certain of their religiously rooted practices.[14] Thus they illustrate a crucial, pervasive issue that remains unresolved in the American polity: The degree and nature of the religious autonomy faith-based organizations legally retain when they enter the public realm. Or, expressing the same question another way: How much religiously based diversity and pluralism are we willing to tolerate in the public square?

In the days ahead this question is likely to loom larger on the public policy stage and to become more, not less, urgent. Initiatives aimed at including faith-based organizations more fully in government funding programs have spanned three presidential administrations. President Bill Clinton on four occasions signed legislation containing "charitable choice" provisions that sought to carve out a role for faith-based organizations in providing needed human services in partnership with government. President George W. Bush created a new White House Office of Faith-Based and Community Initiatives and made his efforts to increase government cooperation with faith-based and other community organizations one of his signature domestic initiatives.[15] President Barack Obama retained the White House office, renaming it the White House Office for Faith-Based and Neighborhood Partnerships, created an advisory council to assist it, and assigned it additional responsibilities. A recent article in *Politico* documented that President Obama has, if anything, increased funding for faith-based organizations: "The story of the Obama administration's large-scale spending on faith-based groups has been largely untold, perhaps because it cuts so sharply across the moment's intensely partisan narrative."[16] Even though it was the Bush administration's faith-based initiative that stirred up the most controversy and news coverage, the fact that three administrations have attempted to include faith-based organizations in the nation's human service network indicates governmental help in funding and in other ways partnering with faith-based organizations is very likely to remain an ongoing feature of the public policy landscape. The issue of the religious autonomy of these faith-based organizations is also very likely to remain, or perhaps to grow more intense.

In addition, a new factor has arisen in recent years that is very likely to raise the issue of faith-based organizations' religious autonomy in a new and compelling manner. This is the gay rights movement and its demands for same-sex marriage and other forms of recognition and treatment on equal terms with heterosexuals and traditional marriages. Not all, but many, faith-based organizations are rooted in religious traditions that reject the moral equivalence of heterosexual and homosexual relationships. Especially in the Roman Catholic, evangelical Protestant, and orthodox Jewish faith communities, one is dealing with moral norms and religiously formed consciences going back thousands of years. These are not fringe religious groups, but major faith communities constituting roughly half of the American population.[17] But many in the gay rights community see distinctions based on sexual orientation as forms of blatant discrimination, no more defensible than distinctions based on race or gender. Also, the academic and media elite for the most part agree with gay rights advocates. In the case of Boston-based Catholic Charities mentioned at the start of the chapter and in many other situations we will see later in this book—especially in chapter 6—this clash is raising bitter conflicts. When faith-based organizations enter the public realm and their religiously based standards clash with those of the gay rights movement, ought the religious autonomy of the faith-based organizations or the goals of the gay rights community prevail? No one should underestimate the looming clash between many faith-based organizations' religious autonomy and the gay rights movement. It will test the nature and the limits of the diversity American society will tolerate.

One final point contributes to the importance of considering the nature and the extent of the religious autonomy of faith-based organizations: namely, the inseparability of individual religious freedom and faith communities' religious autonomy or freedom. W. Cole Durham has put it well:

Protection of the right of religious communities to autonomy in structuring their religious affairs lies at the very core of protecting religious freedom. We often think of religious freedom as an individual right rooted in individual conscience, but in fact, religion virtually always has a communal dimension, and religious freedom can be negated as effectively by coercing or interfering with a religious group as by coercing one of its individual members.[18]

There will be more on this linking of religious communities' religious autonomy and individual religious freedom as this book progresses.

TWO SETS OF QUESTIONS

More specifically, the American polity today is bedeviled by two sets of questions that we have trouble answering. They continue to lead to deep divisions, with each side charging the other with violations of basic freedoms. One set arises when government funding is accepted by faith-based organizations to help fund some of the services they are offering the public: *When in receipt of government funding, how many and what types of religious standards and practices do faith-based organizations retain?* There appears to be a dilemma here. If these faith-based organizations retain the right to exercise fully all of their religiously based practices, government would appear to be funding particularistic religious practices and beliefs that run counter to the beliefs of other Americans. But if faith-based organizations lose their right to act on the basis of their religious distinctiveness, those involved in the organizations lose their freedom to express their religious beliefs, those who wish to receive services in a faith-friendly setting no longer are able to do so, and the diversity we value in theory is lost in practice as the organizations and their programs become indistinguishable from governmental and other secular programs. Clashes of opinion, controversy, and court cases proliferate.

One especially bitter controversy rages over the right of faith-based organizations receiving government funding to take religion into account in their hiring decisions. When President George W. Bush first announced his faith-based and community initiative, many highly respected organizations such as the American Civil Liberties Union, Baptist Joint Committee on Public Affairs, NAACP, National Education Association, and People for the American Way sent an open letter to him contending that a religious organization receiving government funding can no longer consider religion in its hiring decisions. It stated: "Specifically, we seek your commitment that your proposals will make clear that religious institutions that receive public funding for the provision of social services may not discriminate when employing people in taxpayer funded positions based on an applicant's religion or the religious beliefs of the employer."[19] Congressman Bobby Scott (D-VA) stated: "I don't think most people expect that you can apply for a job paid for by the federal government and be told, 'Oh, no, we don't hire people of your religion.'"[20]

During his 2008 presidential campaign, President Barack Obama indicated he would not allow "discrimination" in hiring by faith-based organizations receiving government money, but since assuming the presidency he has not sought to change existing policy that for the most part allows hiring based on religion by faith-based programs receiving government funds. But the controversy remains. A 2009 *New York Times* editorial criticized Obama for leaving "untouched a 2002 presidential directive authorizing religious-oriented programs that receive federal financing to hire and fire on religious grounds." It concluded: "Public money should not be used to pay for discrimination."[21]

Meanwhile, many faith-based organizations have insisted on their right to hire based on religion, believing that if they could not do so they would lose their distinctive religious identity and character and become just like their secular counterparts. In the World Vision case mentioned at the beginning of this chapter, World Vision reacted to the court decision upholding its position in these words: "Our Christian faith has been the foundation of our work since the organization was established in 1950, and our hiring policy is vital to the integrity of our mission to serve the poor as followers of Jesus Christ."[22] An *amicus* brief filed with the court of appeals made this point: "A religious organization cannot answer a divine calling without freedom to define itself and its doctrine, polity, and personnel."[23] In a similar 2004 case involving the Salvation Army of New York City and its right to take religion into account in its hiring, a Salvation Army official declared, "Everything that we do is related to our ministry, and is in fact our ministry." He went on to argue that their employees need to support the mission of the organization: "Why would anyone want to go to work for the Salvation Army if they are not supportive of us?"[24] In these and most other similar cases the courts have ruled in favor of the faith-based organizations and their right to take the religious beliefs of current and prospective employees into account in making hiring decisions, but for many that hardly settles the issue. The debate continues.

Hiring issues are not the only ones that arise when government helps fund certain services faith-based organizations are providing. Unresolved questions have also arisen concerning the extent to which religious elements may be integrated into or be present in the programs supported with tax dollars. There is general agreement that tax dollars ought not to pay for inherently or explicitly religious messages and activities, such as Bible studies, worship services, classes in religious doctrine, or prayer meetings. But those are the easy cases. What about references to God's love for all persons in a government-funded session for persons who have been beaten down by domestic violence and are in need of reassurance of their value and worth? Or what about a counselor in a government-funded program who in response to a question from a recipient of services in a one-on-one counseling session tells about the availability of Sunday worship services? Or what about a cross or other religious symbol in a room where a government-funded nonreligious program is being run? Or simply a poster declaring "God is love." All of these remain contentious issues. The Obama administration appointed a task force to consider such issues and although it was able to reach agreement on some of them, it was unable to reach agreement on the permissibility of the presence of "religious art, scripture, message, or symbols" in rooms where government-funded services are provided.[25] And it never went beyond concluding that government ought not to fund the easy cases of "explicitly religious activities, such as worship, religious instruction, and proselytization" to consider the harder cases of less explicit religious allusions or references.[26]

A second type of controversy has arisen even in the absence of government funding: *Are faith-based organizations bound by general nondiscrimination regulations when their requirements clash with those organizations' religious tenets?* Again, there is no controversy in the case of purely private religious organizations observing or celebrating their core religious ceremonies. No one is arguing that laws against discrimination based on gender ought to be applied to the priesthood of the Catholic Church. But issues arise when the Catholic Church enters the public realm by providing health care in a faith-based hospital or clinic. Should faith-based organizations providing a public service or otherwise operating in the public realm be bound by legal requirements that violate their religious principles or would, in their opinion, undercut their religious character? Or should the law accommodate their faith-based beliefs and practices so they are not forced to act contrary to their beliefs, even if this means some persons may need to go elsewhere for certain services? We cringe at the thought of forcing someone to act in violation of his or her religious conscience. But many also cringe at the thought of someone not being able to take part in certain services he or she sees as being morally acceptable just because someone else believes those services to be morally objectionable.

This issue is at the heart of a case that originated in California and dealt with a 1999 California law that requires all employers that provide prescription drug coverage in their health insurance plans to include contraceptive services. To do otherwise, the law holds, would be to discriminate against women. But providing contraceptive drug coverage goes against the moral standards taught by the Catholic Church, and Catholic Charities sought court protection from the law's requirements on religious freedom grounds. California argued that for Catholic Charities to qualify for a religious exemption it would have to hire mostly Catholics and provide services only to their fellow Catholics, not the general public. Only if Catholic Charities abandoned the public realm and became largely a private religious organization would it win an exemption. Catholic Charities lost in the state courts and the U.S. Supreme Court refused to hear the case. As a result, an analyst working for the United States Conference of Catholic Bishops concluded this was a victory "for those seeking to require health care providers and payers to participate in the delivery of elective reproductive treatment and procedures, even if the provision of such procedures would require the providers and payers to violate their consciences."[27] Should the right of female employees of Catholic Charities—many of whom were not themselves Catholic—to have their health insurance cover contraceptive services or the right of Catholic Charities to act on the basis of their deeply held religious ethical standards take precedence?

Similarly, this was the question at issue in two of the instances mentioned at the start of this chapter. The Christian student club's policy of denying leadership positions to non-Christians and those engaging in a lifestyle contrary to traditional Christian beliefs ran afoul of the school's nondiscrimination standards; the club insisted that without such standards it would be acting contrary to its deepest beliefs and its very character would be undermined. Catholic Charities of Boston stopped its adoption services when Massachusetts' nondiscrimination laws would have forced it to place children with same-sex couples on the same basis as it placed them with traditional husband-wife couples, an action running counter to Catholic moral teaching. In all of these examples a group's deeply held religious beliefs came into conflict with nondiscrimination laws. In such cases, should organizations' religious autonomy or individuals' ability to obtain equal treatment from those organizations take precedence?

This issue leads directly back to the question of how much religiously rooted diversity or pluralism should we as a nation allow in the public square. Should deeply held religious beliefs trump the ability of same-sex couples to adopt children from faith-based agencies that see same-sex relationships as immoral, or should it be the other way around? If some adoption agency—based on white supremacist views it somehow roots in its religious beliefs—would refuse to place children with African-American or mixed white-black families, almost all would say such a claimed religious belief must give way to nondiscrimination laws. But if this is so, can not a same-sex couple claim the same protection? Is there some basis on which one can distinguish these two situations? I believe there is, but such questions are real and deserve a thought-out, careful answer, one they now are often not given. Meanwhile, the debate continues and we as a society seem to come no closer to consensus.

How can we uphold the freedom of faith-based organizations to be who they are and what they are convinced their deeply held religious principles have called them to be without destroying or weakening that which binds us together as one people or denying others services they desire and find morally unobjectionable? Or, more broadly, how can we live together as one people with our deepest differences? Currently we are answering that question poorly or not at all. We lurch from one controversy to another, engendering division and bitterness, while our politicians seek to paper over chasms that remain and our courts go first one way and then the other. But there are answers. This book is based on the premise that we can protect the religious autonomy of faith-based organizations as they act in the public realm while also protecting both our unity as a people and our freedoms promised us as Americans.

A CONFLICT OF THEORETICAL CONCEPTS

One might suppose that the reason for the many conflicts and controversies surrounding the religious autonomy of faith-based organizations in the public life of the nation is because one or more of the various parties in these disputes are narrow-minded and ignorant, dismissive of religious-freedom rights and the First Amendment, or blind to discriminatory practices. Often one side or the other accuses their opponents of such traits. But I am convinced the reason for our differences lies in the differing theoretical concepts, mindsets, or assumptions with which the different sides begin. Nowhere is the old saying, "Where one stands depends on where one starts," more true than in the instance of faith-based organizations and their rightful autonomy. We do not have agreement on concepts and theories that underlie the religious autonomy of faith-based organizations and how they fit into a free, pluralistic society, and thus we disagree on the specific questions highlighted in the prior section.

The positions taken by certain persons and advocacy groups make good sense given the assumptions and theories with which they begin; the positions taken by opposing persons and advocacy groups make equally good sense given the assumptions and theories with which they begin. But because their initial assumptions and theoretical concepts are so different, they end up with vastly different conclusions. What is needed is to begin, not with the conclusions and applications with which different persons and advocacy organizations are reaching, but with the different underlying assumptions and concepts with which, often unself-consciously, they begin. These need to be understood and critiqued.

I will contend that today's assumptions and theoretical concepts lie deeply buried in the eighteenth-century Enlightenment; the American founding era; conservatism and liberalism as they developed in the United States, the church-state consensus that developed in nineteenth-century America and how it was overturned in the twentieth; and the legacy of the 1960s' non-discrimination statutes. There are strengths as well as weaknesses in these American experiences and traditions. But they do not support an agreed-upon, definitive basis for understanding faith-based human service and educational organizations, their place in the network of public services, and the protections and limitations they possess as nongovernmental, public-serving organizations. As a result neither the political left nor the political right has a reasoned position on faith-based organizations and their religious autonomy that is widely accepted and defendable on an equitable, fair basis.

Yet there is a tradition in political and social thought that offers a basis for achieving a better understanding of faith-based organizations, their place in the mix of public services, and their rightful religious autonomy. This is the Christian Democratic tradition and the structural pluralist concepts that underlie it. The Roman Catholic social teaching of subsidiarity and its related concepts, as well as the parallel neo-Calvinist concept of sphere sovereignty, play major roles in structural pluralist thought. When viewing the public policy landscape, structural pluralism sees more than individuals and the state, recognizing a vast array of intermediary structures lying between the individual and the government. These intermediary structures—including faith-based organizations—possess both a legitimate, respected role to play in the public life of the nation and an inherent, genuine, even though limited, autonomy that protects their place in the public square. These concepts have had a large influence in continental Europe but little influence in the United States. If these theoretical concepts and their ways of understanding faith-based organizations and their place in the mix of public policies would be combined with certain American strengths, it is likely that thoughtful, defensible answers to the questions raised in this chapter would emerge.

This book looks to structural pluralism and how it can mesh with the American experience to answer the questions and to resolve the clashes regarding faith-based organizations' religious autonomy considered in this introductory chapter. Doing so requires a careful thinking through of what exactly is at stake, what concepts are relevant, and how to apply these concepts. The need is to give due consideration to the religious autonomy of faith-based organizations deeply involved in the public life of American society, as well as diversity and pluralism, equal opportunities for all, and the opposing of invidious discrimination. The difficult task is determining what is due to whom, so that freedom for all may flourish in a context of respect for those of all faiths and of none. That is what I seek to do in this book.

THE PLAN OF THE BOOK

I seek to develop answers to the questions posed in this introductory chapter in several stages. Chapter 2 demonstrates the importance of the book's topic by documenting the number, size, and impact of faith-based organizations. They are a large part of the American public policy mix. If they would ever be forced out of existence, a huge gap in health, educational, and social services would open up; if they would be squeezed into a secularized mold in tension with their religious nature, religious freedom would be significantly diminished and much of the diversity and pluralism we profess to admire would, in practice, be lost.

Chapter 3 describes and critiques the current legal context within which the American polity seeks to address the issue of faith-based organizations' autonomy. That legal context includes the influence of the eighteenth-century Enlightenment, the American founding era and early nineteenth-century religious currents, the Supreme Court and its church-state jurisprudence, and antidiscrimination laws and their legacy.

In chapter 4 I consider the political left and the political right and why, building upon the legal context discussed in chapter 3, both fail to come up with a theoretical framework and concepts that adequately understand faith-based organizations and their place in the realm of public services. Problems in these assumptions and concepts result in problems and conflicts, as policy makers struggle with defining and implementing the relationship between government and faith-based organizations.

Chapter 5 next considers structural pluralism and its key concepts of subsidiarity and sphere sovereignty. It considers how these concepts have molded the Christian Democratic understanding of pluralism that is common in some other western democracies but is largely new to the United States. It puts forward an understanding of pluralism that, if fully applied and combined with American concepts of limited government and certain aspects of American church-state thinking, would protect the autonomy of faith-based organizations without violating freedom for all.

In chapter 6 I then apply the concepts of structural pluralism and Christian Democracy developed in chapter 5 to faith-based organizations' religious autonomy when operating in the public realm and as partners with government in addressing societal needs. It considers the key controversies now bedeviling governmental partnerships with faith-based organizations, puts forward specific answers to those controversies, and considers how these answers differ from those currently being advocated by the left and the right.

Chapter 2

Faith-Based Organizations and the Network of Human Services

It is easy to come up with moving stories of the good work being done by faith-based organizations, stories of older children who had been languishing in foster care now being adopted by a loving and caring family, of HIV-AIDS sufferers in remote African villages receiving life-saving antiretroviral drugs, and of released prisoners receiving the mentoring and job opportunities that keep them from returning to criminal activities. But such stories do not answer the more difficult question of how widespread are faith-based organizations and the services they provide to persons in need. Are such stories, as heart-warming as they are, the exception to the normal pattern of the delivery of needed services, or are they closer to the norm? This is the question this chapter considers.

This question is vital for the purposes of this book as it explores the extent and nature of the religious autonomy that faith-based organizations possess, and should possess, as they provide services to the public. As will be discussed more fully later, if the rightful autonomy of faith-based organizations is seriously violated, the religious-freedom rights of their staffs and supporters, as well as the recipients of their services, would be violated. Their staff members, financial supporters, volunteers, and recipients no longer could live out, as participants in faith-based services, the faith commitments their religious traditions require—or, at the least, their doing so would be limited and constricted. This means that even if faith-based organizations constitute only a small part of the network of human services, the question of their religious autonomy would still have significance from a theoretical, human-rights point of view. As James Madison wrote in his famous "Memorial and Remonstrance," we ought "to take alarm at the first experiment on our liberties."[1]

If, however, faith-based organizations constitute a significant proportion of the United States' network of human services, the importance of their freedom to live out their religiously inspired beliefs and practices increases exponentially. Then we would no longer be talking about the freedom of a few organizations operating on the margins of the network of human services to live out their faith commitments. Instead, we would be talking about a myriad of organizations and thousands—even millions—of persons who work in, support, and receive services from them. Any violations of religious-freedom rights of faith-based organizations would mean a violation of the religious-freedom rights of many thousands of persons active in them as supporters, volunteers, paid staff, and recipients. Also, if these violations of religious-freedom rights would cause a significant number of faith-based organizations to go out of business, to withdraw from certain areas of service, or to reduce their size, a major portion of the nation's social safety net of human services would be lost. There would be major public policy consequences, as some would go without needed services and private secular agencies and government—which is already under pressure to cut back on its services to those in need—would have to scramble in an effort to find some way to make up for the major gaps now created.

This chapter therefore considers the question of how many faith-based organizations there are today, providing what sorts of services to how many persons. To provide a comprehensive, definitive answer to this question lies beyond the scope of this book. But I will attempt a limited answer to this question by first considering existing research on the role nonprofit and voluntary organizations play in the delivery of human services and the extent and scope of faith-based organizations among those nonprofit and voluntary organizations. Next, I present case studies of the role played by faith-based organizations in three human service areas: international relief and development, adoption and foster care, and prisoner reentry in Michigan. While these case studies do not give definitive answers to the question of the extent of faith-based human services, they do suggest answers and give insight into the role that faith-based organizations play in important human service areas.

FAITH-BASED ORGANIZATIONS IN THE NONPROFIT AND VOLUNTARY SECTOR

Lester Salamon, one of the foremost scholars mapping the nonprofit sector, has referred to the "vast, unchartered network of private voluntary institutions that forms the unseen social infrastructure of American life" and goes on to describe them in these words: "Like arteries of a living organism, these organizations carry a life force that has long been a centerpiece of American culture—a faith in the capacity of individual action to improve the quality of human life."[2] Salamon elsewhere estimated there are, at a minimum, 1.2 million public-serving nonprofit organizations, of which 655,000 are direct services providers, 352,000 are churches, 140,000 are action agencies, and 50,000 are intermediary funding organizations.[3] These nonprofit organizations employ almost 11 million paid workers which constitutes 7 percent of the American work force, more than are employed in agriculture, wholesale trade, construction, or finance and insurance.[4] Most of these workers are employed in health, educational, or social service nonprofit institutions. "One of the more important features of this American approach to social welfare provision is the important role it leaves to private, nonprofit organizations, to nongovernmental institutions that nevertheless serve essentially public, as opposed to private, economic goals."[5]

Many of these nonprofit organizations are faith-based in nature. Salamon has reported that "religious institutions are near the epicenter of American philanthropy: they absorb well over half of all private charitable contributions, and account for a disproportionate share of the private voluntary effort. . . . [N]o account of the U.S. nonprofit sector would therefore be complete without some attention to the religious institutions the sector also contains."[6] A similar point has been made by the nonprofit management expert, Michael O'Neill:

> Religion is a large and important part of the nonprofit sector and has given birth to many other nonprofit institutions: health, education, social services, international assistance, advocacy, mutual assistance, and even some cultural and grantmaking organizations. Directly and indirectly, religion has been the major formative influence on America's independent sector.[7]

Moreover, based on his research, political scientist Steven Rathgeb Smith has reported: "Increasingly, faith-based service agencies are being called upon to shoulder greater responsibility for addressing a myriad of social problems."[8]

Although there are many indications of the large size of the religiously based nonprofit sector, it is difficult to document with confidence the exact number of public service faith-based nonprofit organizations in the United States or their proportion of all nonprofit organizations. What evidence is available indicates that religious congregations and other faith-based organizations constitute a large portion of the American human services safety net. Nonprofit expert Kristen Gronbjerg and Steven Rathgeb Smith have estimated that approximately one-fifth of all nonprofit organizations providing human services are faith-based in nature, an estimate they report is "most likely an underestimate of the extent to which human service organizations have formal religious affiliation."[9]

A number of studies of religious congregations and the human services they provide to both their own members and their broader communities reveal an impressive picture. A comprehensive study in Philadelphia found that some 88 percent of the churches reported providing at least one type of service to the public, with these congregational programs serving an average of 102 persons, of whom thirty-nine were church members and sixty-three were nonmembers.[10] The authors of this study calculated that the annual dollar value of the human services provided by Philadelphia congregations came to some $246,901,440.[11] A similar study of religious congregations in Kent County, Michigan, found 86 percent of the congregations reported that in the previous twelve months they had taken part in social service or community programs or had engaged in some other human service projects.[12] This study calculated that the replacement value of the congregational programs was $95 to $118 million a year.[13] A case study of fifteen religious congregations in the Philadelphia area found that they sponsored a total of 158 social ministry programs.[14] These findings are not the exception, but the norm. A 2007 national survey found: "Almost 70 percent of the congregations around the country provided social services to their members or communities."[15]

A survey of nonprofit relief efforts following the 2005 hurricanes Katrina and Rita in the New Orleans and Gulf Coast areas found that a majority (59 percent) of the nonprofit organizations providing relief were congregations or other faith-based agencies, while 41 percent were secular in nature. The survey also found that the faith-based organizations tended to serve more persons (28 percent of the faith-based organizations served more than five hundred persons while 20 percent of the secular agencies did so.)[16]

University of Chicago professor Scott Allard reports that a three-city survey of the providers of social services found that of the organizations in Chicago providing social services, 20 percent were faith-based nonprofit organizations, while in Los Angeles 18 percent were faith-based, and in Washington, D.C., 30 percent were faith-based.[17] He concluded that "faith-based or religious nonprofit organizations continue to occupy an important position within the contemporary social service-oriented American safety net."[18] In a study I conducted of welfare-to-work programs in Los Angeles, Dallas, Chicago, and Philadelphia, I found that 35 percent of the nonprofit programs were faith-based in nature.[19]

In summary, the evidence from a host of studies clearly indicates that nonprofit, faith-based organizations play an important role in providing human services to the public. If they would disappear overnight, a crisis of the first magnitude would exist in the nation's social safety net.

But the picture painted by the studies I have thus far cited is incomplete. The impact that faith-based organizations are having can be understood more fully by looking carefully at three specific human service areas. That is what the next three sections of this chapter do. In each of these areas I seek to answer these questions:

(1) How many faith-based organizations are actively providing services to how many persons, and what proportion of services in that human service area is provided by them? This question is of obvious importance in judging the relative importance played by faith-based organizations in each of the three human service areas.

(2) Are these faith-based organizations filling a niche that governmental or nonprofit secular agencies would have a difficult time filling? If in terms of the services they provide, the persons they are able to reach, the methods they use, or other unique characteristics, faith-based organizations are filling a service niche others are not or cannot fill, their importance for the nation's human service network increases; if they are not filling any special niche, their reduction in size or even demise would have a smaller adverse societal impact.

(3) Are faith-based organizations largely religious in name only or religious only in the sense of having historic roots in a religious tradition that means little today, or is their religious character something that is alive and meaningful to them in shaping their identity, their motivation for what they are doing, and how they go about doing it? This last question is important both because it affects the extent to which any loss of religious autonomy by faith-based organizations will result in a serious diminution of their religious freedom rights and because it carries implications for faith-based organizations' likely retreat from or reduction in human services if the cost is a loss of their religious identity and practices.

Before turning to specific human service areas, however, one additional point needs to be made, namely that included in the category of "faith-based organizations" are a wide variety of organizations with widely differing ideas of what being a faith-based organization means. One classification scheme has six categories of faith-based organizations based on the amount and explicitness of the religious elements in their programming: faith-saturated, faith-centered, faith-related, faith background, faith-secular partnership, and secular.[20] For some faith-based organizations, their religious beliefs and practices are upfront, explicit, and integrated into their service programming; others may to the casual observer appear to be no different than their secular counterparts with their religious beliefs serving largely as an underlying motivation for their financial supporters, staffs, and volunteers. And even among those with explicit religious elements held in an upfront manner, the religious elements and how they are expressed differ. But this is to be expected. The ability, or freedom, of faith-based organizations to define for themselves the nature and meaning of being faith-based is at the heart of the religious autonomy with which this book is concerned.

INTERNATIONAL EMERGENCY RELIEF AND LONG-TERM DEVELOPMENT

As citizens of a large, prosperous country, many Americans feel an obligation to come to the aid of persons around the world suffering the effects of drought, floods, earthquakes, and other natural or human-caused disasters. Similarly, many feel an obligation to offer help to persons in other countries experiencing long-term, slow-motion disasters caused by disease, unclean water, a lack of education, joblessness, and other consequences of economic underdevelopment. Therefore, there are literally hundreds of nonprofit organizations, both faith-based and secular, working to provide emergency relief and long-term development assistance to peoples around the world. And the United States government—out of both humanitarian and national self-interest concerns—has also sought to provide emergency relief and long-term development aid.[21] This section considers the role played by faith-based organizations in the American people's provision of international relief and development assistance.

Faith-Based Organizations in International Relief and Development

In a well-done, thoroughly researched study, Rachel McCleary of Harvard's Kennedy School of Government has given a thorough picture of American private voluntary organizations (PVOs) active in international relief and development efforts. She writes: "The PVOs—the American Friends Service Committee, the Jewish Joint Distribution Committee, CARE, World Relief, and Catholic Relief Services, to name just a few—perform a vital function. They are the expression of human caring overseas, a compassion that was formalized during World War II and has continued to grow."[22] She found that as of 2005 there were 543 American PVOs active in overseas relief and development work, 364 of which were secular and 179 (33 percent) that were faith-based in nature.[23] She also found that total revenue for PVOs in 2005 was $15.9 billion, and of this amount 46 percent (or $7.3 billion) was revenue received by faith-based PVOs, which indicates that the average faith-based PVO was larger in terms of revenue than the average secular PVO.[24] In 2005, of the ten top PVOs in terms of total revenues, six were faith-based in nature.[25] Clearly, faith-based organizations are major players in the world of nonprofit organizations active in providing international relief and assistance. As indicated by their revenue totals, they deliver almost half of the nongovernmental international assistance. And their size and role is growing, not contracting. McCleary reports that "since 2002 religious PVOs have expanded faster [than secular PVOs], resulting in a nearly equal division of revenue between secular and religious organizations in 2004–5."[26] McCleary has also documented the large amounts of government funding going to both faith-based and secular nonprofit organizations, although it is a greater amount for secular than faith-based organizations. She found that from 1996 to 2005, the share of federal government funding for secular relief and development organizations came to 35 percent of their revenues, and for faith-based organizations it was 14 percent.[27]

A more complete understanding of faith-based organizations in international relief and development work can be gained by looking at two of the largest faith-based organizations and an alliance of faith-based organizations. We met World Vision in chapter 1 already because of a legal challenge to its policy of employing only persons in agreement with its religious commitments. It is a faith-based organization in the evangelical Protestant tradition. Nicholas Kristof, a *New York Times* columnist, has described the size of World Vision, the largest American faith-based international relief and development organization, in these words: "World Vision now has 40,000 staff members in nearly 100 countries. That's more staff members than CARE, Save the Children and the worldwide operations of the United States Agency for International Development [USAID]—combined."[28] According to USAID's *2009 VOLAG Report of Voluntary Agencies*, World Vision's total revenues in 2009 were nearly $1 billion ($957,116,000), with 21.2 percent of those funds coming from government sources.[29] In 2009 it had some 1.2 million donors and its volunteers contributed over one hundred thousand hours of their time.[30] These numbers are only for World Vision USA; a sister organization, World Vision International, has an additional budget of about $1.8 billion, making for a total revenue stream for the two World Vision organizations of nearly $3 billion.

Another large player in the field of faith-based international relief and development efforts is Catholic Relief Services, with an annual budget of nearly $800 million and a staff of nearly five thousand.[31] It is active in seventy-five countries around the world.[32] In 2009, 79 percent of its revenues and in-kind contributions came from government sources, 21 percent from private contributions.[33]

The Association of Evangelical Relief and Development Organizations (AERDO) is an umbrella organization of about seventy-five evangelical Protestant faith-based organizations active in overseas relief and development work. According USAID's *2009 VOLAG Report*, thiry-five members of AERDO were registered with USAID and had revenues of close to $4 billion, which represented a little over 14 percent of the revenues of all faith-based organizations included in the *VOLAG Report*.[34] In addition, the executive director of AERDO has reported that if one adds the revenues of AERDO members who are not registered with USAID, the total revenues of AERDO members, based on the 990 forms they are required as 501(c)(3) tax-exempt agencies to file with the IRS, are about $5 billion a year.[35] Also, AERDO's member organizations often partner with the American government as recipients of financial and in-kind support for their work overseas. In 2009, twenty-eight members of AERDO received over $400 million in government grants and in-kind contributions, which represented almost 11 percent of their total revenues for that year.[36]

It is useful to note the fact that there are also faith-based relief and development agencies in the Jewish and Muslim traditions. American Jewish World Service, for example, had a budget of nearly $40 million in 2009 and specializes in making grants to local, grass-roots organizations working to alleviate hunger, poverty, and disease on the local level in countries throughout the world.[37] Mercy-USA for Aid and Development is a Muslim, United States-based organization dedicated, according to its mission statement, "to alleviating human suffering and supporting individuals and their communities in their efforts to become more self-sufficient."[38] It had total expenditures of over $3 million in 2009, of which $1.2 million came from USAID grants.[39]

In short, nongovernment organizations play a major role in the field of American overseas relief and development efforts, and many of these organizations are faith-based in nature. The largest ones are from the Christian tradition, but there are also those from minority faiths. In addition, many partner with the American government in its overseas relief and development work, receiving financial and in-kind subsidies for their work from the government.

The Added Value of Faith-Based and Other Nongovernmental Organizations

From these numbers it is clear that nongovernmental organizations, including those that are faith-based, play a large role in the American provision of international relief and development efforts. However, there is evidence that their importance is greater than their revenue and expenditure numbers alone indicate. In developing countries, faith-based and other nongovernmental organizations often have existing, trusted, on-the-ground networks down to the village level that the American government and even the host governments do not have. This point was made by Gloria Steele, a senior official in the Bureau for Global Health in the Department of Health and Human Services, in testimony before a congressional subcommittee in 2010:

> Nongovernmental, faith-based, and community-based organizations . . . have strong bases of operations in underserved, rural areas where formal health services are limited. . . . Due to their close contact with local residents, these organizations can facilitate behavior change communication activities to help families prevent and treat malaria. To date PMI [the President's Malaria Initiative] has supported nearly 200 nonprofit organizations, more than 45 of these are FBOs [faith-based organizations].[40]

A concrete example from the implementation of the PMI—begun by George W. Bush and carried forward by Barack Obama—is given on PMI's website, where it describes the role played by EQUIP, a faith-based organization that is a member of the umbrella evangelical association AERDO:

> EQUIP Liberia, a Malaria Communities Program grantee, played a major role in the implementation of a free long-lasting ITN [insecticide-treated mosquito nets] distribution campaign in Nimba County, Liberia, conducted in May-June 2009. EQUIP worked closely with PMI, the Nimba County Health Team, the Ministry of Health, and the national malaria control program to conduct the campaign. . . . EQUIP assisted the County Health team to oversee the distribution of nets from the county level down to communities. Over a period of two weeks, 530 community health volunteers trained by EQUIP Liberia distributed more than 180,000 free ITNs in all six districts of Nimba County, often transporting the bales of nets by foot or even canoe when roads were impassable. Volunteers went from house to house to ensure that each household received three nets and to share information about the importance of using a net to prevent malaria.[41]

Similarly, Kristof has written that it would be a "catastrophe" if American aid would no longer be delivered via faith-based organizations. Why? He uses an example to answer: "In Haiti, more than half of food distributions go through religious groups like World Vision that have indispensible networks on the ground."[42]

In distributing food in the face of a famine, in meeting desperate needs when a natural disaster strikes, in meeting health needs in remote villages, or in coaching small farmers in new, more productive farming techniques, USAID does not have on-the-ground networks in place able to serve as conduits of communication, help, and support. Even the governments of host countries often do not have effective networks in place down to the village level. But nongovernmental organizations (NGOs), including faith-based ones, often have previously established networks in place, marked by working relationships with local clinics, schools, churches, and village elders. These NGOs thereby become a crucial link in the chain of humanitarian outreach that is not captured by figures that only take into account the amount of money they receive and spend.

The Role of Faith in Faith-Based Organizations

A final question to be considered is the nature of the role that religious faith plays in the faith-based organizations involved in international relief and development work. Although each faith-based overseas relief and development agency no doubt answers this question somewhat differently, the evidence indicates that for many faith-based organizations their faith-element is fundamental to who they are and what they do. For them, their mission, as they define it, is not merely a matter of providing humanitarian assistance as any comparable secular organization might, with their religious faith lurking somewhere in the background. Many see their faith element as crucial, even central, to their identity and mission. For them, issues of their religious autonomy, which enables them to determine for themselves the religiously based practices they do and do not wish to follow, is vital. The importance of faith for many faith-based relief and development agencies can be illustrated by looking more closely at the two giants in the international nonprofit field I discussed earlier: Catholic Relief Services and World Vision.

World Vision was involved in the court case cited in the prior chapter concerning several employees who were let go because they no longer met World Vision's religious standards for their employees. They claimed that World Vision was a humanitarian, not a religious organization, and thus did not qualify for an exemption from laws that otherwise forbid employment decisions based on religion. But the federal Court of Appeals for the Ninth Circuit held that World Vision was indeed a religious organization:

> World Vision is a nonprofit organization whose humanitarian relief efforts flow from a profound sense of religious mission. That mission is evinced in the organization's founding documents. Significantly, World Vision continues to act in accordance with those documents, and it explicitly and intentionally holds itself out to the public as a religious institution.[43]

World Vision's website does indeed make clear its Christian commitment:

> World Vision is a Christian humanitarian organization dedicated to working with children, families, and their communities worldwide to reach their full potential by tackling the causes of poverty and injustice. . . . Motivated by our faith in Jesus Christ, we serve alongside the poor and oppressed as a demonstration of God's unconditional love for all people.[44]

In an interview, Steven McFarland, the chief legal officer for World Vision, related the importance of the faith element in the organization:

> Our faith is very important; our mission is very important. . . . It is who we are, the power of God working through our people. We are not just another humanitarian organization, but a branch of the body of Christ. . . . The key to our effectiveness is our faith, not our size. If we would lose our birthright, if we ever would not be able to determine our team, we'd lose our vision and would no longer be a faith-based organization.[45]

Catholic Relief Services (CRS) is another giant in the international relief and development field. It is incorporated separately from the United States Conference of Catholic Bishops, but the bishops' conference legally owns CRS and appoints its board of directors. Its faith commitment is very clear in its mission statement that, in part, declares: "Catholic Relief Services carries out the commitment of the Bishops of the United States to assist the poor and vulnerable overseas. We are motivated by the Gospel of Jesus Christ to cherish, preserve and uphold the sacredness and dignity of all human life, foster charity and justice, and embody Catholic social and moral teaching."[46] Joan Rosenhauer, CRS's Vice President for U.S. Operations, when asked in an interview concerning the importance of the Catholic identity of CRS, responded:

> The leadership team is very conscious of our Catholic identity. The mission statement is based on Catholic social teaching. Every staff person must embrace the ideas that flow from Catholic social teaching, such as the value of all persons and support for the common good. We do training in this—how our work reflects certain values that are rooted in Catholic social teaching. . . . Plus we do not, of course, provide abortions or condoms. We do not hire persons in gay relationships, nor persons in heterosexual relationships outside of marriage.[47]

As seen earlier, the seventy-five members of AERDO collectively are important players in the field of international relief and development. Its members are Christian in a traditional or evangelical Protestant sense. To become a member they must subscribe to a statement of faith that contains such typically evangelical provisions such as "We believe the Bible to be inspired, the only infallible, authoritative Word of God," and "We believe in the deity of our Lord Jesus Christ, in His virgin birth, in His sinless life, in His miracles, in His vicarious and atoning death through His shed blood, in His bodily resurrection."[48] For this association and its members, their faith is an important aspect of their self-identity.

The American Friends Service Committee is another faith-based organization active in international relief and development work. Its website describes its mission in these words: "The American Friends Service Committee is a practical expression of the faith of the Religious Society of Friends (Quakers). Committed to the principles of nonviolence and justice, it seeks in its work and witness to draw on the transforming power of love, human and divine." After detailing more of its mission and some of its core values, it states: "From these beliefs flow the core understandings that form the spiritual framework of our organization and guide its work."[49] Coming out of its Quaker background, the basic thrust of these words differ from that of the organizations in the evangelical and Catholic traditions, but they are no less religious and no less an important part of its understanding of who it is and what its faith compels its members to do.

The key point to be noted in regard to these faith-based organizations active in providing relief and development services around the world—as well as a host of other, smaller organizations—is that even though they define somewhat differently how their faith shapes their work, they nevertheless see their faith as central, not peripheral, to who they are and what they are seeking to do. Their freedom to put their faith at the center of what they are doing and to live out the commands they are convinced God has placed on them is, to them, no small matter. This means that public policy as it deals with their religious autonomy and religious freedom rights—the question with which this book is concerned—is a question of major import to them, their staff members, their volunteers, and their millions of supporters.

ADOPTION AND FOSTER CARE SERVICES

Adoptions and foster care are significant aspects of the human services safety net in the United States—certainly for the children and families involved. In 2007 some 1.8 million adopted children were living in the United States.[50] Of these adopted children, 37 percent had been adopted from foster care, 38 percent were private domestic adoptions, and 25 percent were international adoptions.[51] In 2002, excluding international adoptions, 130,269 children were adopted in the United States.[52] Of these about fifty-four thousand were among related individuals (for example, a grandparent legally adopting a grandchild or a step-father adopting a son or daughter of his wife). This leaves seventy-six thousand domestic adoptions among unrelated individuals—the sort of adoptions one usually thinks of when one reads about adoptions. Of this seventy-six thousand, about 56 percent were handled by government agencies, 22 percent by private, nongovernmental agencies, and 21 percent were arranged among individuals.[53] Among these seventy-six thousand domestic adoptions among unrelated individuals, about forty-six thousand (60 percent) involved "special needs" children, that is, children for whom it is harder to find adoptive families due to their race or ethnicity, being an older age, being part of a sibling grouping, or having a physical, developmental, or emotional disability.[54] In addition to domestic adoptions each year, there are about twenty thousand inter-country adoptions, that is, adoptions by American parents of children from another county, a number that has increased over the past thirty years.[55]

Each year, some 275,000 children enter the foster care system due to their being removed from their homes because of abuse or neglect or due to delinquent behavior, and at any given point in time there are 450,000 to 500,000 children and adolescents in the foster care system.[56] Almost half are placed in licensed foster care families and 15 to 20 percent are in residential facilities.[57] A majority of these children return to their biological families once the issues that led to their being removed from their families have been settled; for others the authorities will terminate parental rights. In the latter case, adoption becomes the preferable option. About 20 percent of the children who exit the foster care system are permanently adopted by new families.[58] In 2008, 24 percent of the children in foster care—or roughly one hundred thousand children—were available for adoption.[59]

This entire area of foster care and adoption services is a labor-intensive, challenging field, marked by both governmental and nonprofit agencies playing active roles. Judgments must be made on the appropriate actions to be taken when neglect, abuse, or delinquency is alleged; adoptive and foster care families need to be both recruited and carefully screened; supportive services and financial payments must be provided for families and residential institutions providing foster care; and biological families where abuse and neglect has occurred require counseling and judgments must be made concerning when either their children can be returned or parental rights must be terminated. Some of these tasks are performed by state government agencies and some by nonprofit agencies, some of which are faith-based in nature (although only official state agencies and the courts can remove children from a home or terminate parental rights). The extent to which states rely on their own governmental agencies or on nongovernmental, nonprofit agencies varies from one state to another. The only generalization is that all states rely on both. Michigan, for example, as of September 2007 had 8,879 children and adolescents in its foster care system. Private, nonprofit agencies were providing care for 5,741 (65 percent) of them and government agencies were providing care for 3,138 of them (35 percent).[60] Of those in licensed foster care homes, 60 percent had been placed and supervised by nongovernmental agencies, and of those in residential treatment facilities, 82 percent were in nongovernmental facilities.[61]

Facilitating adoptions—when that is the appropriate course of action—is crucially important for the children and families involved. All child welfare advocates agree that, as a recent Pew study expresses it, "All children need safe, permanent families that love, nurture, protect, and guide them."[62] Social science supports this conclusion: "Children who live with married parents tend to have higher grades, are more likely to attend college, and experience lower rates of unemployment."[63] This means there need to be families willing to adopt when single mothers conclude they cannot raise a child alone or when children have been removed from their families due to abuse or neglect and the authorities have concluded that parental rights should be terminated. As seen earlier, at any given time, of the nearly five hundred thousand children in the foster care system, about one hundred thousand have been declared eligible for adoption. These children—especially when they have "special needs"—can be very hard to place in loving, welcoming, adoptive families. As a result, some stay in the foster care system until they are eighteen years old (twenty-one years old in some states), often being shuttled from one foster family to another.

In addition, there are international adoptions. There are reliable statistics on the number of children American families adopt from overseas, since each child needs to obtain a visa from the State Department before being admitted to the United States. In 2009 a total of 12,753 children were adopted internationally.[64] Over 40 percent of these children came either from China or Ethiopia. In both of these countries many children are languishing in orphanages—in China due to its government's one-child per family policy combined with cultural norms that favor male children, leading to many female babies being abandoned, and in Ethiopia due to extreme poverty and warfare. Some have sought to denigrate international adoptions as stripping children of their cultural identity. But Scott Simon, the host of NPRs "Weekend Edition with Scott Simon" and the father of two daughters from China, has eloquently answered such objections: "Race, blood, lineage, and nationality don't matter; they're just the way that small minds keep score. All that matters about blood is that it's warm and that it beats through a loving heart."[65] Similarly, *Washington Post* columnist Michael Gerson has written, "It is one of noblest things about America that we care for children of other lands who have been cast aside. . . . After millennia of racial and ethnic conflict across the world, resulting in rivers of blood, America declared that bloodlines don't matter, that dignity is found beneath every human disguise."[66] The fact that two-thirds of all international adoptions are of female children testifies to the low regard in which many cultures hold girls, and to the willingness of American parents to welcome them into their families.[67]

In summary, both the children themselves and society gain when children are adopted into permanent families and when children in foster care experience the love and stability of a family. Also, the over-burdened foster care system gains as children whose parents' parental rights have been terminated are placed into permanent, adoptive homes, leaving case workers with fewer children whose care and progress they need to monitor. Inter-country adoptions do not offer relief to American children and agencies, but from a world-wide perspective they do provide permanent homes for children that often had been languishing in underfinanced, overcrowded orphanages. From a humanitarian point of view, that too is a desirable end. Those agencies—governmental and nongovernmental—that find and train foster care families and place in them children who are in desperate need of care and stability and that recruit families willing to adopt children, screen them for appropriateness, and place children with them, are performing a crucial public service that benefits the children involved, parents longing for a child, and the broader society. They are a crucial part of the human services network working to protect those who are probably the most vulnerable persons of all.

Faith-Based Organizations in Adoption and Foster Care Services

There are reasonably good statistics on the number and percentages of children in foster care who are under the supervision of independent, nonprofit entities. The same is true of adoptions by way of independent, nonprofit agencies. However, it is much harder to find reliable statistics on the number of those independent, nongovernment agencies that are faith-based in nature and the number of foster care children they supervise and the number of adoptions they arrange. There is, however, compelling evidence that the number is significant. Faith-based adoption and foster care agencies do not dominate the adoption and foster care field, but they are an active, substantial part of it.

Taking adoption numbers first, agencies affiliated with Catholic Charities, for example, completed in 2009 a total of 3,794 adoptions, 3,309 of which were domestic and 485 were international adoptions.[68] Bethany Christian Services—the largest faith-based adoption agency in the United States with offices in thirty-two states—is in the evangelical Protestant tradition. In 2009 it completed 1,716 adoptions.[69] Of these, 420 were international and 1,296 were domestic.[70]

This means that these two agencies alone—both of which are faith-based—accounted for nearly one-third of the nongovernmental adoptions in the United States.[71] The National Council for Adoption is an adoption advocacy organization of sixty-two member agencies active in the adoption field. Its president and CEO, Chuck Johnson, reports that thirty of their sixty-two members are faith-based in nature.[72]

In terms of international adoptions, Holt International and All God's Children International are Christian adoption organizations specializing in international adoptions. Together they account for about 911 inter-country adoptions a year.[73] If one adds to those adoptions the international adoptions by Catholic Charities and Bethany Christian Services, these four faith-based agencies alone make possible about 1,843 international adoptions a year, which is close to 15 percent of all international adoptions.

Faith-based organizations are also active in providing foster care to the five hundred thousand children and youths in the foster care system—either in families that have been recruited and trained by them or in residential, group facilities. Again, exact numbers are difficult to document. But the limited numbers that are available indicate that faith-based agencies are a large, crucial—many would say indispensible—part of the foster care system. Nationally, Catholic Charities agencies in 2009 served 34,049 children and youths in the foster care system.[74] Lutheran Social Services is also very active in the foster care field. In 2002—the last year for which accurate figures are available—it served 13,032 children and youths who were in the foster care system.[75] If one combines only the children handled by Catholic Charity and Lutheran Social Services agencies, together they account for almost 10 percent of all children and youths in foster care.[76]

One can also gain some insight into the role played by faith-based organizations in foster care by looking more closely at one state. In Michigan, as of September 2007—as seen earlier—65 percent of the children in the Michigan foster care system were being cared for by nongovernmental agencies, 35 percent by governmental agencies. It is impossible to say exactly what proportion of the 65 percent of the children (or 5,741) in the care of independent, nongovernmental agencies were in the care of faith-based agencies, since neither the government nor the umbrella Michigan Federation for Children and Families organization compile child care statistics by faith-based versus secular agencies. But there is persuasive evidence that a large proportion of those 5,741 children were under the care of faith-based organizations. The head of the Michigan Federation for Children and Families—which includes one-half to two-thirds of all independent agencies providing child and family care in Michigan—estimates that about one-half of its forty plus members are faith-based in nature.[77] In addition, if one takes the number of Michigan children and youths that in a recent year received foster care services from four of the largest, better known faith-based organizations active in foster care activities—the Michigan Catholic Charities agencies, Lutheran Social Services, Bethany Christian Services, and Holy Cross Children's Services—one finds that 4,943 received services from them.[78] One should note that this 4,943 figure and the 5,741 figure are not directly comparable, since the latter figure represents the number of children in foster care at a point in time, while the 4,943 figure represents the total number of foster care children served in a given year. Since many children move in and out of foster care within the course of a year, the actual proportion of foster care children served by these four faith-based agencies is not as large as these two numbers would suggest. For example, Lutheran Social Services supervised a total of 1,380 children in foster care in 2009, but only about 800 of these children were in foster care at any one time. Nevertheless, these numbers demonstrate that faith-based agencies play a very large role in foster care services in Michigan.

In summary, it is clear that faith-based organizations are very active in the adoption and foster care fields and account for a significant number of all foster care provided and all adoptions, domestic and international, in the United States, even if exact numbers are impossible to document. If faith-based agencies were to disappear overnight, a serious gap would open up in the network of agencies that make possible adoptions in the United States—to the detriment of children in need at home and abroad, couples desiring children, and society as a whole due to increased social needs that only intact families can meet. It is hard to doubt Chuck Johnson, the CEO of the National Council for Adoption, when he concluded: "If they [faith-based adoption agencies] would disappear overnight the whole system would collapse on itself."[79]

The Added Value of Faith-Based Organizations

There is some evidence that the importance of faith-based adoption and foster care services goes beyond simply the number of children for whom they provide assistance. Again, it is hard to document the exact numbers, but there is evidence—some statistical and some anecdotal—that faith-based organizations are especially effective in placing special needs children who usually are hard to place in families. Of the 3,794 completed adoptions by Catholic Charities agencies in 2009, 1,721 (45 percent) were of children considered to have special needs.[80] Bethany Christian Services reports that it does not keep track of "special needs" children as a separate category, but that of their 1,716 adoptions in 2009, 541 (or 32 percent) were of older children from out of the foster care system, who by that fact alone would be considered "special needs" children.[81]

There are also anecdotal accounts of churches and faith-based organizations working to find adoptive homes for hard-to-place children. In fact, Lutheran Adoption Service of Michigan in 2006 phased out both inter-country and infant adoption programs in order to concentrate on finding adoptive homes for the six thousand children who were in the Michigan foster care system and available for adoption.[82] The *Denver Post* has reported an adoption success story in which churches are playing a major role: "The number of Colorado children in foster care awaiting permanent adoption has been cut in half by a partnership between churches and government that places parentless kids in 'forever homes.'"[83] The article goes on to report that when in November 2008 the evangelical organization Focus on the Family launched an adoption initiative, there were nearly eight hundred children in foster care awaiting adoption; in early 2010 that number had been cut in half, to 365. The head of the program for Focus on the Family, Jim Daly, explains the effort's motivation this way: "If my Bible math is right, God reminds us forty-seven times to take care of widows and orphans."[84] The One Church One Child organization was founded in the 1970s to reduce the disproportionate number of African-American children in foster care and awaiting adoption in Illinois. Its goal was "to find one family in every African American church in Illinois to adopt one child."[85] Its efforts were reportedly successful in Illinois and it has now spread to thirty-five states.

Even with incomplete data and anecdotal accounts, it is safe to conclude that faith-based organizations are filling an important niche in the adoption and foster care field. Many hard-to-place, special needs children who would not find homes without these faith-based efforts are now finding adoptive homes. That fact is important to note, even though it is impossible to be more precise than that.

The Role of Faith in Faith-Based Organizations

It is also important to note a final point: there is a wide range among faith-based organizations providing adoption and foster care services in terms of what being faith-based means to them in practice. Diversity abounds.

Some, and especially those in the evangelical Protestant tradition, see their faith as being central to who they are and work to integrate it into the services they provide. As noted earlier, Bethany Christian Services is a faith-based organization in the evangelical Protestant tradition and is the largest faith-based provider of adoption services in the nation. The reality of its faith-based character is seen in its mission statement that declares: "Bethany Christian Services manifests the love and compassion of Jesus Christ by protecting and enhancing the lives of children and families through quality social services."[86]

Its president, Bill Blacquiere, when asked if Bethany's faith element is something that shapes the organization and its efforts today, replied: "It is very important to the staff and board that we are a Christian organization. It is very much alive and active in shaping us today. . . . You cannot separate one's Christianity from what you do. We have a faith statement that all employees and board members sign."[87] He went on to explain that Bethany's faith statement is not based on any one tradition within Christianity and that in fact they have Baptists, Catholics, Seventh Day Adventists, and persons from Reformed and independent churches working for them. In light of its evangelical character and beliefs, Bethany, as is the case with Catholic Charities, has a policy against placing children with same-sex couples. An umbrella organization of twenty-three evangelical organizations active in adoption services has the following as its mission statement: "Motivate and unify the body of Christ to live out God's mandate to care for the orphan with the vision to have every orphan experience God's unfailing love and know Jesus as Savior."[88] One hardly needs to point out the explicit religious character of this organization or the religious motivation it articulates.

Lutheran Social Services in America—whose agencies, as seen earlier, are active in the foster care and adoption field—describes its faith-inspired elements in less explicit terms and sees them largely in terms of providing a motivation for what they do. Its website's description of its mission states: "As Lutheran Christian organizations, what compels and sustains us into the future is God's call to love and serve our neighbors."[89] Its board in 2008 adopted a statement that includes among their "Ends Policies," "a spirit of possibility and a will that shapes the future," and "Lutheran social ministry organizations live out their Lutheran identities."[90]

Catholic Charities falls somewhere midway between the evangelical and the Lutheran agencies in the degree to which they are explicit about their faith and how it affects their activities. Catholic Charities' president from 1992 to 2001 wrote an essay that outlined ten ways in which Catholic Charities are genuinely Catholic. Among the ten: its ministry is rooted in the Scriptures, it seeks to meet spiritual needs as well as physical and mental needs, and it operates "consistently with the teachings and values of the Church."[91] He referred specifically to adoption services in pointing out that "the ultimate rationale for our services is our belief in the sanctity of the human person and the dignity of human life. This is reflected, for example, in adoption services."[92] The current head of Catholic Charities, Fr. Larry Snyder, has stated that in their adoption and foster care services they favor traditional, mother-father families, and, while they do make placements with single persons, they do not place children with same-sex couples.[93] This is, of course, in line with Catholic teachings in regard to marriage and family.

The conclusion is that faith-based organizations reflect a diversity of positions as they define what it means to them to be faith-based. And that, I believe, is as it should be, for that is what diversity, pluralism, and religious autonomy are all about.

THE MICHIGAN PRISONER REENTRY INITIATIVE (MPRI)

Beginning in 1973 the United States prison population soared, increasing by 705 percent between 1973 and 2009,[94] resulting in 1.6 million persons being in state and federal prisons by the end of 2009.[95] If one adds together state prisoners, local jail inmates, and federal prisoners, in 2008 one in one hundred American adults was imprisoned.[96] With the increase in the number of prisoners there has, of course, also been a dramatic increase in the money state and federal governments are spending on prisons. From 1988 to 2008 state spending on corrections increased from $11.7 billion to $47.3 billion, more than a four-fold increase.[97] A survey of thirty-four states found that they spend an average of $29,000 per prisoner per year.[98] In California alone, between 1999 and 2008 spending on prisons increased from less than $3 billion to almost $7 billion a year. Its correction budget consumes 9.3 percent of its general fund budget.[99]

Increasing prison populations also mean increases in the numbers of previously incarcerated persons now being returned into society, since 97 percent of all prisoners will be released from prison at some point in time. Nearly 650,000 prisoners a year are released back into society, a number that is likely to increase. This is a 400 percent increase over the 150,000 being released annually in the mid-1980s.[100]

In addition, historically at least 60 percent of released prisoners return to prison within three years of their release.[101] In California, the recidivism rate has been about 70 percent for the past twenty-five years.[102] Thus the increasing numbers of prisoners being released back into society has public safety implications, as well as long-term cost implications since persons who are re-incarcerated after a short time will again become a financial burden on the state.

Michigan is one state in which a large increase in its prison population and consequent huge costs are clearly present. In 1973, Michigan had a prison population of 7,874, which had increased to a high of 51,554 by 2007, an increase of 555 percent, and one of the highest incarceration rates in the nation.[103] Michigan's budget for prisons had topped $2 billion, which was more than it was spending on higher education and consumed over 20 percent the state's general fund budget.[104] This led Michigan to launch in 2005 the Michigan

Prisoner Reentry Initiative (MPRI), aimed at reducing both the state's prison population and its recidivism rate. Michael Thompson of the Council of State Governments has said of this effort: "Michigan has developed one of the most comprehensive statewide re-entry initiatives in the United States."[105] Since it self-consciously seeks to build partnerships between the Department of Corrections and community and faith-based organizations, a more detailed examination will help illustrate the role faith-based organizations are playing in an important public policy area.

The MPRI was an initiative of the administration of Governor Jennifer Granholm, who held office from 2003 to 2010. It grew out of the thinking of several key policy leaders in Michigan, in conjunction with the Council of State Government's Justice Center. The MPRI website proclaims its mission in these words: "The Mission of the Michigan Prisoner ReEntry Initiative (MPRI) is to significantly reduce crime and enhance public safety by implementing a seamless system of services for offenders from the time of their entry to prison through their transition, community reintegration and aftercare in their communities."[106]

More specifically, this initiative has three phases:[107]

- Phase One: Getting ready. Here prisoners, at the beginning of their incarceration, are thoroughly assessed in terms of risks and needs. Based on this assessment a program for each prisoner is developed that seeks to reduce risks and build on strengths.
- Phase Two: Going home. Six months before a prisoner's release, reentry plans are developed that address issues such as housing, employment, and needed community services. Community groups that will be involved with the prisoner after release are already involved (often meeting with him or her). The key here is that this is an integrated plan, not a series of disconnected services.
- Phase Three: Staying home. Here the integrated plan is put into effect, so that the "returning citizen" has the support and assistance that he or she needs. The parole staff and various community providers work together to execute the plan.

In phase two and especially in phase three, extensive use is made of faith-based and other community groups, working cooperatively with parole services and other public agencies. The basic idea underlying MPRI is not to dump ex-offenders into a community with only legal restrictions and obligations enforced by an overworked parole system, but instead to create a network of support and assistance as the ex-offender transitions from prison to life in the community. Services ex-offenders often stand in need of include drug and alcohol counseling, GED preparation classes, and help in obtaining housing and employment. These are in addition to basic services, such as help in obtaining a driver's license or a social security number, a mentor to whom the ex-offender can talk when discouraged, and, for many, a religious congregation that welcomes the ex-offender into its midst and can act as a new family.

In Robert Putman's terms, an ex-offender needs both bonding and bridging social capital.[108] The former refers to ties to family, ethnic, religious, and other in-groups to which a person is linked by birth or membership. With such ties come feelings of belonging, a sense of identity and worth, and emotional and sometimes tangible support. Bridging social capital consists of ties to groups and institutions in the broader community that reach across economic, social class, and ethnic or racial groups. Such ties are important in finding housing or employment and in dealing successfully more generally with the city or community in which one is located. Ex-offenders—probably more so than anyone else in society—lack both bonding and bridging social capital. They have been shut away from society for years and, for many, they were originally led into criminal activity because they were not well integrated into the world of families, work, and other organizations out of which social capital arises. MPRI is intended to create for ex-offenders the social capital that all of us need. This especially is where MPRI looks to faith communities to play a role. As an MPRI policy document begins, "The Michigan Prisoner Reentry Initiative (MPRI) has established very strong connections with Michigan's faith-based and community-based organizations. The MPRI Model . . . establishes the critical role that faith- and community-based institutions must play in order for MPRI's crime-fighting goal to be met."[109]

The early results of the MPRI are encouraging. By 2010, Michigan had reduced its prison population to 44,092, a decline of 14 percent.[110] From 2008 to 2009 alone Michigan reduced its prison population by 6.7 percent, the largest decline among the fifty states except for Rhode Island.[111] Due to the decline in its prison population, Michigan was able to close fourteen of its corrections facilities, at a cost savings of millions of dollars.[112] And, most importantly, this has been accompanied by a reduction in the rate of recidivism. "Before the MPRI, one in two parolees returned to prison within three years. That has improved to one in three. About 2,800 fewer parolees have returned to prison than would have been expected prior to the MPRI."[113] With it costing Michigan over $30,000 a year to house and maintain a person in prison and with fewer persons being returned to prison meaning fewer crimes being committed, everyone gains—the taxpayers who have to pay for prisons, the general public that suffers less crime, and the ex-offenders and their families who now have new opportunities to live productive lives.

The MPRI—while not a silver bullet that solves all crime and reentry problems—is clearly a public policy success. It is also clear that it could not have succeeded without the active support and help of Michigan's churches and other faith-based organizations. It is to this topic that I now turn.

Faith-Based Organizations in the MPRI

Unfortunately, it is impossible to document the exact number and size of faith-based organizations participating in the MPRI, since neither the state Department of Corrections nor independent researchers have broken down community partners by whether or not they are faith-based in nature. But two facts are clear from the testimony of many key players: (1) community groups are key to the initiative and without them it could not have succeeded, and (2) many—if not most—of the community groups active in the initiative are churches and other faith-based organizations. Patricia Caruso, the director of the Michigan Department of Corrections up until early 2011, publically stated that the role played by churches and the faith community in the MPRI have been "critically important," and then went on to explain: "We look at people getting out of prison being welcomed into their community by churches, and in some cases that may be the only support system they have because they may not have a family left to welcome them. It makes an incredible difference."[114]

There are two ways in which faith-based organizations are a part of the MPRI.[115] Some are formal state contractors, who provide certain specified services in return for reimbursement by the state. Others are involved through non-reimbursed programs of help to ex-offenders, beginning when they are still incarcerated and continuing once they are released. Churches and their programs often fall into this second category, and are considered vital since it is important yet difficult for ex-offenders to be integrated into a community of support—or, to put it into sociological terms, to develop both bonding and bridging social capital. Church communities—which can offer mentors, acceptance, contacts into the community, and sympathetic support when times become tough—have the potential to offer the needed help.[116] According to a key policy analyst: "MDOC [Michigan Department of Corrections] recognizes the critical role FBOs play—especially in the 'staying home' phase. To absorb a person back into the community, just to become a part of the community again, with connections and supports."[117] The state went as far as to contract with a person to develop contacts with congregations, encourage them to become involved in prisoner reentry efforts, and to integrate them into the MPRI. This contact person uses a "Healing Communities" tool kit for churches, developed by the Annie E. Casey Foundation and the Progressive

National Baptist Convention, which leads participating churches to be designated "Stations of Hope."[118]

The Comprehensive Prisoner ReEntry Plan adopted by the Department of Corrections provides, "Each local MPRI site must indicate annually the degree to which their plan is engaging the faith-based community and, in addition, establish in their budget how MPRI funds will be used with leveraged state, local and federal funds to support services provided by the faith-based community."[119] Later the same document goes on to testify: "The work being done through local MPRI community sites with faith based non-profits is extensive."[120] Although exact numbers are difficult—indeed, impossible—to uncover, I could go on for pages citing similar testimonies to the extensive, indispensable role played by religious congregations and other faith-based organizations in the MPRI. Examples of faith-based service providers from Wayne and Monroe Counties—which include the city of Detroit—can illustrate the situation that I came across in one area of the state after another: [121]

- Housing services: Lutheran Social Services (Heartline, Inc.), Detroit Rescue Mission Ministries, and Salvation Army Harbor Light
- Workforce development services: Jewish Vocational Services (JVS), Lutheran Social Services, and Detroit Rescue Mission Ministries
- Substance abuse services: Catholic Social Services, Salvation Army Harbor Light, Detroit Rescue Mission Ministries, and Lutheran Social Services
- Mental health services: Detroit Rescue Mission Ministries (which coordinates mental health treatment referrals)
- Family support services: Catholic Social Services
- Life skills: Lutheran Social Services and Detroit Rescue Mission Ministries
- Transportation: Detroit Rescue Mission Ministries and Lutheran Social Services

Research that will document the exact size of the role played by churches and other faith-based organizations in the MPRI is needed, but until such studies are commissioned and conducted all available evidence indicates that their role is major. It would be no exaggeration to say their role is indispensable to the success of the program.

The Added Value of Faith-Based Organizations

The importance of the role played by faith-based organizations in the MPRI goes beyond the simple fact of their active involvement in the initiative. It also rests upon certain unique qualities that faith-based organizations bring to the MPRI table. This point was made especially clearly in a report issued by the MPRI:

> Faith-based institutions have a long history of creating opportunities for teaching and practicing pro-social behaviors. Whether through prayer, religious study, planned social activities, opportunities to volunteer in the community, or simply through companionship, faith-based institutions work hard to improve the social environment, both for their members and their broader communities.
>
> Based on this experience, *faith-based institutions may be able to affect returning prisoners in ways that other programs do not.* Faith communities can help create the conditions for personal transformation, provide inspiration, and motivate individuals to achieve individual goals.[122]

A helpful paper prepared by several scholars for the Annie E. Casey Foundation develops a theory for why houses of worship and other faith-based organizations may be especially effective in enabling former prisoners who are returning to their communities to do so successfully. The authors argue that "numerous practitioners" have concluded: "If existing ministries and service providers offer support for most of the material and social needs of ex-offenders, but fail to address the more intangible religious capital needs for forgiveness, redemption, reconciliation and acceptance, then an important dimension of what it means to be human will have gone unacknowledged and, perhaps, tragically unmet."[123] And, they argue, it is within religious communities that ex-offenders can find the support and acceptance that is crucial. They give the example of an African-American church in Atlanta where one of them attended a service that included a young woman who gave this testimony: "I used to be a streetwalker. The men called 'baby, sweet child, pretty lady.' Then I was arrested and the judge called me a hooker and a criminal. But, now I've been saved and redeemed and God calls me a 'child of God.' My name has changed."[124] For many reasons, it is impossible to imagine a government-run or secular program—no matter how professionally and efficiently run—providing the support that will lead to this sort of testimony.

A 2008 study by the Council of State Governments Justice Center advances this same theme:

> Faith-based and community organizations (nonprofits, grassroots organizations, churches, ministries, other houses of worship, and their affiliated bodies) can supply critical services to people released from prisons and jails. . . . In particular, staff and volunteers at these organizations have been successful at fostering positive and lasting relationships with people released from prisons and jails. These kinds of relationships can be strong motivating factors for people to engage in reentry programs, seek ongoing support, and remain committed to rejecting a life of crime.[125]

This study concluded that for "reentry efforts to be effectual, they largely will depend on the government agencies' ability to establish, develop, and maintain relationships with faith-based and community organizations."[126]

The key point here is that the MPRI's partnership with religious congregations and other faith-based organizations is not merely a matter of utilizing a community asset whose religious character is accidental and inconsequential, but rather it is a matter of utilizing a community asset whose religious character is what helps make it in fact a valued asset in successful reentry efforts.

The Role of Faith in Faith-Based Organizations

The final point of this section is the same one made earlier in other human services areas: the nature and explicitness of faith in the faith-based organizations taking part in the MPRI varies from being very upfront and explicit with day-to-day importance to being more of a background factor helping to shape commitment and motivation. This is true of both churches and non-church faith-based organizations. But faith consistently plays a role, even if that role is defined differently by different entities.

Detroit Rescue Mission Ministries (DRMM) is one of the MPRI subcontractors. As its website indicates, it provides a number of services to returning prisoners, including reaching out to them while still incarcerated in order to develop transition plans for when they are released, finding mentors for them, providing initial housing for them at the mission until they can find more permanent housing, and providing transitional jobs where they can develop good work habits, earn money, and prepare to move into a permanent job.[127] As its name implies, the Detroit Rescue Mission Ministries is deeply rooted in its Christian tradition. Its mission statement is as follows:

> The Detroit Rescue Mission Ministries is a non-profit organization committed to sharing the gospel of the love of Jesus Christ by providing hope to the hopeless, abused, disadvantaged and homeless men, women and children of our community in "rebuilding one life at a time." By ministering to the total person, body, soul and spirit, together we can help them to become faithful Christians discipled into a local church, rehabilitated, employed and living productive lives in restored families.[128]

That its Christian faith is a big part of who they are hardly needs further development.

Other churches and other faith-based organizations, however, have different understandings for what it means to them to be faith-based. Jewish Vocational Services in Detroit, which is also one of the MPRI contractors, describes itself in these words: "JVS is an award-wining metropolitan Detroit nonprofit organization that serves people from all walks of life by providing counseling, training and support services in accordance with Jewish values of equal opportunity, compassion, responsibility and the steadfast belief that the best way to help people is to make it possible for them to help themselves."[129] Its description of its MPRI program (Work Options Reentry Center) does not mention its faith tradition, but one can perceive the presence of the Jewish values mentioned in its just-quoted self-description.[130] Their faith tradition is present, but in contrast to the Detroit Rescue Mission Ministries, it is in the background and more implicit in what it does than explicit.

Pine Rest Christian Mental Health Services in Grand Rapids is another MPRI contractor, providing services in the Grand Rapids area similar to those provided by DRMM in Detroit. It occupies a midpoint between Detroit Rescue Mission Ministries and Jewish Vocational Services in terms of the explicitness with which it links its faith and their public services. In an interview Clifford Washington, Pine Rest's coordination manager for its MPRI program, stated, "This is a ministry, not a job." He himself is an ex-offender, who served fourteen years in a Michigan prison and who insists that "only God made possible what I have now accomplished."[131] He further stated that the Pine Rest CEO is working to make their mission statement real on a day-to-day basis, one that emphasizes their Christian motivations for what they do in a context of professionalism: "Pine Rest Christian Mental Health Services is called to express the healing ministry of Jesus Christ by providing behavioral health services with professional excellence, Christian integrity, and compassion."[132] It further states its philosophy in these words: "We still reflect our faith-based heritage in all we do by providing professional behavioral health services that are rooted in Christian teaching and values."[133]

It is readily apparent that the faith-based organizations active in the MPRI—as we saw earlier is the case with faith-based international relief and development agencies and adoption agencies—are clearly faith-based in more than name alone, even though their understandings of exactly how that faith molds them and their services understandably varies.

In summary, Michigan has been able to reduce its prison population significantly, saving millions of dollars, while reducing recidivism and protecting public safety through a program that makes use of local, community resources. Prominent among these community resources are religious congregations and faith-based organizations, which appear to bring certain unique resources to this task and whose faith plays an important, even if varied, role in who they are and what they do.

CONCLUSIONS

The material presented in this chapter supports three conclusions. One is that there is strong evidence that faith-based organizations play a large role in delivering human services in a range of human service areas. This conclusion is supported by the findings of the various studies mentioned in the first section of the chapter, as well as by the case studies of the role played by faith-based organizations in the three specific human service areas considered in more detail—international relief and development, foster care and adoptions, and Michigan's Prisoner Reentry Initiative.

A second conclusion supported by this chapter is that there is evidence faith-based organizations often fill a niche that either government or large, secular social service agencies would have a hard time filling. This is the case largely for two reasons: first, faith-based organizations often have grass-roots contacts, networks, and structures on which they can call in providing needed services and, second, they have faith-rooted beliefs into which they can tap to motivate and encourage.

A third conclusion is that what it means to be a faith-based organization is determined by the various faith-based organizations themselves, and they vary greatly in how they define what it means for them. For some, being faith-based means they are deeply religious in an explicit, up-front manner; for others it is much more of an unseen, background factor informing their general ethos and serving as a motivation for their staffs, volunteers, and financial supporters; for yet others it lies somewhere in between these extremes, showing itself in some ways and not clearly visible in other ways. "Faith-based" is not a one-size-fits-all category, but is something distinctive to the various faith-based organizations involved in serving the public. And that is not surprising, but expected. The religious autonomy and religious freedom of faith-based organizations as defined and defended in this book is not a call for freedom for a certain type of faith-based organization, but instead is a call for faith-based organizations to be able to determine for themselves what they wish to be, as shaped by their individual histories, religious traditions, and environments. It is a call for pluralism and diversity in the world of human services available to the public.

What lessons can be drawn from these three summary conclusions? Most significantly, these conclusions point to the importance of the religious autonomy issue. If faith-based organizations that seek to serve public needs and, often, to enter into partnerships with government in doing so would have their freedom to define what it means to be faith-based constricted or perhaps even largely done away with, it would have a number of negative consequences. First, it would mean that the religious freedom of their staff members, volunteers, supporters, and recipients would be constricted. Persons whose religiously molded consciences require them to contribute money to or work for organizations that are offering help to those in need in the name of their faith would be limited—perhaps even severely—in their ability to do so. Also, those in need seeking help given in the context of their faith or of a faith community they find attractive would no longer be able to do so, or could do so only to a limited, constricted extent.

Second, given the fact that in some important ways faith-based organizations now fill certain niches in the provision of human services, to the extent they lose their religious autonomy, the ability to fill those niches may also be lost. Potentially, ties to an organization's community of faith and the volunteers, financial contributions, staff members, and supportive networks that are rooted in that community could suffer, perhaps grievously. The unique effectiveness of that organization in meeting human needs could be drastically reduced, as it comes to resemble a host of secular nonprofit and governmental agencies.

Third, some faith-based organizations might very well withdraw from partnerships with government or leave certain areas of human service altogether, if the price they need to pay is to forgo certain standards or practices deeply rooted in their religious traditions. If the choice is violating one's religiously informed conscience or withdrawing from offering a certain service, conscience may very well win out. In the previous chapter we saw that Catholic Charities in Massachusetts stopped doing adoptions altogether due to their being required to place children with same-sex couples. This could happen again and again if faith-based organizations would ever lose their right to live out their faith in providing services to those in need or in other ways become convinced they are being required to violate the very values that gave rise to their existence in the first place.

In a position to be considered later in the book, some may argue there are times we as a polity ought to restrict the religious autonomy of faith-based organizations because there are other values that trump religious autonomy. Whatever one's position on this, it is important to recognize upfront the cost of such restrictions. At the very least, this chapter and the considerations it has spawned demonstrate that the issue of the religious autonomy of public-serving faith-based organizations is much more than a matter for academic debates or Washington, D.C., discussions in think tank offices or over lunches at Old Ebbitt Grill on 15th Street. At stake are the lives of those in need and the religious freedoms we all, at least in theory, prize. Let no one dispute the importance of the autonomy question. That much this chapter has demonstrated.

Chapter 3

The Seedbeds of Attitudes towards Faith-Based Organizations

The Judiciary Committee of the House of Representatives has a Subcommittee on the Constitution, Civil Rights, and Civil Liberties. In late 2010, it held a hearing on the relationship between government and faith-based organizations. Representative Bobby Scott, Democrat from Virginia, declared:

> The most egregious aspect of the so-called faith-based initiative, the right of religious social service providers to discriminate in employment with government funds, remains unresolved. . . . [T]he history of our nation and its First Amendment protections do not and should not allow public funds to be used to proselytize or discriminate. . . . No discrimination with federal funds has been the policy of this government for decades, at least until the so-called faith-based initiative.[1]

At the same hearing, Representative Jim Sensenbrenner, Republican from Wisconsin, took an opposite position:

> Nothing in the Civil Rights Act of 1964 says a religious organization loses its right to staff on a religious basis when it uses federal funds. . . . Members of faith-based organizations should enjoy the same rights to associate with others who share their unique vision that other non-religious groups enjoy. To deny them the same right would be to discriminate against people on the basis that they are religious and have a religious rather than purely secular way of looking at the world.[2]

Two persons could hardly take more diametrically opposite positions on an issue. One says allowing faith-based providers of social services that receive government funding to hire based on their religious faith is discrimination; the other says not to allow them to do so is discrimination. One could suppose that these members of Congress differ so sharply on this issue because one or the other is misguided, ignorant, or has no interest in protecting the freedoms of Americans. Or they may be appealing to different constituencies or perhaps responding to the funders of their election campaigns. But I believe the answer lies elsewhere. Each was operating out of a mindset[3] that acted as a lens through which he viewed faith-based organizations operating in the public realm. That lens led each to the conclusions he held. These differing mindsets and the differing conclusions to which they lead are not limited to members of Congress, but are shared by judges, commentators on public affairs, academics, and the broad American public.

This chapter examines the roots—the seedbeds—of these differing mindsets by considering three key forces that have done much to mold Americans' understanding of faith-based organizations and their place in the public policy realm. I first consider the liberal eighteenth-century Enlightenment and how certain of its features influenced the thinking of the American founders, whose influence continues down to today. In this first section I also consider the nature of religion in the young nation and how it contributed to today's attitudes towards faith-based organizations. I next consider and critique how these underlying ways of thinking have helped shape Supreme Court decisions dealing with church-state relations, which, in turn, have done much both to set the legal context in which faith-based organizations operate and to mold the attitudes Americans hold towards them. Then, I turn to how the 1960s civil rights revolution and the nondiscrimination laws it spawned have had a major impact on—as is the case with Supreme Court decisions—both on the legal context in which faith-based organizations operate and the attitudes Americans hold toward them. Together these three forces have done much to shape the predominant assumptions and attitudes that we as a people bring to the table when we consider faith-based organizations, their role in the delivery of public services, and their religious autonomy. In chapter 4 I consider how these underlying forces and their resulting attitudes have, in more specific terms, molded the sharply different mindsets liberals and conservatives have taken towards faith-based organizations as providers of human services to the public and how these mindsets have led them to the differing policy positions they have taken.

THE LIBERAL ENLIGHTENMENT, THE FOUNDING ERA, AND THE YOUNG NATION

The beliefs and assumptions Americans hold in regard to faith-based social service providers, even today, have been deeply influenced by liberal Enlightenment thinking, the ways it influenced the American founders, and the nature of religion in the founding era and the early years of the nation. This section considers how these forces from America's past have shaped the thinking of Americans towards faith-based organizations. Understanding them is essential to understanding the conflicts and questions we are having problems resolving today.

The Eighteenth-Century Enlightenment in Europe

Classic liberalism arose out of the eighteenth-century Enlightenment, which reacted against both the religious wars that had plagued Europe and the aristocratic, authoritarian political regimes that ignored the needs and desires of the masses.[4] Faced with these challenges, the Enlightenment thinkers emphasized human reasoning over the acceptance of authoritarian structures, whether those of the church, the state, the class structure, or the craft and merchant guilds. It opposed with equal fervor the authoritarian church hierarchies of the day and aristocratic, authoritarian political regimes rooted in a rigid class structure and mercantilist economic policies. The French Revolution embodied these trends, as it opposed a repressive political structure, a rigid class structure, and an authoritarian church. This is understandable, since these entities were mutually supportive, opposing the stirrings of reform that were gathering strength. In place of authority structures the Enlightenment emphasized the ability of human reason, when applied to observing the world of nature and events, to understand truth and to create a better world. The intellectual historian Crane Brinton has described this liberal attitude: "Reason will enable us to find human institutions, human relations that are 'natural'; once we find such institutions, we shall conform to them and be happy. Reason will clear up the mess that superstition, revelation, and faith (the devils of the rationalists) have piled up here on earth."[5] Those who sought to defend existing, rigid ecclesiastical and political structures were to be rejected when their attempts conflicted with the free, independent-thinking, rational individual. Human beings would thereby achieve a level of freedom and happiness here on earth that earlier generations had been taught would only be attained in the afterlife.

Where did this leave the authoritarian political regimes of the day? They were to be freed from the control of the aristocratic classes and made subject to the will of the people, even though Enlightenment thinkers differed on who was included in "the people" and how their will was to be determined. Concerning religion, some leaders of the Enlightenment were completely dismissive of it, as when the leaders of the French Revolution stabled their horses in Notre Dame Cathedral and refused to date their calendar from the birth of Christ. Others held a more benign view of religion, even while opposing the religious hierarchies and structures of their day. They typically saw religion as a purely personal, private matter, and something best kept out of the public realm. But as long as some wished to observe religious practices and rituals in the privacy of their homes or churches, they had no objection and even saw such practices as potentially having the positive effect of making people more law-abiding and peaceful. But the liberal Enlightenment thinkers—with European religious wars fresh in their minds—were united in believing that religion in the public sphere was a dangerous, divisive factor.

Enlightenment thinkers also emphasized the individual over community or the collectivity. The collectivities of their day—the church, political regimes, craft and merchant guilds, and class structures—were oppressive of freedom of thought and action. The free, thinking individual was therefore seen in contrast to the organization or the group; only by breaking the bonds of church, guild, social class, authoritarian governments, and other societal structures could the individual be truly free.

The Eighteenth-Century Enlightenment and the American Founders

The Enlightenment was never a mass movement in the thirteen American colonies or later in the new, emerging nation. In eighteenth-century America, the massive religious revival known as the Great Awakening was a much more powerful movement among the people. But the Enlightenment had a huge influence among the educated elite. The American founders—such as George Washington, Benjamin Franklin, James Madison, and above all Thomas Jefferson—were men of the Enlightenment. They determined much of the intellectual and cultural trajectory of the new nation; their influence on American thinking on both the left and the right is still very much evident today.

The American founders were united in accepting four basic ideas born of the Enlightenment. First, they all made a distinction between the basic tenets of religion that taught morality and kindness towards others and the specific doctrines of the various religious groups present in colonial America. The former were important; the latter unimportant. Typical are Jefferson's words in a 1809 letter to James Fishback:

> Reading, reflection and time have convinced me that the interests of society require the observation of those moral precepts only in which all religions agree (for all forbid us to murder, steal, plunder, or bear false witness) and that we should not intermeddle with the particular dogmas in which all religions differ, and which are totally unconnected with morality.[6]

This emphasis on religion's potential as a uniting force that motivates persons to hold to beliefs and virtues essential for free, democratic government played an especially prominent role in the thinking of founders often referred to as civic republicans.[7] Founders such as George Washington and John Adams typified this attitude. Washington famously stated in his Farewell Address: "Of all the dispositions and habits which lead to political prosperity, religion and morality are indispensable supports. . . . [R]eason and experience both forbid us to expect that national morality can prevail in exclusion of religious principle."[8] Yet it was generalized religion, not religion in its specific manifestations, to which the founders looked.

Second, the American founders saw religious beliefs properly originating not in church authorities and formal creeds, but in individuals and their reason. Nowhere is this more clearly illustrated than in James Madison's famous "Memorial and Remonstrance," when he wrote these words as the first of his reasons to oppose a pending law that would have imposed a tax in Virginia to support the salaries of clergy:

> Because we hold it for a fundamental and undeniable truth, "that Religion or the duty which we owe our Creator and the Manner of discharging it, can be directed only by reason and conviction, not by force or violence." The Religion then of every man must be left to the conviction and conscience of every man; and it is the right of every man to exercise it as these may dictate. This right is in its nature an unalienable right. It is unalienable, because the opinions of men, depending only on the evidence contemplated by their own minds cannot follow the dictates of other men.[9]

"Every man" as the source of religious belief and practice is repeated three times by Madison in one sentence!

But it must be noted that the "reason" of "every man" to which the founders appealed was not abstract or philosophical reasoning, but closer to a common sense, intuitive reasoning. As Jefferson once wrote, "The practice of morality being necessary for the well-being of society, he [God] has taken care to impress its precept so indelibly on our hearts that they shall not be effaced by the subtleties of our brain."[10] This thinking can also be seen when Jefferson penned some of the most famous words ever written: "We hold these truths to be self-evident, that all men are endowed by their Creator with certain unalienable Rights, that among these are Life, Liberty and the pursuit of Happiness." These truths were self-evident to all individuals who with open minds observed and reflected on the world about them and looked into their own hearts.

Third, in an idea that emerged out of the first two ideas just mentioned, the leading American founders saw religion—outside of those universal moral precepts needed for civil peace—as a purely personal, private affair that should be of no concern of government. This thought was expressed by almost every one of the founders in a variety of ways. Thomas Buckley has summarized Jefferson's thought on this point and is worth quoting at length.

> Jefferson considered theological statements, whether made by church councils, creeds, or individuals, to be simply "opinion," based not on reason, but on revelations unacceptable to a thoughtful man. Churches define themselves on the basis of these differences, but they do not affect the public square. Whether you are Calvinist or Arminian, Trinitarian or Unitarian, pray in church or shout under the trees, sprinkle children over the font or dip adults in the creek, it does not touch your life as a citizen. In the Jeffersonian scheme of things, the religious dimension of personal belief was private, absolutely. He repeated it in a multitude of ways.[11]

Most of the American founders held views similar to this.

Fourth, the founders were united in having a strong commitment to the individual and individual rights at the expense of collectivities. They consistently extolled the individual and clearly had thought through and defended the freedoms and rights of individuals in numerous ways, but social structures tended not to enter their thoughts. Individuals loomed large in their thinking; collectivities did not. As already seen, churches and their leaders—outside of their contribution to civil peace and a general contribution to morality—were largely dismissed as irrelevant to the public life of the nation. John Witte and Joel Nichols quote from a letter Jefferson wrote John Adams and then note, "Such views were also based on the assumption that a person is fundamentally an individual being and religion is primarily a matter of private reason and conscience, and only secondarily a matter of communal association and corporate confession."[12] In fact, when the founders did refer to groups and organizations they almost always saw them as posing dangers. In his Farewell Address, George Washington warned against the danger of parties, which included both political parties and what today we call interest groups:

> I have already intimated to you the danger of parties in the state, with particular reference to the founding of them on geographical discriminations. Let me now take a more comprehensive view, and warn you in the most solemn manner against the baneful effects of the spirit of party, generally.
>
> This spirit, unfortunately, is inseparable from our nature, having its root in the strongest passions of the human mind. It exists under different shapes in all governments, more or less stifled, controlled, or repressed; but, in those of the popular form, it is seen in its greatest rankness, and is truly their worst enemy.[13]

James Madison, in his famous Federalist #10, also expressed the typical attitude of the day when he warned against "factions," and in so doing revealed his emphasis on the individual and dismissal of collectivities. He defined factions only in negative terms: "By a faction, I understand a number of citizens, whether amounting to a majority or minority of the whole, who are united and actuated by some common impulse of passion, or of interest, adverse to the rights of other citizens, or to the permanent and aggregate interest of the community."[14] He thereby defined factions in terms of opposition to the interest of the community, that is, the public interest or the common good. His worldview could not conceive of a faction—a group or organization—that could act to promote the broad public interest or the common good. Both Washington and Madison, along with the other founders, placed free individuals, with their common sense reasoning abilities, at the center of their political and social worldview.

In doing so the founders ignored what was literally under their own noses. Barry Shain has pointed out that a crucial part of the social picture during the colonial and founding eras was the existence of a very strong "local communalism."[15] In many ways, the villages with their congregations, family structures, and moral standards and practices were both communal and autonomous. As Shain has written concerning eighteenth-century America: "Most men and women continued to live within overlapping and concentric circles of family, congregation, neighborhood, parish, town, and county. This formed a thick communal network that made possible a good life."[16] This local communalism contributed positively to the new, emerging society and nation by helping make prosperous, growing towns and communities possible. But the leading founders simply took local communities and their social structures for granted, as just the way things were, and never really saw them as an important, contributing part of the American fabric. Influenced by liberal Enlightenment individualism, their thinking jumped directly from the individual—who was to be freed from the shackles of traditional authorities and groups and made into an autonomous, freely and rationally choosing citizen—to the nation, or at the least to the colony and later the state. They failed to see social collectivities as circles within which most persons live their lives and as the incubators of free, contributing citizens. Therefore, they never saw the need for their political and social theories to take social collectivities into account and assign them a role in the public life of the nation. Americans have struggled ever since to see organizations and groups as an important part of the fabric of society and relevant to public purposes, instead of as somewhat dangerous and potentially subversive of the public good.

Religion in the Founding Era and the Young Nation

The Great Awakening, beginning in the 1740s, was marked by itinerant preachers, mass religious meetings, and a surge of religious fervor, almost always outside of the "respectable," mainstream churches of the day. It resulted in a resurgence of evangelical religion in the colonies and in the explosive growth of new religious groups, especially Baptists and other new dissenting groups. Then, in the early decades of the nineteenth century, the young nation experienced the Second Great Awakening, marked by large religious camp meetings, a popularizing of the Christian faith, and the explosive growth in the numbers of believers and churches.[17] As historian Nathan Hatch relates: "The wave of popular religious movements that broke upon the United States in the half century after independence did more to Christianize American society than anything before or since."[18] The growth in churches, clergy, and believers was largely not among the well-established churches, such as Congregationalists, Episcopalians, and Presbyterians, but among newly arising churches and groups of churches, such as the Methodists, Christian Churches and Disciples of Christ, and various Baptist groups. Hatch reports that in a sixty-year period, from 1784 to 1845, the Methodists grew from a mere fourteen thousand members to over a million members, with almost four thousand itinerant preachers and 7,700 local preachers.[19] The Second Great Awakening especially flourished among the settlers of the newly opened frontier west of the Appalachian Mountains.

Given these vigorous religious movements—resulting in a renewal of faith and huge numbers of new, transformed, and revitalized believers—one would expect these dedicated believers and their leaders to have had a major impact on the founding era's and the new nation's ways of thinking, especially as they related to the role of religious faith and religious groups in society. But the undeniable fact is that they did not. Their failure to do so helps explain the attitudes that are still prevalent today towards faith-based organizations. Thus the story of why they failed to influence the intellectual life of the new nation is an important one for our purposes.

The Great Awakening of the eighteenth century did provide much of the popular impetus for disestablishing the traditional Congregational and Anglican churches and for fulfilling the founders' vision of church-state separation and religious freedom for all. Robert Bellah and his colleagues have noted: "It was undoubtedly pressure from the dissenting sects, with their large popular following, on the one hand, and from that significant portion of the educated and politically effective elite influenced by Enlightenment thought on the other, that finally led to the disestablishment of religion in the United States."[20] But, as Witte and Nichols point out, the new, evangelical churches "developed only the rudiments of a political theory. Most Evangelicals were content with a state that created a climate conducive to the cultivation of a plurality of religions and that accommodated all religious believers and religious bodies without conditions or controls."[21] They go on to point out that it was the "Enlightenment movement in America [that] provided a political theory that complemented the Evangelical theology of religious liberty."[22] This means the theoretical basis on which the religious groups gained their freedom was the Enlightenment-influenced pattern of seeing religion as an individual, private affair. Under the founders' assumptions, individuals were free to choose, teach, celebrate, and propagate their religious beliefs, but except for teachings of generalized morality and right conduct, those beliefs were to be kept purely private, with no implications for the public life of the nation. The historian Sidney Mead has described the result:

> It is hard to escape the conclusion that each religious group accepted, by implication, the responsibility to teach that its peculiar doctrines, which made it distinct from other sects and gave it its only reason for separate existence, were either irrelevant for the general welfare of the nation-community, or at most, possessed only an indirect and instrumental value for it. It is no wonder that a sense of irrelevance has haunted religious leaders in America ever since.[23]

Nor did the Second Great Awakening lead to political and social theories that defined a public role for religion and religiously based organizations. Two of its features help to explain why. First, it was an antielitist, populist, grass-roots religious revival. Hatch has described it well: "Christianity was effectively reshaped by ordinary people, who molded it in their own image and threw themselves into expanding its influence. Increasingly assertive common people wanted their leaders unpretentious, their doctrines self-evident and down-to-earth, their music lively and singable, their churches in local hands."[24] Second, in its antielitist nature, it appealed to a common sense rationalism that believed the village blacksmith could find religious truth and understand and interpret the Bible as well as—and probably better than —the most learned theologian. In Hatch's just-quoted description he refers to "self-evident" doctrines, that is, religious doctrines that were self-evident to reasonable, thoughtful persons using their common sense. Historian Mark Noll has referred to the evangelical dependence on "intuitive common sense, which was everywhere considered the basis for reliable knowledge."[25] Others have referred to a "Common Sense rationalism" that marked American religion of the era.[26] In this, the evangelical, revivalistic religion of the young nation shared a trait with the rationalism of the American founders—both looked to a common sense that found truth in what one could observe as being self-evident.

These two characteristics of the Second Great Awakening—its populist, antielitist nature and its reliance on common sense rationalism—made Christianity widely popular among the common people and imbued it with a down-to-earth flavor that relied on self-starting, popular leaders and undercut the authority of well-established, institutionalized churches. These characteristics had results whose importance is hard to overstate. Noll has expressed it succinctly: "The very character of the revival that made evangelical religion into a potent force in North America weakened its intellectual power."[27] With a revivalism that emphasized personal experience and the emotionalism of powerful preaching and popular singing, and with a theology that was reduced to a common sense, intuitive understanding of the Christian Scriptures, little room was left for theological reflection or political analysis. The very features that made the Christianity of the Second Great Awakening hugely popular also rendered it weak intellectually. Thus, when Christianity surged in numbers and potential influence in the young nation, and would have been in a position to develop social and political concepts informed by its faith, it failed to do so. The nineteenth century produced many notable preachers and revivalists—Francis Asbury, Alexander Campbell, Lorenzo Dow, and Charles Finney—but produced few, if any, notable theologians who are still read today.

The Legacy of the Founding Era and the Young Nation

The assumptions and patterns of thought that emerged out of the founding era and the early nineteenth century form a legacy that continues to exert a strong influence today on how we as a nation view faith-based organizations in public life. Three are especially important. Each poses certain problems that contribute to today's confusions and conflicts in regard to faith-based organizations and their religious autonomy.

First, *Americans tend to think not in terms of faith communities, but in terms of individuals and their religious beliefs and attachments.* The legacy of the founding era and the young nation rightly sees and protects individual religious rights—the right of individuals to choose and practice their religious faith—yet it fails to give sufficient weight to the fact that individual religious freedom is inescapably bound up with communal religious freedom: a failure to protect the latter means the denial of the former. With very few exceptions, religion is not simply a matter of individual choice and belief but is rooted in communities of faith and traditions stretching back for centuries. The faith of Orthodox Jews, for instance, is not something that persons create and practice as individuals. Rather, their faith integrates them into a millennia-old tradition and places them into a specific community of faith, with distinctive beliefs, norms, social interactions, and patterns of behavior. In addition, communities of faith almost without exception are embodied in concrete organizations: in churches, synagogues, mosques, denominations, missions, schools, and human service organizations that are independently organized yet deeply rooted in specific faith communities. Attempts to protect the religious freedom of individuals without protecting the religious freedom of the faith communities and religious associations within which faith is given birth, nurtured, practiced, and passed on from one generation to the next make no sense. Yet the legacy of the founding era and the young nation have left Americans ill-equipped to understand the role organized religious groups and their faith-based organizations play in securing and protecting religious freedom.

A second aspect of the legacy that emerged out of the founding era and the early days of the nation is *an assumption that religion, other than a generic civic faith, is a purely private matter, with no real role to play in the public realm of public policies and issues.* It is hard to overstate the importance of this legacy. The American founders accepted religious pluralism as something good, not something to be opposed. Today we still accept and even celebrate the religious pluralism of American society. And references to a broad, generic God that protects and guides the nation are not only acceptable, but expected. But when religion seeks to enter the public policy world in its distinctive, particularistic forms, it is seen as a danger and a threat—somewhat like the proverbial bull that has wandered out of his pasture and into a china shop. The attitude that Stanley Fish once described continues to find support in the United States:

> When the liberal citizen exits the private realm and enters the public square, he or she is supposed to leave religious commitments behind and function as a stripped-down entity, as an abstract-not-full personage, who makes political decisions not as a Jew or a Christian or a Muslim but as what political scientist Michael Sandel calls an "unencumbered self," a self unencumbered by ethnic, racial, gender, class or religious identities.[28]

As a result, persons who bring religion into public discussions and debates are quickly challenged not on their logic or the improper use of religious beliefs or categories, but on the very act of using religious beliefs or categories in political discussions and debates.

For example, when in 1999 George W. Bush in one of his presidential campaign debates responded to a question by saying Jesus Christ was his favorite political philosopher, many reacted with raised eyebrows, embarrassment, or outright incredulity. The *New York Times* columnist Maureen Dowd characterized Bush's response in these words: "When you take something deeply personal and parade it for political gain, you are guilty either of cynicism or exhibitionism."[29] She went on to dismiss Bush's opponent in that election, Al Gore, for stating he was a born-again Christian: "Mr. Gore has sunk to the same level on religion."[30] This columnist assumed the only motive for candidates for public office to bring their religious faith into their campaigns was to cynically manipulate the voters. Her mindset could not conceive of any legitimate role for religious faith in public life. Dowd went on to praise President John Kennedy for having "vowed to keep a wall between church and state: 'I believe in a president whose views on religion are his own private affairs.'"[31] Religion is all right and free to flourish in one's private life; it is not to be brought into our leaders' public lives. The only religion that is seen as fully legitimate in the public realm is a tamed, generic, consensual, civil religion, marked by general references to a God whom "we trust" and can be called upon at times of national crisis or stress, and to whom politicians can refer when they need to burnish their religious credentials. We shall meet this attitude many times in later chapters.

There are, however, two ways in which viewing religion as a purely private matter is historically, factually inaccurate if taken as a description of reality. First, all of the major religious voices in the United States today—Catholicism, mainline Protestantism, African-American Protestantism, evangelical Protestantism, Reform Judaism, Orthodox Judaism, and Islam—in fact see their faiths as highly relevant to the public policy issues of the day. They speak to issues of poverty, war and peace, health care, HIV-AIDS, immigration, natural disasters at home and abroad, and global climate change and other environmental challenges.

Documents from both the evangelical Protestant and Roman Catholic traditions—the two largest religious traditions in the United States—also make the needed point. A document officially adopted by the National Association of Evangelicals states: "We also engage in public life because Jesus is Lord over every area of life. . . . To restrict our stewardship to the private sphere would be to deny an important part of his dominion and to functionally abandon it to the Evil One. To restrict our political concerns to matters that touch only on the private and the domestic spheres is to deny the all-encompassing Lordship of Jesus."[32] This document later goes on to state that "we owe each other help in time of need" and points out: "Though the Bible does not call for economic equality, it condemns gross disparities in opportunity and outcome that cause suffering and perpetuate poverty, and calls us to work toward equality of opportunity."[33] Similarly, a document put out by the United States Conference of Catholic Bishops states: "In the Catholic Tradition, responsible citizenship is a virtue, and participation in the political life is a moral obligation. . . . We are called to bring together our principles and our political choices, our values and our votes, to help build a better world."[34] It later goes on to insist: "A basic moral test for our society is how we treat the most vulnerable in our midst. . . . Scripture gives us the story of the Last

Judgment and reminds us that we will be judged by our response to the 'least among us.'"[35]

A second way in which American religion is, in practice, not simply a personal, privatized affair is that throughout American history, faith-based groups have been active in providing a variety of educational, health, and other human services to the public. The famous nineteenth-century French observer of American life and government, Alexis de Tocqueville, wrote in an often-quoted passage:

> Americans of all ages, all conditions, and all dispositions constantly form associations. They have not only commercial and manufacturing companies, in which all take part, but associations of a thousand other kinds, religious, moral, serious, futile, general or restricted, enormous or diminutive. The Americans make associations to give entertainments, to found seminaries, to build inns, to construct churches, to diffuse books, to send missionaries to the antipodes; in this manner they found hospitals, prisons, and schools. If it is proposed to inculcate some truth or to foster some feeling by the encouragement of great examples, they form a society.[36]

What is often missed is that many of the examples Tocqueville gave here are religious associations and what we today would call faith-based human service organizations. In addition, chapter 2 of this book documented the many faith-based organizations that continue today to play a vital role in the provision of needed services to the public.

In short, now and through American history faith communities have been active in the public realm by advocating for certain public policies and by providing relief, help, education, and healing to the public. Factually, in practice, religion is not a purely private, personal affair, but has clear and distinct public facets to it. Yet this public face of religious faith continues to struggle to find a fully accepted place in the United States' public square. Pluralism and diversity, when religiously based, are thereby often wrongly limited in the public life of the nation.

These first two legacies, when combined, lead to a third: namely, *the lack of a thought-out, carefully considered theory that defines the place of religion and religious associations in the public life of the nation.* Such a theory would define the place of religious communities and organizations in securing religious freedom for all, the relationship between organizational religious freedom and individual religious freedom, and the rightful, legitimate role that religion, religious organizations, and religious beliefs can and should play in the public life of a democratic, pluralistic nation. The founders assumed religion, outside of generalized principles of morality, was irrelevant to and even dangerous in the public realm; the leaders and the multitudes generated by the First and Second Great Awakenings were content as long as their freedom to preach and form churches was protected. Their popularized, intellectually thin version of Christianity—while helping the popularity of their faith—worked against the formation of theoretical insights that defined and defended their position in the public realm.

As a result, one of the paradoxes of American life even today is that most faith traditions believe their faith speaks to the public policies being pursued by the government and that a wide variety of religious congregations and innumerable faith-based human service organizations continue to thrive. But they do so without a thought-out, explicitly articulated theory or set of ideas that supports their role in the public life of the nation. In terms of the patterns of thought typical of most Americans—and especially the academic and media elite—faith-based public policy positions and faith-based human service organizations are rendered, as it were, orphans. There is no rich vein of political and social theories, concepts, or political traditions that faith-based organizations can draw upon to define their place in public life and defend their right to an institutional autonomy that guarantees their religious freedom rights.

THE SUPREME COURT, CHURCH-STATE RELATIONS, AND FAITH-BASED ORGANIZATIONS

The Supreme Court and its decisions on church-state relations in general and on faith-based organizations in particular are a crucial part of the context within which faith-based organizations operate and their religious autonomy is defined. In its decisions, the Supreme Court both reflects and molds popular and elite attitudes towards church-state relations generally and, more specifically, the religious freedom rights of both individuals and faith-based organizations. This section examines how the legacy bequeathed the nation by the founding era and the young nation continues to be reflected in the Supreme Court and its decisions. But it also considers how the answers given by the American founders was to a different question than the one being raised today by faith-based organizations and their place in the mix of public services. The result is a threatened diminution of religious freedom and competing lines of reasoning among Supreme Court decisions.

The Strict Separation, No-Aid-to-Religion Standard

In a seminal 1947 case, Everson v. Board of Education, Justice Hugo Black, writing for the Supreme Court majority, declared in ringing words:

No tax in any amount, large or small, can be levied to support any religious activities or institutions, whatever they may be called, or whatever form they may adopt to teach or practice religion. Neither a state nor the Federal Government can, openly or secretly, participate in the affairs of any religious organization or group and vice versa. In the words of Jefferson the clause against establishment of religion by law was intended to erect "a wall of separation between Church and State.". . . That wall must be kept high and impregnable.[37]

He later went on to claim that the Court would not allow the "slightest breach" in that wall.[38]

Note the near absolute language. *No tax in any amount, large or small* could be used to support *any* religious institutions or activities. Religion was to be a private matter, unsubsidized by the state, and with a wall between them. The position originally expressed by the American founders such as Madison and Jefferson—who were cited and quoted in the decision—clearly guided the Court. The Supreme Court thereby laid down no-aid-to-religion as a bedrock principle and as an end in itself. It is hard to overstate the subsequent influence of this decision and the language Justice Black used.

In a series of decisions in the 1960s and 1970s, the Supreme Court took hold of this strict separation, no-aid-to-religion language and insisted the First Amendment was violated whenever the government would either subsidize religious organizations or would itself support or encourage religion. Most of these decisions involved K-12 education. One of the key cases dealt with state government funding programs for religiously based K-12 schools in Rhode Island and Pennsylvania. These states sought to get around the no-aid-to-religion strictures of the Everson decision by providing funds only for teaching "secular" subjects. But in 1971 the Supreme Court struck down both states' programs. It declared that the teachers in the religious schools might be able to "segregate their religious beliefs from their secular educational responsibilities" but it would be difficult for them to do so and "the potential for impermissible fostering of religion is present."[39] Given this fact, the states would constantly have to monitor classrooms to assure that subsidized subjects did not have any religious content, and that would lead to an unhealthy entanglement of church and state. The continuing impact of the American founders' Enlightenment thinking can be seen in the Court's insistence that religion must be kept a private matter: "The Constitution decrees that religion must be a private matter for the individual, the family, and the institutions of private choice."[40]

The Supreme Court has if anything been even stricter in ruling against a series of attempts to introduce some form of religion into the public schools. In the 1960s, it found both a simple, religiously generic prayer used in New York schools and the reading of the Bible and use of the Lord's Prayer in public schools to be unconstitutional.[41] In the latter case, Justice William Douglas clearly invoked the no-funding-of-religion principle when he wrote in a concurring opinion that "public funds, though small in amount, are being used to promote a religious exercise. Through the mechanism of the State, all of the people are being required to finance a religious exercise that only some of the people want and that violates the sensibilities of others."[42] In later decisions, the Court held that a prayer at a public school graduation ceremony, a student-led prayer prior to a school football game, and even a moment of silence at the beginning of the school day were all unconstitutional.[43] The Court has also ruled against the teaching of creation accounts in science classes and the posting of the Ten Commandments in public school classrooms.[44]

But this is far from the complete story. The Supreme Court has also frequently approved as passing First Amendment review a number of laws and programs that would appear to offer support, recognition, or financial support to religious institutions or practices. It has approved financial aid to religiously based colleges, tax credits for money parents spend to send their children to faith-based schools, vouchers to parents of children that can be used pay for their education at faith-based schools, a municipally owned crèche displayed during the Christmas season, prayers at the start of legislative sessions by a state-paid chaplain, and the display of the Ten Commandments on the grounds of a state capitol. It has done so while still attempting to maintain the no-aid-to-religion as a bedrock principle by the use of three additional principles or standards.

One such principle is the sacred-secular distinction that the Supreme Court rejected as unworkable in the case of K-12 education. This principle says that if a faith-based school or other organization separates out certain secular programs or activities from its religious ones, government may fund the secular ones without violating the First Amendment. It is on this basis that the Supreme Court in three separate decisions approved funding for religiously affiliated colleges and universities.[45] The money was only going to support the teaching of secular, nonreligious subjects. Similarly, the Court approved programs that loaned state-paid, purely secular textbooks to religiously based K-12 schools and granted funds to faith-based programs seeking to reduce teenage pregnancies as long as the money was only going to secular aspects of the programs.[46]

A second basis on which the Supreme Court has sometimes upheld financial support for faith-based organizations while still upholding the strict separation, no-aid-to-religion standard is the direct versus indirect distinction. The Court has upheld the constitutionality of a number of programs that resulted in government funds going to faith-based organizations, as long as the government was not directly disbursing the money to the organizations, but the funds were instead finding their way to the organizations by an indirect process based on the choices of private individuals. In 1983, the Supreme Court approved a tax credit program in Minnesota for expenses parents incurred in sending their children to K-12 schools, whether public or private schools (including religiously based schools). Justice William Rehnquist wrote in the Court's majority opinion: "Where, as here, aid to parochial schools is available only as a result of decisions of individual parents no 'imprimatur of State approval,' can be deemed to have been conferred on any particular religion, or on religion generally."[47] The most important Supreme Court decision based on the direct-indirect distinction occurred in 2002 when the Court, in a close 5 to 4 vote, approved a voucher program in Cleveland, Ohio, that granted low-income parents of children in failing schools certificates that paid for their education in alternative nonpublic schools, most of which were faith-based. The Court largely based its decision on the direct-indirect distinction: "Our decisions have drawn a consistent distinction between government programs that provide aid directly to religious schools, and programs of true private choice, in which government aid reaches religious schools only as a result of the genuine and independent choices of private individuals."[48]

The Supreme Court has also allowed some limited forms of cooperation and acknowledgment of religion in spite of its no-aid-to-religion standard, as when it held constitutional a paid chaplain who offered prayers at the beginning of Nebraska legislative sessions and a nativity crèche as part of a Christmas display in Pawtucket, Rhode Island. [49] It did so on the basis of a third consideration (calling it a principle is too strong), namely, long traditions, the innocuous nature of these recognitions of religion, and—in the case of the crèche—the presence of other nonreligious Christmas season symbols which distracted from any religious message present. The Court seemed to be saying that in these cases the religious character of the challenged action was overshadowed by long tradition or secular elements that were also present. No one would really take their religious message all that seriously. This idea was once articulated in embarrassingly clear terms by Justice William Brennan in a dissenting opinion: "I would suggest that such practices as the designation of 'In God We Trust' as our national motto, or the references to God contained in the Pledge of Allegiance to the flag can best be understood . . . as a form a 'ceremonial deism,' protected from Establishment Clause scrutiny chiefly because they have lost through rote repetition any significant religious content."[50] That which is religious is, by a wave of the judicial pen, rendered nonreligious.

The Equal Treatment, Neutrality Standard

What has been related thus far is, however, only part of the story of Supreme Court church-state jurisprudence. There is another entire line of reasoning

that the Supreme Court has since the 1980s increasingly relied upon in decid-
ing church-state cases. This is the equal treatment, evenhandedness, or neutrality standard (it has gone by various names).

In a mark of the difficulty the Supreme Court has had in dealing with
church-state issues, the 1947 Everson decision that enshrined the wall of
separation in Supreme Court jurisprudence and articulated the no-aid-to-
religion standard in clear, near-absolute terms—both of which have had
an enormous influence in subsequent law and popular attitudes—was also
the first decision that clearly articulated this counter line of reasoning. The
specific issue at stake in the Everson case was the constitutionality of New
Jersey subsidizing the transportation of children to attend faith-based K-12
schools. Thus it is more than a little ironic that after the ringing words we
saw earlier declaring that any and all aid to religion and religious organizations is a violation of the Establishment Clause, the Supreme Court approved
New Jersey's subsidy for the transportation of children to religiously based
schools. It did so on the basis of the neutrality principle, which it described in
these words: "[New Jersey] cannot exclude individual Catholics, Lutherans,
Mohammedans, Baptists, Jews, Methodists, Non-believers, Presbyterians,
or the members of any other faith, because of their faith, or lack of it, from
receiving the benefits of public welfare legislation."[51] It went on to state that
the First Amendment "requires the state to be a neutral in its relations with
groups of religious believers and non-believers; it does not require the state to
be their adversary. State power is no more to be used so as to handicap religions than it is to favor them."[52] And this standard was to be followed even
if a state's actions in some way benefited religion or religious institutions.
The Court thereby upheld New Jersey's subsidizing of bus transportation of
children to faith-based schools on the grounds that this was a general public
benefit, available equally to all children and their parents.

Although the no-aid principle tended to dominate Supreme Court decisions
in the 1960s and 1970s, things began to change in the 1980s, and today the
no-aid and the equal treatment, neutrality principles are vying for dominance.
An important case that first gave renewed impetus to the equal treatment,
neutrality line of reasoning was a 1981 case in which the Court held that a
religious student group at the University of Missouri at Kansas City could not
be denied access to on-campus meeting rooms that all other students groups
enjoyed.[53] It did so on the basis that the university, once it had created a setting where students groups could organize and use campus facilities, could
not exclude religious groups. Equal treatment would have to prevail. In a
similar case, the Court ruled that a parent-initiated, voluntary after-school
religious club for elementary school students could not be excluded from
using school facilities, as long as the school allowed other community groups

to use its facilities.[54] Again, equal treatment or neutrality among religious and secular groups and activities trumped a rigid no-aid to all things religious.

The most important case in this line of reasoning was a 1995 case in which the Supreme Court, in a 5 to 4 decision, held that when the University of Virginia established a policy of funding a variety of student publications, it could not exclude a publication that was clearly religious in nature. It did so on the basis that offering funds to a wide range of nonreligious publications but refusing to fund religious ones amounted to unconstitutional discrimination. Justice Sandra Day O'Connor, in a concurring opinion, accurately defined the question at issue: "This case lies at the intersection of the principle of government neutrality and the prohibition of state funding of religious activities."[55] The Court majority decided this case on the basis of governmental neutrality, not no-aid-to-religion. Justice Anthony Kennedy, speaking for the Court majority, articulated the neutrality principle in unmistakable terms:

> A central lesson of our [prior] decisions is that a significant factor in upholding governmental programs in the face of Establishment Clause attack is their neutrality towards religion. . . . We have held that the guarantee of neutrality is respected, not offended, when the government, following neutral criteria and evenhanded policies, extends benefits to recipients whose ideologies and viewpoints, including religious ones, are broad and diverse.[56]

The opinion went on to declare: "The governmental program here is neutral toward religion."[57]

Writing for the four dissenting justices, Justice David Souter saw clearly that the neutrality principle, which the five majority justices followed, clearly clashed with the no-aid-to-religion principle, which the dissenting justices would have followed. His dissent begins with these words: "The Court today, for the first time, approves direct funding of core religious activities by an arm of the State."[58] He also saw that the Court's position was based on neither the sacred-secular distinction nor the direct-indirect distinction discussed earlier: "Even when the Court has upheld aid to an institution performing both secular and sectarian functions, it has always made a searching enquiry that the institutions kept the secular activities separate from its sectarian ones, with any direct aid flowing only to the former and never the latter."[59] One can question the accuracy of Souter's claim that in previous cases the Court had *always* used the sacred-secular distinction and had insisted that *no* direct aid could be used for religious purposes, but he certainly is accurate in pointing out that in this case those two distinctions were not being followed. The Court majority followed the neutrality, equal treatment, evenhandedness principle, and in doing so it gave that principle—which is in competition with the wall of separation, no-aid-to-religion principle—one of its clearest articulations.

There have been other cases upholding this same neutrality principle. For instance, as seen earlier in the Cleveland school voucher case of 2002, a key element was the indirect nature of the government funds going to religiously based schools. But the Court also relied upon neutrality in its reasoning: "In sum the Ohio program is entirely neutral with respect to religion. It provides benefits directly to a wide spectrum of individuals, defined only by financial need and residence in a particular school district. It permits such individuals to exercise genuine choice among options public and private, secular and religious."[60]

Legal scholar Jeffrey Rosen has stated that "the era of strict separation is over" and has referred to "the collapse of the wall of separation."[61] He went on to contend: "The Supreme Court is on the verge of replacing the principle of strict separation with a very different constitutional principle that demands equal treatment for religion."[62] Rosen, while not inaccurate, may have overstated the situation. The Supreme Court has usually applied the neutrality line of reasoning only in cases where the freedom of expression was somehow at issue, and rarely in cases where the issue dealt with faith-based human service agencies and their right to receive government funding or recognition on the same terms as their secular counterparts. Nor, as we will shortly see, has the neutrality, equal treatment principle gained the same level of notice and acceptance among the American public and academic and media elites as has the no-aid, wall-of-separation principle. Nevertheless, the neutrality line of reasoning has been increasingly used by the Court in recent years and has the potential to replace the no-aid line of reasoning as the key standard for judging the constitutionality of programs that help fund the educational and human service programs of faith-based organizations.

The Accommodationist Standard

There is a third standard, one that the Supreme Court has never embraced, but one that some justices on the Court have advanced and—as we will see in the next chapter—many on the political right have supported. This is what has been termed the accommodationist position. It argues that there is no constitutional, First Amendment problem when government recognizes or supports religion, as long as it is recognizing or supporting a generalized religion that does not favor one faith over another. Justice William Rehnquist in 1985 once expressed this position in a dissenting opinion: "The Establishment Clause did not require government neutrality between religion and irreligion nor did it prohibit the Federal Government from providing nondiscriminatory aid to religion. There is simply no historical foundation for the proposition that the Framers intended to build the 'wall of separation' that was constitutionalized in Everson."[63] Rehnquist went on to conclude: "Nothing in the Establishment Clause of the First Amendment, properly understood, prohibits any such generalized 'endorsement' of prayer."[64]

The accommodationist position, although popular among many conservatives—especially within what has been termed the religious right—has not gained much support among Supreme Court justices, and those justices opposed to the strict separation, no-aid-to-religion position have in recent years tended to rely upon the equal treatment, neutrality standard, not the accommodationist standard.

In summary, there are today three competing lines of reasoning struggling for dominance on the Supreme Court. One takes a strict church-state separation and no-aid-to-religion as *the* bedrock principle for guiding church-state relations, including government's relations with faith-based human service organizations. A line of reasoning gaining acceptance on the Court in recent years argues the key guiding principle should be the equal treatment or neutrality principle that says government ought not to favor one religion over another or neither secular nor religious points of view or organizations over the other. A third line of reasoning that has sometimes been put forward—the accommodationist—says that government may favor and even support religion, as long as it is a generalized support that does not favor any particular religious tradition. This book argues that if the religious autonomy of faith-based organizations is to be protected, the Supreme Court and the American polity need to follow the equal treatment, neutrality principle, not the strict separation, no-aid-to-religion position nor the accommodationist position. But first we need to recognize and understand why the strict separation, no-aid principle continues to exert a strong pull on the American people—especially among the academic and media elites—and why it is an inadequate standard for protecting religious freedom for all in today's world. These are the topics of the next two sections.

The Continuing Strength of the Strict Separation, No-Aid-to-Religion Standard

A recent study reported of the general public, when asked if they favor a high wall of separation between church and state, that majorities in the 60 to 70 percent range agreed, and that nearly one-half to two-thirds thought there should be no government help for religion.[65] The study also revealed that among academic, business, media, and government elites the support for no government help for religion and for a high wall of separation was even higher—in the 80 to 95 percent range.[66] Thomas Jefferson's "wall of separation"—which was raised to a principle of constitutional interpretation in the

Supreme Court's Everson decision—has come to be deeply embedded in the American understanding of church-state relations. In spite of the neutrality standard to which the Supreme Court has increasingly turned in recent years, it is still the strict separation, no-aid standard that dominates in the *New York Times* editorial offices and, for the most part, the elite law schools and academic departments. It remains an ingrained part of the American attitude on matters of church and state.

There are three reasons why the wall of separation, no-aid-to-religion standard continues to resonate so well in the American polity. One is its clear, vivid, unambiguous nature. If government is not to favor one religion over another and is to stay out of the conflicts and squabbles among the multitude of religions and religious organizations in the United States, it should simply stay on its side of the wall. If it does not try to intervene in religious matters or favor or aid one religious group or another, it will remain neutral on matters of religion. What could be simpler or clearer? As we will shortly see, matters in fact are neither simple nor clear, but there is a surface simplicity and clarity that is appealing.

A second reason explaining why the wall of separation, no-aid-to-religion position resonates so strongly with Americans is that it seems to line up well with the position of key American founders discussed earlier—persons such as James Madison and Thomas Jefferson. It was Jefferson himself who first used the phrase, "wall of separation," in an 1802 letter to the Danbury Baptists.[67] Madison famously wrote that "the same authority which can force a citizen to contribute three pence only of his property for the support of any one establishment [of religion], may force him to conform to any other establishment in all cases whatsoever."[68] And the American founders, as we saw earlier, were deeply influenced by Enlightenment thinking that failed to see religion as rooted in communities of faith and embodied in organized structures. They saw religion—outside of support for a generalized sense of morality and good conduct—as a purely individual, private matter and of no concern of government. Thus to ignore the role of collectivities in the lives of the faithful and to wall religion off from government would do no harm to religion, since it operates in an individual, private sphere. This attitude is still prevalent in the United States today.

A third factor encouraging the wall of separation, no-aid-to-religion attitude lies in the fact that—as originally applied to churches and clergy in their practice and dissemination of their core religious teachings, celebrations and rituals—it proved in practice to be beneficial to government and religion both. It spared the United States many of the religious conflicts other nations have endured and probably contributed to the vitality of religion in the United States down to today. When, at the founding and in the early days of the nineteenth century, American governments got out of the business of trying to support churches or clergy, it proved to be good for both the nation and for religion.

All three of these considerations have worked to ingrain into the American political culture the idea that both the state and religion are better off when there is a wall between them and government stays out of the business of trying to aid and abet religion, and religion does not look to government for validation and support. At this point the conclusion seems obvious. The wall of separation, no-aid-to-religion principle has served us well and is good for both religion and society. There is no more to be said. Case closed. Or so it would seem.

The Inadequacy of the Strict Separation, No-Aid-to-Religion Standard

But there is much more to be said and the case is anything but closed. Understanding why is crucial for grasping the nature and extent of the religious autonomy of faith-based organizations, especially when they are working in partnership with government. Therefore, this section carefully explores problems with the strict separation, no-aid-to-religion standard as the bedrock principle supporting religious freedom. Basic to these problems is one observation and two changes in the factual situation from two hundred or even seventy-five years ago. All three points are of vital importance.

The observation is this: *a total or absolute separation between church and state has never existed and is neither possible nor desirable.* Even the most ardent strict separationist does not advocate this. When a church catches fire, the city's fire department rushes to put it out, thereby saving churches huge amounts on their fire insurance; similarly, police departments provide traffic control and protection for churches and religious events. Cities in a sense subsidize churches, synagogues, mosques, and nonprofit faith-based organizations by providing them not only fire and police protection but also services such as water and sewage. Also, churches and other centers for worship must meet local fire and safety building codes, enforced by local building inspectors. Clergy and other religious officials can be prosecuted for crimes such as embezzlement or child abuse. Church-based child care centers must meet state and local standards for such centers. When a well-known religious leader such as the Pope visits a city or massive religious rallies are held, police provide security and traffic control. Faith-based organizations can qualify for 501(c)(3) nonprofit status, but they must apply to the Internal Revenue Service for that status and must meet various government-imposed standards to achieve it. Also, as seen earlier, churches and religious leaders often speak out forcefully for or against certain public policies being pursued by the government, exercising what is often called a prophetic voice that speaks truth to power. Now, and throughout American history, there have been interactions of many and varied types between church and state. No one argues against this.

This leads to a very basic question: By what standards can—and should—we judge what are proper and improper interactions between church and state? No one objected when in 2008 the police provided security for the Pope when he celebrated the mass in Yankee Stadium; all would object if New York City government would subsidize the utility bills at St. Patrick's Cathedral or pay the salaries of its priests. But on what basis do we rule one type of subsidy in and the other out? The wall-of-separation, no-aid-to-religion standard has no clear answer. To the extent it insists on a total separation and an absolute no-aid answer, religious persons and organizations would be denied protections and services all other persons and organizations enjoy; to the extent it allows protections and services to religious persons and organizations it seems to go against its own standard with weak explanations for why and no guidance on how far such protections and services may go.

In addition, two changes in the factual situation have occurred since the emergence of Jefferson's and Madison's strict separation, no-aid-to-religion standard. As a result, the answer given at the American founding and largely adopted by the Supreme Court in the mid-twentieth century was a response to a different situation than the one now present in the early years of the twenty-first century. One change is that *the deepest, most consequential religious divide in American society today is no longer between various religious traditions, but between persons who hold to traditional religious beliefs and practices and persons who hold to secularized beliefs and practices.* The most important religious divides are no longer between the religious categories that used to be crucial in American society: Catholics versus Protestants, certain Protestant denominations versus others, or Christians versus Jews. These old religious divides are being replaced—to simplify a bit—by a religionist versus secularist divide. Sociologist James Davison Hunter has written that "the secularists . . . represent the fastest growing community of 'moral conviction' in America."[69] He went on to point out that the most basic, emerging religious division in the United States is between religiously traditional Catholics, Protestants, and Jews and more modernist, secularly-oriented Catholics, Protestants, and Jews—plus those of no religious faith.[70] The Pew Forum on Religion and Public Life found in 2010 that a little over 16 percent of the population is not affiliated with any particular religion, leading it to observe: "They thus comprise the fourth largest 'religious' tradition in the United States, nearly approximating the number of members of mainline Protestant churches."[71] In 1993 already *Newsweek* magazine estimated that roughly 30 percent of the population can for most intents and purposes be considered secular.[72] A more recent study also found that a little over 30 percent of the population was largely secularized in the sense that they neither attended religious services regularly nor engaged in personal, private prayer.[73]

One ought not to assume that all persons falling in the 30 percent "secular" camp are secular in the sense of being atheists or agnostics and with no use for religion. Instead, among them are those with nominal religious affiliations and those who are unaffiliated with any religion but who believe in God and consider themselves "spiritual" in an individual, personal sense. The Pew Forum found that almost 6 percent of the population has no religious affiliation yet consider themselves to be religious.[74] Thus in labeling about 30 percent of the population as being secular, I am using the term loosely to include both those who are secular in an explicit, thought-out sense and those who could be considered "functionally secular" in the sense that traditional, organized religion does not play a significant role in their lives and systems of belief.

On the other side of the divide are those who are religious in a traditional sense, whether Catholic, Protestant, Jewish or of some other religion. They belong to an organized religious body, attend religious services regularly, and engage in such religious acts as private prayer and reading of sacred scriptures. One study has estimated that about 38 percent of Americans belong to a religious congregation, attend religious services, and engage in private prayer.[75]

The changing nature of the religious divisions in the United States carries with it an enormous but often unrecognized significance for church-state principles. The strict separation, no-aid-to-religion principle would be reasonable if the only question was maintaining governmental fairness or evenhandedness between different religious traditions and groups (all would be treated the same), but problems arise when it is applied to a society where the deepest and most consequential religious divide is between traditional religionists and persons who, broadly speaking, are secularists. Traditional religionists are put at a disadvantage by the strict separation, no-aid standard (their beliefs and organizations are not able to be accommodated or aided by the government) as compared to the secularists (their beliefs and organizations are able to be accommodated and aided by the government). I will develop this point more fully later, but first a second change in the factual situation from earlier years must be considered.

This second crucial change in the situation from the founding era is that *the strict separation, no-aid-to-religion principle that emerged out of the founding era was an answer to a different question than the one the United States faces today.* At the time of the American founding the issue was whether or not government ought to fund and in other ways favor either a particular denomination and its clergy or churches and their clergy generally. The issue was the funding of churches and clergy in their core religious rituals and ceremonies, conducted for their own members. Those colonies—and soon to become states—with established churches not only financially supported certain churches but also passed regulations that favored them or in some ways regulated them. James Madison's famous "Memorial and Remonstrance" was written in opposition to a proposal introduced into the Virginia legislature by Patrick Henry that would have imposed a tax to broadly fund churches and clergy. The position urged upon the emerging nation by James Madison, Thomas Jefferson, and others was that the government should neither fund nor regulate the churches. Church and state were to be separate. Although the new Constitution and its quickly-added Bill of Rights did not forbid the states from having established churches, most did not, and by 1833 the last state to have an established church abandoned this practice. Today no one doubts the wisdom of the separation of church and state of this nature. Government is neither to fund nor regulate religious congregations and their clergy in their core religious celebrations and rituals. Madison and Jefferson—not the position advocated by Patrick Henry—prevailed and both religion and government are the better for it.

But the issue the United States is facing today is not that of the funding or regulation of religious congregations in their core religious rituals and ceremonies but of the funding and regulation of religiously rooted organizations that are providing educational and other human services to the general public. These faith-based organizations providing public services are usually not churches or other religious congregations. Instead, they are usually parachurch or other independent organizations but with roots in a certain religious tradition or faith community (often with their own 501(c)(3) status).[76] These faith-based organizations are providing public services that are similar or parallel to those the government itself, secular nonprofit agencies, and for-profit companies are offering the public. There are, for example, hospitals run by faith-based organizations, cities and counties, secular nonprofit groups, and for-profit firms. The same is true of drug and alcohol rehab programs, spouse abuse shelters, welfare-to-work programs, and many other human service organizations and programs.

But does it make any difference that in the past two hundred years the church-state question has shifted from the funding and regulation of churches and other religious congregations in their core religious practices conducted for their own members to the funding and regulation of parachurch organizations providing a host of human services to the public? It makes an enormous difference.

Taking the regulatory function of government first, government has an obligation to protect the public's health and safety by regulating, in one way or another, hospitals, health clinics, drug treatment programs, homeless shelters, adoption agencies, child care centers, and other such human services agencies, and programs. A Catholic hospital should not be allowed to permit an unlicensed physician to perform surgery; a Jewish child care program should not be allowed to hire a convicted sex offender as a care giver; an evangelical Protestant homeless shelter should not be allowed to serve meals from an unsanitary kitchen. No one disputes the need for such regulations of faith-based providers of services to the public. Even in the case of religious congregations, some government regulation is recognized as good and acceptable. For example, no one challenges the right of local governments to insist on clearly marked exits in a church or synagogue sanctuary or on electrical systems that meet local building codes. Yet government regulation of religious congregations has been minimal. Congregations do not even have to file annual reports with the Internal Revenue Service, as do other nonprofit organizations. In that way we continue to follow the standard laid down in the founding era.

The central question that remains unresolved and continues to be a source of intense debate concerns parachurch and other faith-based human service agencies providing services to the public, not churches and other religious congregations in their core religious rituals and celebrations. The question being posed today concerns the extent to which the regulatory arm of government can and should reach them. As seen in chapter 1, the form this question usually takes today concerns government regulations that require a faith-based organization to provide services or to act in ways that are contrary to its deeply held moral convictions. To put the question in more general terms: Should faith-based organizations be exempted from nondiscrimination and other regulatory rules if obeying them would require them to violate their religiously rooted beliefs? This is a question the leaders of the American founding era two hundred years ago never faced. Jefferson's "wall of separation" metaphor—which would seem to free faith-based organizations from government's regulatory reach—is an inadequate basis for an answer. It was the answer to a different question.

In addition, whenever government insists that a faith-based organization must provide certain services that run counter to its religious conscience, it is coming down on the secular side of the deepest, most consequential religious divide in American society today—that between traditional religionists and secularists. Whenever a faith-based organization gives in to the regulatory efforts of government and goes against its own religiously based standards, it is being secularized under government pressure; if is resists those pressures it either faces fines or other penalties or—more likely—must stop offering a certain service or even go out of business. Secularly based human service agencies often chafe under the regulatory reach of government but do not face the same pressures as do faith-based organizations seeking to hold to certain faith-inspired standards.

The eighteenth century's answer to that time's church-state controversy is frequently invoked in the case of funding of faith-based organizations by the government. But does this answer—that has worked well in case of religious congregations in their central religious ceremonies and rituals—work equally well in the case of parachurch and other faith-based organizations providing public services? It does not. When it comes to religious congregations in their central religious practices and ceremonies there are no organizations engaged in similar or parallel activities to those of the churches and competing for the allegiance of the people. There is, in effect, a closed universe (congregations, clergy, religious denominations) and the decision the new nation arrived at was that no one in that universe should be funded.

Now, however, many still seek to apply the no-aid, strict separation position even though the circumstances are vastly different. Today, the government itself, secular nonprofit organizations, for-profit organizations, and faith-based organizations—all four—are actively engaged in providing a wide variety of human services. They are in competition with each other for staff, clients, supporters, and government grants and contracts. Also, government often helps fund the programs of faith-based, secular nonprofit, and for-profit organizations. This situation, in which the government is actively involved with human service organizations as a funder, was unknown at the close of the eighteen century when the no-aid-to-religion standard emerged.

As a result, were the strict separation, no-aid-to-religion standard to be applied to government funding of faith-based organizations, it would fail the test of full religious freedom for persons and organizations of all faiths and of none. It ends up favoring the nonreligious over the religious and exerting pressure on the religious—whether individuals or organizations—to become less religious. In striking a balance between the two sides in the deepest, most consequential religious divide in the United States today—that between traditionally religious persons and organizations and secularized persons and organizations—government ends up putting its large thumb on the secularized side of the scales. When government itself, secular nonprofit organizations, for-profit firms, and faith-based nonprofit organizations are all providing the same type of services, to fund or in other ways to favor only the first three of these types of programs and not the fourth would put the faith-based programs at a clear, government-created disadvantage.

And this is precisely the result to which the wall of separation, no-aid-to-religion standard leads when applied to faith-based human service organizations. It allows government to fund (and in fact it does fund) its own programs, and there is no constitutional barrier to its funding secular nongovernmental programs, both for-profit and nonprofit. But under the no-aid-to-religion standard it would not be able to help fund the very same programs of faith-based organizations. Former Court of Appeals judge and legal scholar Michael McConnell was correct when he wrote: "In the marketplace of ideas, secular viewpoints and ideologies are in competition with religious viewpoints and ideologies. It is no more neutral to favor the secular over the religious than it is to favor the religious over the secular."[77]

In summary, in spite of the continuing popularity of the strict separation, no-aid-to-religion standard and in spite of its working well in the case of religious congregations in their core religious celebrations and rituals, in today's world there are questions it was never intended to answer. Is it appropriate to impose regulations on a faith-based organization that require it to go against its deeply held beliefs? Is it appropriate for government not to help fund the services of faith-based organizations, if it is funding similar services being offered by competing secular organizations? More on these questions as this book progresses.

The Supreme Court and Freedom of Association

In several cases that have come before it, the Supreme Court has developed the concept of the freedom of association. Although the Court has not applied this concept widely, it does relate directly to the autonomy of associations and the limits of that autonomy. Thus it is important to consider it briefly. The Constitution does not, of course, explicitly provide for the freedom of association. Instead, the Supreme Court has held that this freedom emerges out of other First Amendment rights, such as the freedom of speech, press, and assembly. The Court clearly articulated the freedom of association in a 1958 case. During the struggle by African-Americans to win their basic rights—a struggle often marked by violence and threats—the state of Alabama had demanded that the NAACP turn over its lists of members and donors. The NAACP, fearing intimidation, refused to do so. The Supreme Court used the freedom of association to rule the NAACP did not have to comply with Alabama's demand:

> Effective advocacy of both public and private points of view, particularly controversial ones, is undeniably enhanced by group association . . . . It is beyond debate that freedom to engage in association for the advancement of beliefs and ideas is an inseparable aspect of the "liberty" assured by the Due Process Clause of the Fourteenth Amendment, which embraces freedom of speech. . . .

> Of course, it is immaterial whether the beliefs sought to be advanced by associa-
> tion pertain to political, economic, religious or cultural matters, and state action
> which may have the effect of curtailing the freedom to associate is subject to
> the closest scrutiny.[78]

It is hard to argue against the proposition that to advance beliefs, whether "political, economic, religious or cultural," it is often advantageous for like-minded persons to band together.

However, if a group of persons associates together based on some shared characteristic (such as a shared interest, gender, age, race, or religion), it necessarily means it needs to exclude those who do not possess that shared characteristic. Thus the right to associate implies the right to exclude. This raises the difficult question of the nature and extent of the right to exclude. This issue was addressed by the Supreme Court in 1984. The state of Minnesota had required the Jaycees, an all-male organization of young businessmen, to admit otherwise qualified women who had applied for membership. The Minnesota Jaycees claimed this state requirement interfered with its members' freedom of association. The Court, in an opinion written by Justice William Brennan, first reiterated the freedom of association in strong and clear language:

> There can be no clearer example of an intrusion into the internal structure or
> affairs of an association than a regulation that forces the group to accept mem-
> bers it does not desire. Such a regulation may impair the ability of the original
> members to express only those views that brought them together. Freedom of
> association therefore plainly presupposes the freedom not to associate.[79]

But the Court then went on to rule that the Jaycees had "failed to demonstrate that the [Minnesota] Act imposes any serious burdens on the male members' freedom of expressive association"[80] and that Minnesota had a compelling state interest—an often-used test that is usually difficult to meet—in allowing women access to the Jaycees. It therefore ruled Minnesota could constitutionally require women to be admitted to the organization.

In 2000, the Supreme Court considered the same question and this time ruled in favor of the organization and its freedom of association. This case concerned the Boy Scouts of America and their right to exclude a gay assistant scoutmaster—and gay members more generally. The Court ruled by a 5-to-4 vote that the Boy Scouts could exclude gays in spite of a New Jersey law that held such exclusion to be illegal discrimination. Chief Justice William Rehnquist, who wrote the majority opinion, began by summarizing the current state of the Court's jurisprudence on the freedom of association:

The forced inclusion of an unwanted person in a group infringes the group's freedom of expressive association if the presence of that person affects in a significant way the group's ability to advocate public or private viewpoints. But the freedom of expressive association, like many freedoms, is not absolute. We have held that the freedom could be overridden "by regulations adopted to serve compelling state interests, unrelated to the suppression of ideas, that cannot be achieved through means significantly less restrictive of associational freedoms."[81]

The opinion next noted that the Boy Scouts believe "homosexual conduct is inconsistent with the values it seeks to instill in its youth members,"[82] and then went on to conclude that New Jersey's law that required the Boy Scouts to accept a gay person as a leader ran "afoul of the Scouts' freedom of expressive association."[83]

On the other hand, in the case of the Christian Legal Society student group on the campus of the Hastings College of Law, discussed earlier in chapter 1, the Supreme Court rejected the claim of freedom of expressive association the students had put forward. The Court held the strength of the assertion of this right was weakened since the "CLS [Christian Legal Society] may exclude any person for any reason if it forgoes the benefits of official recognition."[84] The ability of Hastings to penalize the student group by taking away advantages all other student groups enjoyed due to alleged discrimination, was not blocked by the group's freedom of association.

Nevertheless, the Supreme Court's line of reasoning in freedom of association cases offers a basis for a legal, constitutional defense of the religious autonomy of faith-based organizations. In his quotation at the beginning of this chapter, Representative Jim Sensenbrenner made reference to the freedom of association to defend the right of faith-based organizations to hire on the basis of religion when he said: "Members of faith-based organizations should enjoy the same rights to associate with others who share their unique vision that other non-religious groups enjoy."[85] Legal scholar Kent Greenawalt has made the needed point: "A religious body may accept only those who accept the tenets or practices of the religion. . . . Should a legislature ever attempt to forbid a church from using religious criteria for membership or to forbid a political organization from using political criteria, such a law would strike at the very core of associational identity; courts would declare it invalid."[86] After the Supreme Court's 2010 decision dealing with the Christian Legal Society student group, one ought not to be too certain laws such as Greenawalt cites would be held invalid by the courts, although Greenawalt seemed to be thinking here and elsewhere in his essay in terms of churches and other religious congregations, not faith-based human service and parachurch organizations. Nevertheless, the principle he articulated can be the basis for asserting faith-based organizations' freedom of association as a legal basis for defending their right to determine their membership.

Summary

The record of the Supreme Court's jurisprudence as it relates to faith-based organizations and their religious autonomy is troubling, but it also contains some bases for defending faith-based groups' religious autonomy. The troubling part is the strict wall-of-separation, no-aid-to-religion thinking still prominent on the Supreme Court and its continuing pull among the academic and media elite and even among the general population. This thinking has served the nation well in regard to protecting the religious autonomy of churches and other religious congregations, preventing both stifling regulations and funding that could undermine their spiritual mission. But when applied to faith-based human service and educational organizations, it results in deep inequities and can lead to basic interferences with their religiously rooted practices. On the other hand, the neutrality, equal treatment line of reasoning that has been gaining importance in Supreme Court jurisprudence and the Court-enunciated right of freedom of association offer bases for defending the religious autonomy of faith-based organizations. The first does not insist on the secularization of organizations as the price for receiving the same government funding that similar or parallel nonreligious organizations are receiving; the latter offers a basis on which to defend the ability of religiously motivated persons to form organizations that pursue distinctive practices rooted in their shared religious beliefs.

Even though Supreme Court jurisprudence has established a foundation for protecting the religious autonomy of faith-based human service organizations without violating the religious freedom rights of others, that foundation is neither fully developed nor widely accepted. Advocacy groups such as the American Civil Liberties Union and Americans United for the Separation of Church and State regularly rail against the neutrality, equal treatment standard, as do the editorial writers for the *New York Times* and other elite opinion leaders. The equal treatment standard tends to be viewed as a form of aiding religion, not as a means of treating religiously based and secularly based groups and beliefs in an evenhanded manner. Even when it has prevailed before the Supreme Court, it has more often than not been by close 5-to-4 votes. The concept of freedom of association has been applied in only limited situations, and most recently the Court refused to apply it in the case of the Christian Legal Society student group on the campus of the Hastings College of Law.

The need remains for a standard by which the religious freedom rights of all are respected: faith-based organizations providing faith-inspired and faith-guided services to the public; governmental, nonprofit, and for-profit programs offering similar services to the public; the beneficiaries of these programs who may or may not desire religious elements to be integrated into the services they are receiving; and citizens of a wide diversity of religious faiths and of none who are asked to support these programs with their tax dollars and who may desire certain services a faith-based organization may believe in good conscience it cannot provide.

NONDISCRIMINATION MEASURES AND FAITH-BASED ORGANIZATIONS

In addition to the legacy of the Enlightenment-influenced American founding era and the religious developments in the early nation, and in addition to Supreme Court church-state jurisprudence, there is a third important factor that has deeply affected American attitudes towards faith-based organizations and their autonomy. It consists of the tradition of nondiscrimination laws designed to protect the American people in all their diversity from arbitrary, irrational discrimination. In the 1960s and since, the United States has enacted a series of laws designed to assure all Americans—whatever their race, color, gender, religion, or handicapped status—equal opportunities in employment, education, voting, housing, and receipt of services. These laws—long overdue and now widely accepted—have helped mold the American way of thinking about faith-based organizations and their responsibilities in a land of equal opportunities for all where irrational distinctions and discriminations are now legally banned.

The 1960s Nondiscrimination Civil Rights Laws

The long, sad story of Jim Crow laws and racial discrimination designed to keep African-Americans in a separate, subservient position in American society is sufficiently well-known that it does not need to be repeated here. For years Senate Democrats from the states of the former Confederacy used the filibuster and their generalized political clout to stop all civil rights legislation, even something as basic as a law that would have made lynching a federal offense. In the post-World War II era, led by NAACP's legal arm and a number of Supreme Court decisions, public schools were mandated to end the policy of segregation. But it was not until the 1960s, with Martin Luther King, Jr., rallying African-Americans to march from their churches and into the streets, combined with the overreaction of white power structures, that the political establishment began to move. Led by President John F. Kennedy and, after his assassination, by an even more forceful President Lyndon Johnson, Congress passed a series of civil rights acts that banned discrimination based on race, color, religion, sex, and national origin.[87] The big breakthrough came when the Senate broke a determined filibuster and enacted the Civil Rights Act of 1964. That act banned discrimination based on race, color, religion, sex, and national origin in public accommodations such as hotels and restaurants and in employment and conditions of employment. It also sought—to a large degree unsuccessfully—to strengthen voting rights for African-Americans. This Civil Rights Act, which was bitterly opposed and passed with great difficulty, made passing subsequent antidiscrimination civil rights acts through Congress, while still difficult, less so.

In 1965 the Voting Rights Act was passed. It provided for strong enforcement mechanisms for voting rights that other acts had sought to protect. Next was the 1968 Fair Housing Act, passed in the wake of the assassination of Martin Luther King, Jr. It prohibited discrimination in the sale and rental of housing based on the same five categories of race, color, religion, sex, and national origins. Then in 1990 Congress passed, and President George H. W. Bush signed, the Americans with Disabilities Act, which included a person's status in terms of mental and physical disabilities as a covered group protected from arbitrary discrimination.

These four acts—with a number of subsequent amendments to meet situations where experience demonstrated need for modification—completed the legal changes that were needed to ensure equality of opportunity for persons of all racial, ethnic, and religious groups, men and women on an equal basis, and persons irrespective of mental and physical handicaps. This is different, of course, than claiming that racism, sexism, and other biases do not still exist and negatively affect the actual opportunities many Americans possess. But these acts clearly put the law on the side of equality of opportunity.

An additional important observation is that all of these acts took into account that, while the general rule was there could be no discrimination against the covered categories, certain exceptions were warranted in the case of religion, if Americans' right to religious freedom was to remain uncompromised. No one would advocate that the Roman Catholic Church should be forced to hire women as priests, or a Jewish congregation to hire a Baptist as its rabbi. Therefore, the original 1964 Civil Rights Act provided in Section 702 that religious organizations would not be subject to Title VII (the section barring employment discrimination) in the case of employees responsible for religious activities. And then in 1972 Congress broadened this exemption with these words: "This subchapter shall not apply to . . . a religious corporation, association, educational institution, or society with respect to the employment of individuals of a particular religion to perform work connected with the carrying on by such corporation, association, educational institution, or society of its activities."[88] In other words, religious organizations were given exemption to the employment provisions of the act as they relate to nondiscrimination based on religion. In 1987, the Supreme Court unanimously upheld the constitutionality of the Section 702 exemption for religious organizations in the case of Corporation of Presiding Bishop v. Amos. Writing for the Court, Justice Byron White concluded that "as applied to the nonprofit activities of religious employers, §702 is rationally related to the legitimate purpose of alleviating significant governmental interference with the ability of religious organizations to define and carry out their religious mission."[89] This decision was made all the more impressive not only by the fact that it was reached unanimously by all nine justices but also by the fact that it did not involve a clearly religious worker directly involved in a church ministry, but a maintenance worker at a church-owned gymnasium.

The Legacy of Nondiscrimination Laws

One legacy of the movement that led to the adoption of nondiscrimination laws is that it came to be recognized that discrimination practiced by private individuals and organizations can be as destructive of persons' freedom as when government practices discrimination. One reason the passage of the 1960s civil rights laws was accompanied by much controversy was that the forms of discrimination against which they were aimed often involved discriminatory practices of private employers: hotels and resorts, country clubs, real estate companies, banks, and more. This means that outlawing discrimination by nongovernmental organizations came to be accepted as part of the understanding of freedom for all Americans. This affects faith-based organizations by creating standards that they, along with all other associations and institutions, must follow.

A second and probably more important, even if indirect, legacy of nondiscrimination laws emerges out of the fact that although most of the antidiscrimination civil rights acts were bitterly opposed when first adopted—and this was certainly true of the three acts adopted in the 1960s—they have come to be fully accepted and even celebrated as being in the best traditions of America. Martin Luther King, Jr., can be described as an American icon, and his birthday has been enshrined as a national holiday. In 2006, Congress passed and President George W. Bush signed a twenty-five year extension of the Voting Rights Act with little controversy. In common, everyday usage, "discrimination" became a negative term of disapproval, and to successfully label persons or organizations as engaging in discrimination is to condemn them. Thus the word "discrimination" today is often used in political rhetoric to condemn or to discredit an organization or program. In the two quotations cited at the beginning of this chapter, both the congressman who favored and the congressman who disfavored government partnerships with faith-based organizations used "discrimination" and "to discriminate" to discredit persons taking the opposite position.

However, the negative, pejorative use of the word "discrimination" is only one way in which the word can be used. When one says of someone that she has "discriminating taste," we are saying something positive about her—that she recognizes and opts for quality when she sees it. When a law firm hires as attorneys only persons who have a J.D. degree and have passed the bar exam, it is in a sense discriminating against all non-lawyers. It is noting distinctions and favoring those with certain characteristics and disfavoring those without them. But no one registers a complaint, since these distinctions are rationally related to the job opening being filled. Similarly, the 1990 Americans with Disabilities Act does not require an employer to hire someone who is physically or mentally unable to perform the job, unless with reasonable accommodations they would be able to do so.[90] And as seen earlier, the 1964 Civil Rights Act that banned religious discrimination in hiring exempted religious organizations from this requirement, recognizing that religion-based hiring by a religious organization is rationally related to its nature and purpose. Discrimination only becomes negative when it makes arbitrary, irrational distinctions based on prejudice, as when an entire category of persons (women, African-Americans, Hispanics, those with a handicap) is rejected and held to be unqualified.

But what happens when certain nondiscrimination standards clash with other standards rooted in religious beliefs going back hundreds, if not thousands of years? Faith-based organizations differ widely in what standards of belief and practice it is important for them to uphold in employment and other practices. How much autonomy should faith-based organizations have in determining for themselves what distinctions are rationally related to their nature and goals?

It is unwarranted to equate a faith-based organization's conclusion that upholding certain standards related to the religious beliefs or life-style choices of their employees is essential to their religious character and the fulfilling of their mission with arbitrary, invidious distinctions based only on prejudice. Yet what is an arbitrary, invidious distinction and what is upholding religiously rooted standards is often in the eye of the beholder. We as a society need certain criteria, or standards, by which to judge what practices of faith-based organizations are truly discriminatory in an irrational, inappropriate sense, and which are rationally related to their faith and their faith-inspired missions. Or putting it differently, we need agreed-upon concepts and theories that define the place of faith-based organizations in the public life of the nation and thereby define how much diversity we ought to allow among faith-based organizations as they seek to follow their religious beliefs in the public realm.

CONCLUSIONS

This chapter has considered key forces that have molded the attitudes, assumptions, and legal concepts and precedents Americans bring to the issue of the religious autonomy of faith-based organizations, that is, their freedom to determine for themselves their religious identity and beliefs and to act on the basis of that identity and those beliefs. These forces are highly problematic for the religious autonomy of faith-based organizations, but they also contain some bases to defend their religious autonomy.

Among the problematic forces are the founding era and the early years of the nation, which bequeathed a legacy that sees religion—in its particular manifestations—as largely a matter of individual choice and private belief and devotion, with no real role to play in the public life of the nation. The nature of religion in the founding era and the early nation—although in one sense strong and vigorous—was weak intellectually and did little to develop theoretical concepts that defined and defended communal religious life. The Supreme Court's jurisprudence built on this legacy and decreed religion to be an individual, private matter that was to be walled off from government and not aided. More recently, the American civil rights struggle and the resulting nondiscrimination laws have established a heritage that says government has the duty to protect persons from perceived discrimination, whether originating in government itself or nongovernmental groups.

Nevertheless, there are also aspects of the American heritage that have the potential to support the religious autonomy of faith-based organizations. One is the continued existence of a healthy, vigorous associational life in the United States. From colonial times to de Tocqueville and even today, American society has been marked by a host of independently organized, often local, nonprofit organizations and associations, many of which are faith-based in nature. They continue to flourish. Also, the neutrality, equal treatment line of reasoning that is gaining strength in the Supreme Court's jurisprudence offers the basis for defending the right of faith-based organizations not to be treated worse than their secular counterparts. And the Court's doctrine of freedom of association offers the grounds for defending the right of faith-based organizations to define and act upon who they are.

Taking the problematic and the positive features of the American heritage together, they mean the American polity has never developed and come to agreement on a set of concepts and theories that define and protect the religious autonomy of faith-based organizations. What is needed is a more systematic theory, or set of concepts, that will bring these disparate strands together and build upon them. I seek to contribute to this effort in this book. But first we need to look at how the more theoretical and historical factors covered in this chapter work themselves out in the day-to-day political arena of political debate and the seeking of partisan advantage. This I do in the next chapter.

Chapter 4

The Partisan-Political Landscape Today

The historic and legal patterns and the resulting attitudes and assumptions to which they have led described in the previous chapter have a practical, immediate relevance to today's world of public policy debates. They do much to explain the positions taken today by persons and organizations on the left and on the right of the political spectrum, and thereby help to explain why liberals and conservatives are clashing on issues of faith-based organizational religious autonomy. They also demonstrate the need for a rethinking of the assumptions and concepts both sides are bringing to today's public policy debates.

In this chapter, I describe and critique how both the political right and political left today view faith-based organizations offering services as a part of the human services network—and how those views lead liberals and conservatives to differing policy positions. Both the Left's and the Right's understandings of faith-based organizations and their place in the mix of public policies fail to provide a firm, thoughtful foundation for the religious autonomy of faith-based organizations. This chapter first describes how the political left views faith-based organizations and then it does the same for the political right. In both cases it first considers how the forces described in the prior chapter lead to certain underlying perspectives that have shaped the mindsets with which the Left and the Right view faith-based organizations as public actors, and then it considers how these differing mindsets have shaped the more specific policy positions the Left and the Right have taken towards faith-based organizations. It also critiques both the underlying perspectives and the public policy positions of the Left and the Right.

FAITH-BASED ORGANIZATIONS AND THE LEFT

This section considers the political left as it reacts to and relates to faith-based organizations that are providing public services.[1] In short, the progressive left tends to ignore them as though they do not exist or sees them either as potentially dangerous and divisive or as potentially helpful in meeting societal needs, but only if they play down or surrender much of their religious character. What is missing is a set of theoretical concepts that assigns faith-based organizations a legitimate, respected role in the provision of needed public services. The Left thereby fails to possess a genuine understanding of a rightful independence or autonomy that belongs to faith-based organizations. This section develops and documents these observations.

The Left's Mindset towards Faith-Based Organizations in the Public Realm

There are five factors that underlie and work to mold how liberals view faith-based organizations and the place their educational and human service programs have in the mix of the nation's public policies. The first is *a strong emphasis on the free, autonomous, choosing individual.* This view clearly has its roots in the eighteenth-century Enlightenment and the founding era with their emphasis on the individual and individual freedom. "Pro-choice" is a term associated with the Left's position on abortion, but the Left is also "pro-choice" on other issues as well, from flag-burning as a form of political protest to the availability of what many consider pornography to same-sex marriage. The pro-choice position on such issues is, of course, a pro *individual* choice position, one that insists that individuals be free to make their own choices. "Keep your laws off my uterus," as the abortion rights bumper sticker proclaims. This liberal vision is one of the free, autonomous individual, able to make his or her own way in a world where the dictates of law and tradition are seen as often inappropriately constraining the ability of human beings to be truly free—free to make their own decisions and chart their own course in life. Respect for group and community norms gives way to the individual; the consequences of individuals' choices for others are played down—such as for women pictured in pornography or near-pornography or performing at strip clubs, or for families seeking to teach sexual values that are undercut by an entertainment industry that assumes teenage sex is normal.

Individual freedom is certainly a valid and important commitment, but to divorce individual freedom from the social groups and organizations within which all of us live our lives is to ignore the context within which individual freedom is nurtured and lived out.[2] We are not autonomous individuals, making individual choices in a moral and value-free vacuum, but embedded individuals—embedded in families, neighborhoods, religious congregations, friendship groups, associations, and many other social structures. To focus only on the individual and ignore the communities within which we find meaning and live our lives is to isolate individuals from the context in which they live and thrive. It is impossible to preserve individual freedom without preserving freedom for the communities within which we live our lives. Yet this basic fact is often ignored by the Left.

A second factor underlying the Left's thinking about faith-based organizations and their autonomy is *a suspicion of traditional values and religion when they enter the public square, especially in their particularistic manifestations.* Again, the influence of the Enlightenment and the founding era can be seen, as well as that of the failure of dominant religious groups in the nineteenth century to think through and articulate a vision of religion's place in the public square. This second underlying force consigns religion to the private realm of religious congregations in their worship activities and rituals and of individual, private prayers and devotions. Vague, consensual references to God and religion are seen as sufficiently innocuous to be allowed into the public realm. But more specific, particularistic religious beliefs and ideals are seen as dangerous when they enter the public realm, and thus can best be kept locked up at home or in the church.

This attitude can be seen in the reasoning underlying the no-aid-to-religion, wall-of-separation principle that we saw in the previous chapter the Supreme Court took to church-state issues in the post–World War II years—reasoning the Left has enthusiastically supported. In defending and explaining its no-aid decisions, the Supreme Court has often referred to the divisiveness of religion and the danger it poses to public peace and unity. In the 1971 decision noted in chapter 3 that held aid to religiously based schools unconstitutional, the Court declared divisions based on religion are "a threat to the normal political process" and "tend to confuse and obscure other issues of great urgency," and that such divisions conflict "with our whole history and traditions."[3] The patronizing language of the Court clearly reveals an underlying mindset that sees religion in the public square as something that is out of place and dangerous: political divisions along religious lines are something other than the "normal political process" and distract from issues "of great urgency." Religion in the political process is abnormal and unimportant. In 2002, the liberal Supreme Court justice Stephen Breyer (appointed by President Bill Clinton), in a dissenting opinion dealing with vouchers for low-income students that could be redeemed at both secular and faith-based schools, approvingly reviewed earlier Supreme Court decisions that had cited religious divisiveness as a key danger American society is facing. He then went on to declare the voucher program would "inevitably pose problems that are divisive. Efforts to respond to these problems not only will seriously entangle church and state . . . but also will promote division among religious groups."[4] Religious pluralism in the public square is seen as posing special dangers, dangers that are not present in other societal divisions, such as those between labor and management, different regions and ethnic or racial groups, or the host of other differences that mark any society. Thus, religion must stay on its own side of the wall, that of private belief and observance.

Additional examples of liberals' suspicion or antagonistic attitudes towards religion in the public realm are easy to find. Rick Warren is an evangelical pastor of a southern California megachurch, author of *The Purpose Driven Life* which has sold 30 million copies, and described by *The Economist* as "America's favorite pastor."[5] But when President Barack Obama asked him to offer an invocation at his inauguration he was met by a storm of criticism from liberals. John Nichols, the Washington correspondent for the liberal *Nation* magazine, used terms such as "self-promoting," "fundamentalist," "authorizes discrimination," and "backward thinking" to describe one of the best-known and most popular religious leaders in the United States.[6] Also recall the example cited in the prior chapter of the *New York Times* columnist, Maureen Dowd, who heavily criticized both George W. Bush and Al Gore in their 2000 presidential campaigns for mentioning their religious faith as taking "something deeply personal and parad[ing] it for political gain."[7] She could not conceive of candidates' religious faith as being something with a public facet that might be relevant to their public policy views.

The Left's suspicion includes not only religiously based values and positions but also traditional values more broadly. One example was given by a *New York Times* essayist in 2010: "Liberals hated almost everything about George W. Bush's presidency, but they harbored a particular animus toward a minor domestic policy priority: abstinence-based sex education."[8] Also, it is the Left that has led the charge in support of same-sex marriage and quickly sees censorship when the Right raises questions about the nontraditional moral standards being portrayed in movies, on television, in video games, and in books and magazines. It is instructive that in these instances, about the only argument that seems to carry weight with the Left is that minors should be shielded—or at least they and their parents forewarned about—the contents of such media. The unstated assumption is that if one is eighteen years or older, an "everything goes" policy should mark what persons are able to view or read.

An ingrained suspicion of religion in the public realm and a desire to limit it to the private sphere does violence to religion as it is today and has been practiced down through the centuries. As seen in the prior chapter, almost all religious traditions claim a public relevance that involves public policy advocacy and providing services and help to those in need. To ignore or trivialize the public aspect of religion is to close one's eyes to reality and to lay the groundwork for doing serious damage to the religious freedom of the faithful as they act as individuals or as members of organizations rooted in their faith-traditions. Yet this is what the Left either fails to recognize or, when it does recognize it, sees it as a dangerous aspect of religion and that must be limited and carefully hedged about, not celebrated as a part of the freedoms and diversity we claim to cherish.

This leads to the third underlying factor that has helped shape the liberal mindset towards faith-based organizations: *seeing government as a potentially positive force for social change and improvement.* This factor does not emerge out of Enlightenment thinking. In fact, it is a reversal of Enlightenment thinking. The Enlightenment, arising out of an era of authoritarian governments dominated by aristocratic classes and inflexible church hierarchies, could not conceive of governments being agents of change and greater democratization. But that gradually changed during the nineteenth century. A number of reform movements sprung up that attempted to use, often with success, the powers of government to bring about social reform and change. William Wilberforce led an effort to abolish by force of law the British slave trade and later slavery in all British colonies; Lord Shafesbury in England fought for legislation to reform the working conditions in mines and factories; American abolitionists worked to legally abolish slavery; and Jean-Jacques Bourcart worked for the reform of child labor laws in France.[9] Out of these efforts, and those of many others, reformers came to see that political power, when wrested away from the conservative, aristocratic classes, could become an agent of reform and change. In the United States, these tendencies were strengthened and then confirmed by the work of such progressive politicians as William Jennings Bryan, Theodore Roosevelt, Woodrow Wilson, and, above all, Franklin D. Roosevelt. The well-known Democratic speaker of the House of Representatives, Tip O'Neill (1912–1994), once clearly illustrated this characteristic of American liberals when he wrote: "I'm still a bread-and-butter liberal who believes that every family deserves the opportunity to earn an income, own a home, educate their children, and afford medical care. That is the American dream and it's still worth fighting for." And how was this dream to be achieved? "In my view the federal government has an obligation to help you along the line until you achieve that dream."[10]

As a result, beginning in the late nineteenth century, and certainly from the early twentieth century onwards, a fundamental aspect of the Left's thinking has been an optimistic view of the power of government as an agent for social change and for addressing inequalities and other wrongs liberals see in

American society. It means that the Left tends to look to government and government agencies as a primary means—perhaps even *the* primary means—to
deal with education, health, and other social needs. This becomes more fully
the case when the needs being addressed are those of the poor and others on
the margins of mainstream society. Therefore, liberals see a primary means
for dealing with human needs and services as being government agencies and
programs; faith-based agencies and programs tend to be ignored or, at the
most, to be seen as secondary and auxiliary to government efforts. A 2008
New York Times editorial revealed this perspective with striking clarity when
it criticized President Bush's efforts to subsidize the social services being
provided by faith-based organizations as "a policy that violates the separation of church and state and turns a governmental function into a charitable
donation."[11] It assumed that social services are a "government function"
and looking to faith-based organizations as partners in providing them as an
instance of government surrendering a function that properly belongs to it.

The Left's optimistic assumptions concerning the potential of government to be a positive agent for change in society have been, in many ways,
confirmed by experience. There are a host of historical instances where government by its efforts brought about improved conditions. Think of antitrust
laws that have helped maintain the free enterprise system, of Social Security that has greatly reduced poverty among the elderly, of a host of labor
protections laws that have raised wages and protected workers from injury
and death, of civil rights laws that have eliminated many forms of invidious
discrimination aimed at African-Americans and women, and of environmental protection laws that have made our air and water cleaner. But the very
success of such efforts as these carry with them the danger of assuming that
government is the answer to all societal problems or that government action
is always to be preferred over other potential courses of action. Liberals are
not wrong to look to government for improvements in societal conditions,
but they are wrong when they so emphasize government's ability to meet
social needs that they assume there is no role—or only a marginal role—for
other entities. Government can be and often has been effective in meeting
societal needs; it is also limited in what it can do and accomplish. It is well
suited to do some things, and ill suited, or less well suited, to do other things.
Recall chapter 2 and the niches it pointed out faith-based organizations can
fill better than government agencies in international relief and development
work, adoption and foster care efforts, and prisoner return programs. Liberals fail when they look too confidently or too exclusively to government
agencies and programs for meeting societal needs.

A fourth underlying factor helping to shape how the left views the public
role of faith-based organizations is *its embrace of the strict church-state*

separation, no-aid-to-religion standard. In chapter 3 we saw this is one of two lines of reasoning the Supreme Court has relied upon in its church-state decisions. Even though the Court has been moving away from it in recent years, it has given the Left's more generalized, underlying predispositions of thought reinforcement a greater focus, and blessed them with constitutional support. This principle has become a mainstay of liberal thought, reflected by many liberal commentators, judges, advocacy groups, academics, and office holders. For example, the Cleveland school voucher case mentioned in chapter 3 involved a program that allowed low-income students to opt out of dysfunctional schools and attend alternative public, faith-based, or secular nonpublic schools and which the Supreme Court upheld in part on the basis of neutrality reasoning. The *New York Times* editorially dismissed this program as "a serious retreat from this nation's historic commitment to maintaining a wall between government and religion."[12]

Meanwhile, the competing neutrality, equal treatment standard has been largely ignored by the Left or seen as no more than the latest attempt of conservatives to chip away at church-state separation. One searches in vain the leading liberal periodicals and commentators for expressions of positions that even take seriously the attempt of the neutrality standard to treat religious and nonreligious persons and entities in an even-handed manner. This was the case in the just-cited *New York Times* editorial, which never even considered the equal treatment, neutrality line of reasoning that is gaining acceptance on the Supreme Court and to which the Court's opinion in this case made reference. Liberals tend not even to ask which principle affords superior protection for those of all religions and of none but assume that the separationist, no-aid principle is the one to be followed. Supreme Court decisions based on the neutrality principle are seen as aberrations that one can safely ignore. Or it may be a matter of hoping that if one ignores this line of judicial reasoning in time it will just go away. As I argued in chapter 3, the strict separation, no-aid standard has serious defects when applied to today's issues surrounding faith-based organizations providing services to the public. At the beginning of the next chapter, I will argue that the neutrality principle is in fact a surer guarantee of religious freedom for all than the no-aid, strict separation principle. Yet the presuppositions of the Left make it blind to even the possibility that, in today's world, neutrality might be a better response than wall-of-separation, no-aid-to-religion reasoning to evaluate government's partnerships with faith-based organizations.

A fifth and final factor underlying liberals' approach to faith-based organizations is *the legacy of the nondiscrimination statutes of the 1960s.* As seen in the prior chapter, these laws, although bitterly opposed at the time of their enactment, have become a part of the widely accepted public policy landscape. These laws asserted individual, not organizational or group, rights. Indeed, they sought to guarantee individual rights against state and local governments, private employers, and nongovernment organizations such as country clubs and labor unions. Although the political right has come to accept these laws, it was the Left that led in their passage. The Left's commitment to individual rights and government as a means by which social change can come about was reinforced and raised to a level of increased importance in the Left's thinking by its successful drive for nondiscrimination laws.

This has influenced how the Left thinks about faith-based organizations, as it views them through an antidiscrimination lens. When the Left sees a faith-based organization not hiring someone of a religious faith different than its own, or when it refuses to hire a gay counselor or an abortion rights advocate, or when it refuses to offer the full range of "reproductive services," it is easy for many liberals to see the same sort of discrimination the Left fought to overcome in the recent past. This tendency is made more powerful in the Left's thinking because of its previously-noted view of religion as a purely personal, private affair with no—or a very limited— role in the public realm. If religion is a purely personal, private affair with no relevance to the world of human services, then faith-based organizations that take religion into account in their practices are engaging in invidious discrimination, much like racial and gender discrimination that was made illegal years ago.

Even though the nondiscrimination statutes of the 1960s and their subsequent refinements are one of the great success stories of twentieth century America, this does not mean they can be applied indiscriminately to every-and-all situations where "discrimination" is alleged. As argued in chapter 3, some distinctions and actions based on those distinctions are rational and worthy of being defended; others are not. Yet liberals are quick to assume that any distinction among persons is another case of irrational discrimination. The exception written into the 1964 Civil Rights Act that allows religious congregations and other faith-based organizations to take religion into account in making employment decisions is generally ignored as a rational and appropriate provision that protects the religious integrity of those organizations. Note the statement of Representative Bobby Scott at the beginning of chapter 3. Especially when coupled with the assumption of the personal, private nature of religion and a no-aid understanding of church-state separation, it is easy for liberals to assume that when religious organizations make religious distinctions—as some do in their hiring policies or in other practices they either follow or refrain from following—they are engaging in invidious discrimination, indistinguishable from previously banned racial, ethnic, and gender discrimination.

The need is for certain criteria, or standards, by which to judge what practices of faith-based organizations are truly discriminatory in an irrational, inappropriate sense, and which are rationally related to their faith and their faith-inspired missions. This, for the most part, the Left has not even attempted to do, but has assumed that any distinction that would be inappropriate for a secular nonprofit organization to make is equally inappropriate for a faith-based organization.

In summary, rightly or wrongly—or better, sometimes rightly and sometimes wrongly—the five underlying factors discussed in this section have together worked to mold a mindset—an interrelated set of concepts, attitudes, assumptions, predispositions, and values—that has led today's liberals to certain positions in regard to faith-based organizations and their place in the delivery of important human services. This mindset functions for the Left as a lens through which it views faith-based organizations, their place in the network of human services, and their partnerships with government in providing those services.

Applications of the Left's Mindset towards Faith-Based Organizations in the Public Realm

It is not much of an exaggeration to say that the Left's mindset means there is really no place or room for faith-based human service providers in its thinking. The Left possesses no ready categories or concepts with which to understand them and their role in the public realm. The individual and individual rights are certainly important; so are governments and the programs and reforms they enact. The Left often has debates within itself in terms of when individual rights should be trumped by certain societal values. It places the right to choose to obtain an abortion on one side of the line; the right to choose to own an automatic assault rifle on the other. It also debates what new government programs are truly needed in light of various priorities and limited finances. In both cases the Left has a language it can use to discuss and debate such issues and to defend the conclusions it reaches. Most liberals thereby see public policies and programs to deal with societal needs as emerging out of an interplay between individuals and their rights on the one hand, and government and its potential to improve societal conditions through the programs it enacts on the other hand.

However, when it comes to faith-based organizations and their programs of service to the public, liberals have a hard time fitting them into categories with which they are accustomed to dealing. The Left does not have the concepts or even the language to analyze and react to faith-based organizations that are both truly religious and truly public-serving. By viewing faith-based organizations and their provision of human services through lenses created by the five underlying factors just discussed, the Left forces them into a Procrustean bed rooted in its understandings concerning society and the role of government and its public policies in meeting human needs. With no concepts that encompass faith-based organizations that are providers of human services to the public, faith-based organizations either must be religious organizations similar to churches and other religious congregations and thus outside the scope of government partnerships, or they must be similar to the other, secular organizations in the public arena. Entities that are truly religious and truly public just do not fit the categories with which it is accustomed to dealing. The Left thereby fails to understand faith-based organizations for what they are: religious organizations that are operating in the public realm by providing services, not primarily to their own members, but to the general population—and thus a part of the network of public services. As a result, the Left has developed public policies related to faith-based, public-serving organizations in three related, but somewhat different ways, all of which possess clear inadequacies. I consider each of these three applications in turn.

First, sometimes liberals *simply miss the presence and relevance of faith-based organizations as an important part of the network of human services.* It is like a car salesperson who witnesses a car accident and is later able to describe in detail the makes, colors, and model years of the cars involved but will not recall any details about the clothing worn by the persons involved. Meanwhile, a clothing salesperson who witnesses the same accident will recall the details of the clothing worn by the persons involved in the accident but will be unable to recall any details concerning the cars involved. We all see, remember, and take into account that with which we are acquainted and can sort into categories familiar to us. This also applies to most liberals, whose mindset does not encompass faith-based organizations as a significant part of the network of human services. They are not on the Left's radar screen.

For example, this was the case in President Barack Obama's 2010 State of the Union address. Towards the beginning of his address, he had this sincere, deeply moving tribute to the American people:

> They share a stubborn resilience in the face of adversity. After one of the most difficult years in our history, they remain busy building cars and teaching kids, starting businesses and going back to school. They're coaching Little League and helping their neighbors. One woman wrote to me and said, "We are strained but hopeful, struggling but encouraged."
>
> It's because of this spirit—this great decency and great strength—that I have never been more hopeful about America's future than I am tonight. Despite our hardships, our union is strong. We do not give up. We do not quit. We do not allow fear or division to break our spirit. In this new decade, it's time the

American people get a government that matches their decency; that embodies their strength.[13]

What is missing throughout this speech, outside of a brief tip of the hat to Little League baseball, is any reference to the 12 percent of the American workforce and some 1.5 million organizations that we saw in chapter 2 make up the nonprofit sector of American society. From Obama's perspective they were not worth mentioning as contributing to meeting the enormous problems America faced in 2009 and were continuing into 2010. Obama does have a White House Office of Faith-Based and Neighborhood Partnerships, but when he can give a seventy-minute speech on the state of the nation that emphasized the strengths of American society without mentioning the faith-based and neighborhood organizations with which government is partnering, one comes away with the suspicion that they do not loom large in his view of how to deal with America's challenges.

And this is not a lone exception. One searches in vain the speeches and websites of well-known, leading liberal political leaders and organizations for meaningful references to faith-based organizations and their role in the provision of services to the needy. A February 2010 position paper the liberal Center for American Progress released is instructive. It was entitled "Doing What Works: Building a Government that Delivers Greater Value and Results to the American People" and was coauthored by a leading liberal activist, John Podesta.[14] In many ways it is a thoughtful, insightful twenty-page essay on how to improve government processes and services. But what is missing is almost any reference to faith-based organizations or, for that matter, to the independent, nonprofit sector at all. Even when it talks about the importance of experimentation and innovation it ignores the possible lessons to be learned from the nonprofit sector and only thinks of "state and local governments [that] provide a unique opportunity in this respect."[15] It does have a brief reference to community-based antipoverty programs, but only to warn that they often do not share information with each other, which can "cause efforts to be misdirected or duplicated."[16] Similarly, one can find in the policy statements and advocacy documents related to the 2009–2010 struggle for health care reform almost no mention of the role to be played by the thousands of faith-based hospitals, clinics, and hospice organizations.[17]

To miss the large world of faith-based social service, health care, international aid and relief, and educational services is to ignore a large component of the network of human service agencies in the United States. Chapter 2 documented this component of the network of human services and the often indispensable work it is doing. To ignore or marginalize a host of agencies that are helping to meet pressing societal needs distorts the public policy-making process seeking to meet those needs, and harms both the agencies that are doing vital work and the hundreds of thousands of persons they are helping and the additional persons they potentially could help.

A second application of the Left's mindset towards faith-based organizations in the public realm leads some liberals *to insist faith-based organizations have no real role in the provision of public services or, when they do, their religiously rooted practices must be eliminated or fenced about with safeguards.* If faith-based, public-serving organizations are not private religious organizations, similar to religious congregations, they must be similar to other public-serving nonprofit organizations providing secular services. Those are the only two categories recognized by the Left's mindset. Thus faith-based, public-serving organizations either have no genuine role to play in the provision of public services or, if they do, steps must be taken assure they act like similar secular organizations. This conclusion is fed by the Left's suspicion of religion and religious values when allowed into the public square and its acceptance of the strict separation, no-aid-to-religion standard.

Some liberals fear faith-based organizations as dangerous manifestations of intolerant religion that will pursue heavy-handed proselytizing of the recipients of their services. They suspect such proselytization will interfere with the recipients' free choice of religion and will impose outmoded values that at best are irrelevant to the problems the recipients are facing and at worst will interfere with their making headway. For example, when President George W. Bush first announced his faith-based initiative in 2001, the *Los Angeles Times* published an essay by Bart Kosko entitled, "The Problem with Faith-Based Funding is Faith Itself."[18] In it the author warns that the "faithful have all too often been willing to die or kill for their notions of spiritual right and wrong" and that faith "undermines critical thinking."[19] In a 2009 *New York Times* essay, Susan Jacoby warns that recipients of services from a faith-based organization are "a captive audience" and, "It cannot be easy to say no to a proselytizer if saying yes means a warm bed in a homeless shelter, extra help for a child or more privileges while serving jail time."[20]

More often, however, the Left will not simply oppose governmental financial partnerships with faith-based organizations, but will insist either that all religious elements must be removed or that a number of redundancies must be built into such funding programs to assure that the beneficiaries of such funding are protected several times over from being exposed to any religious elements. Also, this position insists that when a faith-based organization provides a certain type of service to the public, it must provide all such services, even those that go against its deeply held, religiously based moral standards. A faith-based program providing public services must be made to fit into the category of secular agencies providing secular services.

In the case of financial partnerships, the American Civil Liberties Union has held that government may partner with faith-based organizations, but only if they secularize themselves: "The government already can and does work collaboratively with faith-based organizations. It has long granted tax dollars to religious social service providers . . . that operate their social services in a secular manner."[21]

This position holds that when religious elements do remain in a faith-based program, the beneficiaries of those programs must be protected from unwanted religious messages. First, beneficiaries must be able to opt out of a program sponsored by a religious entity and receive services from a secular program; second, no religious elements may be included in the services that the beneficiaries receive; third, the religious commitments and beliefs of potential employees may not be taken into account in hiring decisions; fourth, any passive religious symbols or pictures must be removed from the room where the government-funded services are offered; and fifth, any religious elements that may still be present in the program must be purely voluntary and offered at a different time or in a different location than the government-subsidized program.[22] A February 2010 open letter to President Obama from an organization tellingly calling itself the Coalition Against Religious Discrimination and signed by many mainstream liberal organizations clearly calls for such conditions to accompany any subsidies going to programs run by faith-based organizations.[23] Recipients of government-subsidized services in faith-based organizations must be protected from exposure to religion by a series of firewalls.

In discussing whether or not faith-based organizations must provide services that run counter to their religious beliefs, the American Civil Liberties Union has declared: "When, however, religiously affiliated organizations move into secular pursuits—such as providing medical care or social services to the public or running a business—they should no longer be insulated from secular laws. In the public world, they should play by public rules."[24] The underlying assumption is that religion is a purely personal, private matter, and thus when a faith community forms an organization to provide needed services to the public, it has left its religious character behind and is now engaging in secular activities, just as any other secular organization. Thus a Catholic hospital can be forced to provide contraceptive and abortion services and an evangelical Protestant adoption agency to place children with same-sex couples.

This second position that often characterizes the Left comports well with a mindset that emphasizes individual rights, assigns religion a purely private role (seeing it as posing dangers or abandoning its religious nature when entering the public realm), and believes the First Amendment wisely insists government only support completely secularized programs. However, to demand the elimination of all religious elements from faith-based programs and to demand a series of firewalls to protect persons taking part in the programs of faith-based providers to assure they are shielded several times over from any unwanted religious elements is unnecessary and potentially damaging to the cause of religious freedom of faith-based organizations and their staffs, volunteers, supporters, and recipients of their services. Surely the First Amendment means that no one should be forced to face proselytizing pressures or be exposed to gentler religious messages against their will, nor should faith-based organizations be favored over secular agencies in any distribution of government funds for which they are eligible. Here the Left is correct. But when this principle is pursued to the exclusion of all others and is seen as so basic that faith-based programs receiving government funds must either become thoroughly secular in nature or a number of redundancies must be built in to protect beneficiaries from unwanted religious messages, no matter how subtle or passive, the very principle of religious freedom the Left is seeking to promote can end up being violated.

Think in terms of an example. Say there is a faith-based domestic violence shelter that because of its good work is partially funded by a grant from the city. A woman entering it was sexually abused as a child. At school, due to her troubled life at home and a dysfunctional school, she failed one class after another. When an older man entered her life and showed her the attention she had previously lacked, she moved in with him. But he betrayed her trust and proved to be physically and emotionally abusive. In desperation she comes to the shelter seeking help. The counselor to whom she is assigned went through some of these same experiences at an earlier point in her life. She was able to turn her life around by her own inner strength and a loving church community. She now works at the shelter as a way of living out her faith and in obedience to the biblical command to care for the "least of these." For her, doing so is as much a religious obligation God has placed on her as church involvement and personal prayer. In such a situation may this counselor assure the woman, who has been beaten down and wronged by life at almost every turn, that God made her and loves her and has a plan for her life that is good? To answer this question with a simple "No" is inadequate. It would ignore the religiously rooted obligation that the counselor feels and that led her into counseling work in the first place. And assuming the victim has, at the least, a general belief in a benevolent God who has created and cares for her and the rest of the world, she would likely welcome and find comfort and the beginning of the recovery of a healthy self-esteem in what the counselor wants to share with her. In such a case, would not denying what both the counselor and the victim desire and what would help a victim who has been grievously wronged pose serious religious freedom issues? The answers in all such circumstances are not easy, but the insistence on a complete removal of all religious elements—including something as passive as a religious picture on the wall—is surely too easy an answer. Yet the liberals' mindset blinds them to such subtleties.

Similarly, if religious commitments are no protection from faith-based organizations being forced to provide services that run counter to their deeply held beliefs, their religious freedom rights would clearly be violated. We can see this in the case of individual rights. A society that would force a physician to perform an abortion that she views as morally equivalent to murder sounds more like a totalitarian than a free democratic society. What almost all would see as a moral horror suddenly becomes acceptable when a faith community and its organization is at issue. This is where emphasizing individual rights over communities and communal rights and failing to take into account faith-based organizations that are genuinely religious and genuinely public-serving lead.

Also, it is important to recognize that insisting on the removal of all religious elements from faith-based programs and insisting faith-based providers of public services provide the same services as secular providers would do violence to a diversity of programs and providers. A sameness would replace pluralism. A diversity of agencies, programs, and approaches to needed services is a good thing. It provides choices to those seeking services. In dealing with extremely complex situations, there usually is no one treatment modality that is demonstrably the most effective. Thus allowing for a mix of programs—some large, others small and more personal; some run by persons of the same racial, ethnic, or religious background as the recipients of services, others run by professionals not of the same backgrounds; some secular, others religious—is a good thing. To achieve this, we as a society must be willing to tolerate differences in programs and providers. Yet the Left's attempt to force faith-based programs into secular molds leads to a uniformity that undercuts diversity and pluralism.

A third application to which some liberals' mindset leads is similar to the second application, but differs in that these liberals see faith-based organizations in a more positive light. This application *sees faith-based organizations as potential allies in meeting pressing human needs, but sees their religious character as not all that important and something that can be played down or limited without doing any real harm.* Under this perspective, liberals recognize the public good that faith-based organizations are doing and support government working in partnership with them, even helping to fund them. They are aware and appreciative of what faith-based organizations are doing and are genuinely desirous of making a space for them in the public realm. They are hesitant to force them into practices that run counter to their religiously rooted beliefs. But their mindset has not equipped them with the concepts or categories with which to articulate and defend a public role for faith-based organizations. They are caught between their recognition of the important contributions faith-based organizations are making to society on the one hand, and their own underlying, ingrained presuppositions and their fellow liberals' more negative, suspicious attitude towards faith-based organizations as public entities on the other hand. Thus they end up compromising or waffling on the place of faith-based organizations in the mix of human services and the terms and conditions under which government may partner with them. These liberals lack clearly defined categories and principles to defend such partnerships, and thus their support often appears weak and vacillating. They see faith-based agencies as running positive programs that are really the same as those of their secular counterparts, but with a little religion available on the side for those who wish it and with religion serving as an underlying motivation for their employees and volunteers. Implicitly, if not explicitly, they assume the religious elements of faith-based programs can largely be removed from their programs without doing any real harm to the public good they are providing. These persons often end up being accused by their fellow liberals' of compromising fundamental principles and by faith-based organizations of seeing their religious aspects as tangential and dispensable.

President Barack Obama appears to view faith-based organizations in this light. Coming out of his community organizing days in Chicago, when churches played a major role in his efforts, he has a genuinely positive view of faith-based organizations as providers of human services and of government working alongside them as partners. During his 2008 campaign he declared: "Now, I know there are some who bristle at the notion that faith has a place in the public square. But the fact is, leaders in both parties have recognized the value of a partnership between the White House and faith-based groups."[25] As president, Obama created an Office of Faith-Based and Neighborhood Initiatives, as well as an advisory council attached to it. He charged that advisory council with these words: "Instead of driving us apart, our varied beliefs can bring us together to feed the hungry and comfort the afflicted; to make peace where there is strife and rebuild what has broken; to lift up those who have fallen on hard times."[26]

Clearly, Obama and other liberals taking this perspective view faith-based organizations and their efforts in providing human services in a positive light. But they also seem to hold to a belief that the religious aspects of faith-based organizations can be dispensed with or marginalized without negatively impacting the services they are providing. In the same campaign speech from which I quoted above, Obama made clear that in his view the separation of church and state means the religious elements in faith-based programs that partner with government must be segregated out from the secular services, with government only funding the secular services. He also seemed to say that any faith-based program receiving government funds would not be able to take religion into account in its hiring decisions, although once in office he has disappointed many of his liberal supporters by continuing to allow faith-based organizations receiving government funding to use religious criteria in hiring. Yet tellingly he has done so without articulating a rationale for religion-based hiring, only saying that decisions will be made on a case-by-case basis. It is noteworthy that after almost three years in office his administration had found no specific case where a government-funded faith-based provider could not take religion into account in hiring. Obama seems to recognize and respect faith-based organizations and the services they provide and wishes to include them in his call for an "all hands on deck" approach to meeting human needs, but coming out of a liberal background and mindset, he lacks a set of concepts or principles with which to define and defend that inclusion. Thus he compromises and waffles as he seeks to protect faith-based organizations without alienating his more purely liberal supporters.

This third application to which some liberals' mindset leads them results in a generally favorable attitude towards faith-based organizations and their provision of services to the public. It allows space for some limited religious elements in faith-based organizations' programs. This is to the good. But this approach faces a huge tension: it wants to accommodate faith-based organizations and their contribution to the public good, but it lacks principled guidelines either to guide them or to allow them to defend in a principled manner what they are doing. By default they continue to hold to much of the Left's assumptions and beliefs regarding faith-based organizations that are in tension with what they are seeking to do. An approach marked by improvisation and what appears to be waffling and pragmatic compromises results.

In summary, liberals vary in the degree to which they recognize and take into account faith-based organizations and the degree to which they view them favorably or with a deep-seated suspicion, but the underlying problem is that as a whole they do not have a framework of theoretical concepts that assigns faith-based organizations a role *as faith-based organizations* in the mix of public human services. They simply have no category in which to fit them. As a result, seemingly irresolvable dilemmas emerge. If government partners with, perhaps even helping to fund, programs of faith-based organizations without requiring them to secularize the programs it is funding, what happens to church-state separation and individual religious freedom? Government would be funding activities with religious elements embedded in them and one citizen's tax dollars would be going to help subsidize programs of a religious faith not her own. On the other hand, if government refuses to fund any programs of faith-based providers or only those of providers who agree to give up key religious elements in their programs—even while it is funding nonreligious or secular programs—is this not discriminating against faith-based programs and using tax dollars to pressure faith-based organizations to give up their programs' religious elements? And if government regulations would force a faith-based organization to offer services it believes on the basis of its religious faith to be morally wrong, can this be distinguished from government regulations that would force an individual to act contrary to his religious beliefs? I believe there are answers to these questions, answers that respect in practice the diversity and pluralism we claim in theory. I will offer these answers in subsequent chapters, but the tensions I just described— while not true dilemmas—are indeed real.

FAITH-BASED ORGANIZATIONS AND THE RIGHT

Support for faith-based initiatives is usually seen as a conservative, Republican position, perhaps even a position championed by the highly conservative religious right. However, even though the Right is more supportive of the work faith-based organizations are doing and is more protective of their religious autonomy than is the Left, it too does not have a reasoned, thought-out understanding of faith-based organizations *as faith-based organizations* nor a positive conception of their place in meeting needs in society. The Right is not much more successful than the Left in possessing a set of concepts and assumptions with which to understand the faith-based sector and the rightful autonomy of its members as they take their place in the nation's network of human services. As I did with the Left, in this section I will first consider underlying factors that have shaped conservatives' mindset towards faith-based organizations as providers of human services, and I will then demonstrate how conservatives apply the resulting mindset to issues surrounding the place of faith-based providers in today's mix of human services.[27]

The Right's Mindset towards Faith-Based Organizations in the Public Realm

There are four underlying factors shaping the Right's mindset towards faith-based organizations as providers of human services to the public. The first one is *a deep-seated suspicion of governmental power*. This factor can be traced back to the eighteenth-century Enlightenment and the American founders and their deeply felt suspicion—even opposition—to powerful, authoritarian government and their exaltation of the free, autonomous individual. Even today, the founders' influence can be seen in a strong libertarian strain in the American right. The less government, the better is its watchword. As President Ronald Reagan was fond of saying, "Government is not the solution to our problems, government *is* the problem."[28] This force within conservatism pushes for lower taxes, even in the absence of reduced government spending, in an effort to "starve the beast" as it is often put, and thereby in the long run driving down the scope and power of government. As the taxing and regulatory reach of government expands, the freedom of individuals will contract; as the taxing and regulatory reach of government contracts, the freedom of individuals will expand. The Tea Party movement that came to prominence in 2010 is clearly in this wing of conservatism. The mission statement of the Tea Party Patriots reads: "The impetus for the Tea Party movement is excessive government spending and taxation. Our mission is to attract, educate, organize, and mobilize our fellow citizens to secure public policy consistent with our three core values of Fiscal Responsibility, Constitutionally Limited Government and Free Markets."[29] Conspicuous by its absence is any mention of social issues, such as abortion and same-sex marriage. One of the leaders involved in the Tea Party movement has stated: "I think social issues may matter to particular individuals, but at the end of the day, the movement should be agnostic about it. . . . To include social issues would be beside the point."[30]

The Cato Institute is a Washington think tank that also clearly embodies this way of thinking. Although the media usually refer to it as a conservative think tank, its own website explicitly rejects this label and instead suggests:

> "Classical liberal" is a bit closer to the mark, but the word "classical" connotes a backward-looking philosophy. . . .
> The Jeffersonian philosophy that animates Cato's work has increasingly come to be called "libertarianism" or "market liberalism." It combines an appreciation for entrepreneurship, the market process, and lower taxes with strict respect for civil liberties and skepticism about the benefits of both the welfare state and foreign military adventurism.[31]

The well-known support by the Right for free enterprise and lower taxes and opposition to further government regulation of business grows out of this underlying attitude or force in its thinking, which one can trace back to classical, or Enlightenment, liberalism.

The antigovernment, libertarian leanings the right inherited from the eighteenth-century Enlightenment—as I also noted earlier is the case with the Left's mindset towards faith-based organizations—stresses individual freedom and autonomy at the cost of recognizing the importance of the social groups and communities in which all human beings are embedded. The Right is helped—as we will shortly see—by its Burkean conservative element, which serves as a partial corrective to the Enlightenment's individualism that by itself would lead to an unrelenting libertarian, suspicion-of-government attitude. Yet the influence of this individualistic factor on the conservatives' mindset works against recognizing the legitimate, rightful role of associations, organizations, and communities in meeting needs present in society. Both the Left and the Right tend to focus on the individual and the government. The Left is suspicious of government regulation and power in some settings and sees it as an ally for progress in other settings; the Right is also suspicious of government regulation and power in some settings and sees it as an ally in protecting important values in other settings. But they differ on the settings in which governmental power and regulation are to be favored and in which they are to be opposed. The Left tends to be suspicious of governmental power and regulation in settings it defines as private, personal behavior (for example, abortion) and sees it as a source for progress in settings it defines as societal improvement (for example, protecting the natural environment). Meanwhile, the Right tends to be supportive of governmental power and regulation in settings it views as involving important personal and social values (for example, abortion and national defense) and views it as a danger in settings where it runs counter to the free enterprise system (again, environmental protection laws serve as an example).

This means the Left and the Right clash on when and how much government power should be supported and when and to what degree individuals should be left free to make their own choices. Most of the debates between the Left and the Right come down to debates over what should be left to individual choice and control and what should be assigned to government for its regulation and control. The key point for our purposes here is that both sides in these debates tend to miss the host of intermediary social structures—families, neighborhoods, religious congregations, associations, and nonprofit service organizations—that lie between the individual and government. Neither the Left nor the Right has a clearly recognized, articulated, theoretical place for these intermediary social structures in its thinking. They loom larger on the Right's radar scope than they do on the Left's because of the influence of Burkean conservatism on the Right—to be considered shortly—with its emphasis on traditional values and established social arrangements. But even the Right does not have an explicitly defined, theoretical place for them in its thinking. Much of the Right's understanding of the place of faith-based organizations and its defense of them comes down to pragmatic considerations, that is, seeing them as means to achieve certain conservative goals, not as having a role and value in their own right. More on this later.

A second underlying factor that has also been key in molding the Right's mindset as it relates to faith-based organizations is *a traditional conservatism that emphasizes traditional values and approaches societal change slowly and carefully.* Just as the Left has elements of Enlightenment thinking modified by a nineteenth-century tradition of seeing government as a potential agent of reform, so the Right has its libertarian tendencies inherited from the Enlightenment modified by a traditional conservatism. It is this additional factor in conservative thinking that makes the libertarian Cato Institute uncomfortable with the conservative label.

Traditional conservatism is most often associated with Edmund Burke (1729–1797), a British philosopher, writer, and member of Parliament.[32] He famously was one of the few voices in British public life that supported the Americans in their revolution against British rule, but was strongly opposed to the French Revolution. His reasons for supporting one revolution and not the other do much to reveal his underlying thought. He saw the American Revolution as being waged in support of the traditional rights of British subjects, rights rooted in British history and customs; he saw the French Revolution as asserting rights rooted, not in history or tradition, but in human reason and attempts to remake society by human will. In his famous *Reflections on the Revolution in France* he wrote: "We are afraid to put men to live and trade each on his own private stock of reason; because we suspect that this stock in each man is small, and that the individuals would be better to avail themselves of the general bank and capital of nations, and of ages."[33] Burke, in contrast to the Enlightenment thinkers, saw human reason as an untrustworthy guide. A surer guide was the accumulation of human experience as embodied in history, traditions, and institutions that have evolved over time. Therefore, Burkean conservatives emphasize that change should come slowly, in evolutionary fashion, not by sweeping legal and social changes. And they respect religiously based and other traditional values, since they have been tested by time and are important in shaping flawed human beings into citizens who will prove to be responsible contributors to society.

Russell Kirk is the best known American proponent of this facet of conservatism. In his highly influential 1953 book, *The Conservative Mind*, he stated that "the essence of social conservatism is preservation of the ancient moral traditions of humanity. Conservatives respect the wisdom of their ancestors . . . ; they are dubious of wholesale alteration. They think society is a spiritual reality, possessing an eternal life but a delicate constitution: it cannot be scrapped and recast as if it were a machine."[34] Kirk goes on to list six basic principles of conservative thought. Notably absent from both his formulation of conservatism quoted above and the six principles he lists is any reference to a libertarian, the-less-government-the-better principle or exultation of the free enterprise system freed from government regulation. Instead, Kirk's emphasis—as was Burke's—was on respect for the wisdom of the past embodied in the institutions and moral structures of the day and a deeply felt distrust of schemes to scrap the practices and patterns embedded in society and of human efforts to design something entirely new. Current practices should grow and evolve over time, not be uprooted and replaced with what today's opinion judges to be better.

With traditional, Burkean conservatism in mind, suddenly the Right's opposition to abortion and same-sex marriage and its friendliness to religion and religious traditions, even when they require active governmental intervention, become understandable. Thus, the Right has tended to be highly critical of the Supreme Court's strict separation, no-aid-to-religion principle, seeing it as undercutting the traditional values crucial to a free, healthy democracy. Also, the Right's strong support for efforts to support the police in their fight against drugs and other criminal activity, for long prison sentences for those convicted of crimes, for the death penalty for first degree murder, for the teaching of abstinence in teen sex education classes, and for a strong national defense become explainable as a part of the conservative approach to the issues of today. These all mean a stronger, more active government; they also all mean a defense of traditional values—including those that are religiously based—and a defense of society against outside forces that would destroy and disrupt.

Both of these first two factors that underlie the Right's mindset towards faith-based organizations—an Enlightenment-inspired fear of big government and a Burkean conservative faith in well-established, traditional institutions, values, and practices—can be seen in how the Heritage Foundation, probably the leading conservative think tank in Washington, D.C., describes itself: "Founded in 1973, The Heritage Foundation is a research and educational institution—a think tank—whose mission is to formulate and promote conservative public policies based on the principles of free enterprise, limited government, individual freedom, traditional American values, and a strong national defense."[35] The less-government, Enlightenment-inspired facet of the Right is seen in its commitment to free enterprise, limited government, and individual freedom; its Burkean, traditional conservative facet is seen in its commitment to traditional values and a strong national defense.

The influence of Burkean conservatism—with its emphasis on the importance of religion and other traditional values, as well as the communities that give them birth and nurture them—serves as a healthy corrective to the individualism bequeathed by the Enlightenment. It recognizes that human beings and human reason are flawed and can be turned to selfish, destructive ends, if not restrained by societal conventions forged and tested over time—and sometimes reinforced by law. The Right's commendable respect for and desire to defend the place of religion in society and in faith-based organizations can be traced back to this factor. Nevertheless, there are problems. Traditional, Burkean conservatism tends to see religion and traditional values in a positive light because it sees them as contributing to a healthy society, not because they are necessarily rooted in truth and possess a value in their own right. This aspect of conservatism was on full display when President Dwight Eisenhower once famously said: "In other words, our form of government has no sense unless it is founded in a deeply felt religious faith, and I don't care what it is."[36] From the outset, traditional conservatism thereby infuses the right with a certain pragmatic cast that primarily views traditional values and institutions as useful, perhaps even essential, for a stable, peaceful society.

It is also important to recall that Burkean conservatism does not defend a static society, but recognizes the importance for traditional societal values and ways of doing things to develop and evolve over time. This is good. Some traditional values should change, as happened in American society in the past fifty years with attitudes towards racial segregation, interracial marriages, and gender roles. But Burkean conservatism itself does not contain principles by which to evaluate what traditional values should and should not change. The Right thereby at times is in the position of initially opposing certain social changes or reforms, seeing them being adopted over its opposition, and after the passage of time fully embracing them.

These marks of Burkean conservatism leave faith-based organizations and the services they provide in a vulnerable position, without clear standards or principles by which to defend themselves and their autonomy. Their position and protections can be challenged by claims that they in fact are not contributing as much as expected, in pragmatic fashion, to a healthy society—or that a healthy society could exist without them. Or they may lose the basis for their independence and autonomy, if societal values evolve over time in such a way that leaves them vulnerable. Now, for example, societal values would largely defend on the basis of freedom of conscience the right of a Catholic health clinic to refuse to provide abortions, but if societal values would over time evolve to the point where abortion was nearly universally recognized as a right, the current grounds now supporting the right of that Catholic clinic to refuse to do abortions would be eroded.

Also lacking are standards or principles by which to judge when government and its regulations or programs are needed and when government should defer either to individuals or to the many informal groups and formally organized associations lying in between the individual and the government. Traditional conservatism thereby tends to encourage an indiscriminate wariness of government as a force for change, rather than developing defensible standards or principles to judge the proper role of faith-based organizations operating in the public realm and how to apportion their place and government's place.

These first two factors underlying the Right's mindset are reflected in and reinforced by two additional factors. One is *a generalized appreciation of religion and a genuine respect for its role in society.* This factor emerges from the Burkean, traditional wing of conservatism. Among the traditional values that knit Americans together into communities and a nation, religion is seen as one of the most important. It is seen as a crucial basis on which such virtues as selflessness, a concern for others, law abidingness, and accepting family and community responsibilities are rooted. It sees religion as an important part of the American heritage and as having played a key, positive role in the American story—from George Washington to Abraham Lincoln to Martin Luther King, Jr. In this the Right embraces the idea that democratic society can only flourish among a moral people, whose morality is taught and strengthened by religious traditions and observances.

Thus the Right rejects a public realm stripped of all religious symbols and references. It favors prayers at the start of public ceremonies, the posting of the Ten Commandments in certain public places, presidential proclamations of national days of prayer or thanksgiving, and other such acknowledgments of religion. Conservatives—with their respect for religion and their belief that it has an important role to play in a stable, free, and prosperous society—instinctively lean in the direction of supporting religious symbols and references that signal a place for religion in the public square. This means conservatives reject strict separation, no-aid-to-religion interpretations of the First Amendment. Many favor the accommodationist position that would allow government to recognize and even support religion, as long as it is recognizing or supporting a generalized religion that does not favor one faith over another. They agree with Justice William Rehnquist, who, as seen in the prior chapter, once insisted in a dissenting opinion: "Nothing in the Establishment Clause of the First Amendment, properly understood, prohibits any such generalized 'endorsement' of prayer."[37]

Conservatives are correct in respecting the contributions of religion to the well-being of society and more specifically in challenging the strict separation, no-aid-to-religion standard the Supreme Court has often followed. However, their generalized respect for religion faces the same problems as their support for traditional values more generally. This respect is based more on tradition, long-standing practices, and religion's contributions to a stable, peaceful society than on its being rooted in certain principles that defend religion's rightful place in a pluralistic society. Thus, as tradition and established practices evolve and as persons question religion's contribution to society or are able to demonstrate that stable, peaceful societies can exist without religion (witness Sweden and other secularized societies of Western Europe), the basis for respecting religion and for opposing the strict separation, no-aid position melt away.

Also, the accommodationist position that supports governmental recognition and support of religion generally, as long as it is not favoring any one religion specifically, has its problems. In one respect this position has the same problem as the strict separationist position. Both give insufficient weight to the fact noted in chapter 3 that the sharpest religious divide in the United States today is between traditional religion in its various manifestations and a largely secular ethos or worldview. The strict separationist would in effect have government take the side of the secularists; the accommodationists the side of the religionists. In either case, government is being less than neutral on the greatest, most consequential religious divide in American society today. The point made by Michael McConnell in his quotation from chapter 3 is equally applicable to the strict separationist and the accommodationist positions: "In the marketplace of ideas, secular viewpoints and ideologies are in competition with religious viewpoints and ideologies. It is no more neutral to favor the secular over the religious than it is to favor the religious over the secular."[38]

A fourth factor underlying the right's mindset towards faith-based organizations is *a belief that government is not a trustworthy agent for social change*. It emerges from a fusing of the libertarian suspicion of governmental power and the Burkean conservative suspicion of rapid social change. The libertarian predisposition sees government itself as a threat to individual freedom, and the Burkean predisposition fears that human beings are too imperfect and too limited to construct new answers to enduring social problems and then enact those answers into law. To try to do so is to engage in human arrogance and hubris. The health care reform program that was strongly pushed by the Obama administration and passed by Congress in 2010 over adamant conservative opposition is an example of an issue where both wings of conservatism came together in opposition to a major public policy initiative. The Right has also been opposed to strong new regulations of the banking industry and legislative or executive branch efforts to limit carbon emissions in an effort to limit global climate change. All these are seen as attempts to enact new government policies that would force sharp breaks with well-established practices that, while not perfect, are functioning reasonably well. Enacting new policies such as these is seen as an unnecessary tampering with established patterns that are likely to result in more harm than good. In the case of faith-based organizations, this factor leads the Right to oppose attempts to impose new standards and regulations on faith-based providers of services, fearing that government meddling in their practices will interfere in the very thing that makes them effective.

History teaches that this fourth factor shaping the Right's mindset towards faith-based organizations in the public square has often been correct—but also often wrong. Prohibition, the war in Vietnam, President Lyndon Johnson's war on poverty, and many government-to-government foreign aid programs stand as examples of government programs that most now agree failed to live up to expectations. However, the Social Security program enacted in 1936, the civil rights laws of the 1960s, and President George W. Bush's PEPFAR (President's Emergency Plan for AIDS Relief) are all now seen as successes that lifted persons out of poverty, changed attitudes toward race and equality of opportunity, and saved thousands of lives. Again, what the Right lacks are standards or yardsticks by which to judge which proposed programs are likely to succeed and which ones are not. When it comes to faith-based programs and the potential for partnerships between government and faith-based organizations, the Right can offer a generalized caution, or suspicion, towards such partnerships but few standards by which to judge which ones under what conditions and circumstances are likely to succeed and which ones are not.

In summary, the mindset of the Right in relation to faith-based providers of public services is shaped by the four factors discussed in this section: an Enlightenment-inspired suspicion of governmental power and authority; a Burkean conservative respect for tradition and a suspicion of human efforts to forge new answers to persistent problems; a generalized respect for religion and a rejection of the strict separation, no-aid-to-religion line of Supreme Court reasoning; and a rejection of government as a trustworthy agent of social change. These four factors have led to a mindset—an interrelated set of attitudes, assumptions, predispositions, and values—that conditions how the Right—as does the Left's mindset for liberals—views and understands faith-based organizations. This mindset functions as a lens through which conservatives react to and view faith-based organizations as providers of public services. The next section considers how their doing so works itself out in more specific commitments and policy applications.

Applications of the Right's Mindset towards Faith-Based Organizations in the Public Realm

Growing out of the conservative mindset are four crucial applications that the Right makes in regard to faith-based organizations providing human services to the public. Together they mean that, although the Right is more favorable to faith-based organizations providing public human services, it does not have much more of a clearly, self-consciously thought out theoretical framework into which it can fit faith-based organizations than what the Left has.

First, somewhat surprisingly, *the presence and relevance of faith-based organizations in the public life of the nation are often missed by the Right,* even if not as frequently as they are by the Left. Earlier I mentioned President Obama's 2010 State of the Union address and how in it he ignored faith-based and other nonprofit organizations and their potential role in meeting the challenges American society was facing. The Republican response that evening was given by Robert McDonnell, the Republican governor of Virginia. He did not mention faith-based organizations any more than Obama did.[39] Outside of a passing reference to families, the Republican response looked only to free enterprise, individual efforts, and needed governmental actions. McDonnell stated: "We must enact policies that promote entrepreneurship and innovation, so America can better compete in the world. What government should not do is pile on more taxation, regulation, and litigation that kill jobs and hurt the middle class." He then went on quote the Enlightenment liberal, Thomas Jefferson, as describing the ideal when he wrote: "A wise and frugal Government which shall leave men free to regulate their own pursuits of industry . . . and shall not take from the mouth of labor the bread it has earned." The traditional, Burkean wing of conservatism only came out in a call for a strong national defense and a tip of the hat to religion by a brief quotation from the Bible. But any reference to faith-based organizations—or any nonprofit organizations—were as absent from his address as they were from Obama's. The Right's emphasis on free, autonomous individuals making their way in a competitive, free market system, leads it largely to miss the importance of faith-based organizations—as well as the nonprofit sector generally—in the provision of public services to those in need.

To formulate and evaluate public policies and miss the existence and actual and potential contributions of faith-based organizations in meeting public needs is to look through lenses that distort and block part of the public policy landscape. The Right's thinking in terms of individual freedom versus government regulation and control leads it often to ignore this entire sector lying in between the individual and government. Admittedly, sometimes individual conservative thinkers and especially the leading conservative think tank, the Heritage Foundation, think in terms of the faith-based and other organizations in the nonprofit sector,[40] but in perusing the statements, writings, and websites of leading conservative policy advocates and politicians, one is struck by the absence of references to the nonprofit and faith-based sector as serious players in the provision of public services. The Republican response to the 2010 State of the Union address by Robert McDonnell cited above is close being to the norm.

Second, the Right, lacking a thought-out set of concepts that assigns faith-based providers a legitimate place in the mix of human services, usually *sees and seeks to defend them in pragmatic terms—as a practical means to reduce the size and scope of government or to achieve more favorable results than government-run programs can.* Jim Towey was the head of President George W. Bush's White House Office of Faith-Based and Community Initiatives from 2002 to 2006. He once defended using faith-based organizations to meet human needs with these words:

> I went to the Bowery Mission in New York City, a homeless shelter that has been on the Lower East Side for 122 years. It has lots of caring volunteers, lots of community connections. The work they do is impressive. Under its nine-month program the recidivism rate is 7 percent. The City of New York has 12,000 shelter beds; some of the city-run shelters are over a thousand beds each. Think about the quality of life in those kind of facilities. They look like little more than prisons. And the recidivism rate back into the shelter system is 90 percent.[41]

Towey contrasted a faith-based program with a government-run program and saw the faith-based one as having much better outcomes.

Similarly, Michael Tanner of the Cato Institute has confidently asserted: "No one denies that private charities, especially faith-based ones, can transform lives and help lift people out of poverty and despair. Indeed, private charities are more effective than government welfare programs in fulfilling those roles."[42] Similarly, when George W. Bush in 1999 was just beginning his campaign for president, he made a speech that committed his administration to helping faith-based organizations in the work they were doing with these words:

> In every instance where my administration sees a responsibility to help people, we will look first to faith-based organizations, charities and community groups that have shown their ability to save and change lives. We will make a determined attack on need, by promoting the compassionate acts of others. . . . This will not be the failed compassion of towering, distant bureaucracies. . . . We will take this path, first and foremost, because private and religious groups are effective. Because they have clear advantages over government.[43]

Towey, Tanner, and Bush all contrasted the effectiveness of faith-based organizations with the presumed ineffectiveness of government agencies. They saw faith-based and other charitable programs as being able to take over for government-run programs and doing a more compassionate, effective job.

This view grows out of the Right's respect for religion and the traditional values that religion supports, combined with the Right's ingrained distrust of government. Religion is a part of the fabric of society that has evolved over many years, thus one would naturally expect providers that come out of a religious tradition to be more successful in working with those in need than would government programs with no religious elements at all and based on the latest social science research findings. Faith-based programs uphold what conservatives see as the moral bedrock of American society as a whole, as well as qualities in individuals that lead to success, such as a sense of personal responsibility and a strong work ethic. Thus, conservatives tend to readily attribute spectacular success levels to faith-based programs. Their underlying mindset leads them to expect such results.

Similar to a belief in the greater effectiveness of faith-based programs compared to government-run programs is the pragmatic belief that relying more fully on faith-based programs to provide for those in need is an effective strategy for reducing the size and reach of government. Conservatives who resonate closely with the libertarian facet of conservatism often take this position. For instance, Marvin Olasky, editor of *World* magazine and prominent policy wonk usually associated with the religious right, once wrote: "It is time now, however, to talk not about reforming the welfare system—which often means scraping off a bit of mold—but about replacing it with a truly compassionate approach based in private and religious charity."[44] He saw faith-based organizations and other nongovernmental entities as a means to get government out of the welfare business.

Given the presumed clumsy, stumbling efforts of government, all will gain to the extent faith-based programs can supplement, and perhaps fully replace government programs. Tanner in the essay from which I quoted above concludes by urging, "Budget hawks, advocates of religious freedom, and the faith-based community itself should join together and get government out of the charity business."[45] Even conservatives who do not go as far as Olasky and Tanner often view faith-based organizations favorably due to their presumed ability to reduce the role and reach of government by providing services previously delivered by government agencies.

In short, the Right's suspicion of government and its respect for religion and traditional values lead conservatives to support a robust role for faith-based providers of human services, but it does so not on principled grounds but on the pragmatic grounds that they can do a better, more effective job than can governmental human service providers and that relying on them can reduce the size of government.

But there are problems with this position. It leaves faith-based organizations open to challenge on pragmatic grounds. From the Right's point of view, faith-based organizations are to be admired, government is to partner with them whenever possible, and their religious elements ought to be protected because they are more effective in meeting the needs of the public than other ways of doing so. However, if ever it could be demonstrated that faith-based programs—either as a whole or, more likely, certain specific ones—are no more or even less effective than government-run or other secular programs, the basis for defending their role in providing human services, either alone or in partnership with government, would disappear. In fact, social science research is beginning to find that faith-based programs tend to have only slightly better outcomes than their secular counterparts.[46] More seriously, if it could ever be demonstrated that a given faith-based program has just as good outcomes with its religious elements removed as when they are present, the case for protecting their religious elements disappears. If there is no principled, religious-autonomy basis for protecting the religious freedom rights of faith-based organizations, they are put in a position of constantly having to prove that their religiously based practices are important for the effectiveness of the services they are providing.

Similarly, when the Right views faith-based organizations as a means to shrink the size of government, they are again being seen as a means to a desired end, not as possessing a legitimate role to play in society in their own right. If one could ever figure out an even better way to reduce the size of government, the rationale for relying on faith-based organizations to meet public needs would disappear. In addition, this offers no basis for defending the religious-freedom rights of faith-based organizations, since a program stripped of its religious elements may be able to take over for government-provided services—thereby reducing the size of government—just as well as one that maintains its distinctive religious elements. Also, if it would turn out that faith-based organizations were unable to meet the needs of those the government had stopped serving, the whole effort would be viewed as a failure. And that would almost inevitably be the case if the role of government would ever be reduced drastically, since the level of government efforts and expenditures outstrips those of the nonprofit sector many times over. The role and value of faith-based organizations—and other nonprofit organizations— would be tied to their ability take over government's role in meeting human need, surely a losing proposition.

The Right's mindset that respects traditional values and religious beliefs as important aspects of a stable, healthy society leads it *to support protecting the faith elements in faith-based organizations and their programs.* This position is rooted in the Right's generalized respect for, and recognition of, the importance of religion in a healthy society, and in its rejection of the strict separation, no-aid-to-religion interpretation of the First Amendment in favor of an accommodationist position that sees no constitutional problem in government's encouragement of religion as long as it does not favor one religious group over another. This position can be clearly seen in an open memo two staff persons at the conservative think tank, the Heritage Foundation, wrote to Barack Obama upon his election in 2008:

> Our Constitution rightly forbids establishing an official national church, but it does not call for the separation of religion from politics. . . . From our earliest days as a nation, religion and morality have been "indispensable supports of good habits, the firmest props of the duties of citizens, and the great pillars of human happiness." . . . Forcing faith-based organizations to abandon their religious identity and religious integrity whenever they partner with the federal government to serve the needy would be a major mistake.[47]

Later—in the context of medical procedures such as abortion, abortion training, and sterilization—they urged Obama to "ensure the availability of federal conscience protections that free physicians and other medical professionals to serve patients without violating their religious beliefs."[48] It has largely been conservative organizations and public figures that have taken the lead in defending the right of faith-based organizations—even when receiving government subsidies for their programs—to take religion into account when hiring staff and in other ways to allow certain religious elements to remain in faith-based programs. It was conservative Republican Jim Sensenbrenner who, in the quotation at the beginning of chapter 3, defended the right of faith-based organizations to take religion into account in their hiring. And conservatives have defended the ability of faith-based organizations to engage in practices based on their religious beliefs that others have labeled discriminatory, such as the right of faith-based organizations not to provide abortions and to take lifestyle choices—such as same-sex relationships—into account in hiring staff.

There is much to commend in the Right's mindset that leads it to view faith-based organizations through the lens of traditional values and a respect for religion. Again and again, Republicans and others on the Right have been in the forefront of political battles to protect the ability of faith-based organizations to act on the basis of their faith. That is to be commended. But two weaknesses mark the Right's efforts to defend the place of religion in the work of faith-based organizations.

One weakness rests on the fact that not every religiously rooted aspect of every faith-based organization should be defended. Imagine, hypothetically, a grab bag of faith-based organizations with the following practices: refusing to provide services to African-Americans; insisting it hire only staff members who are supportive of its religiously based mission; using messages of God's love and care to encourage and lift up those beaten down by their life experiences; using severe corporal punishment on children in order to discipline them; threatening a drug-dependent person with hell-fire if he or she does not remain drug-free; offering a Bible study for program participants; having a crucifix in the room where free flu shots are being administered to the elderly; and firing an employee who is discovered to be in a same-sex relationship. The question is this: Which of these religiously based practices should faith-based organizations be free to pursue and which ones should they not? Also, to what extent is the appropriate answer dependent on whether or not the faith-based organization is receiving government funds? The problem is that the Right's generalized support for religion having a legitimate role in the public realm, and therefore also in the programs and activities of faith-based organizations providing services to the public, does not offer a ready answer. What are needed are standards, guidelines, and tests to determine which of the listed situations faith-based organizations should be able to follow and which not—and to be able to defend clearly one's answers.

The second weakness in conservatives' attempts to protect the religiously based practices of faith-based organizations relates to their frequent support of the accommodationist position on church-state separation. They are right to reject the Left's no-aid separation as *the* proper interpretation of the First Amendment, but in substituting a generalized favoring of religion over secularism—that is, an accommodationist alternative—they face the same charges of a discriminatory position as the strict separationists do. The answer to a non-neutral favoring of secular perspectives and practices ought not to be a non-neutral favoring of religious perspectives and practices.

The ingrained suspicion of government within conservatism leads the right to a fourth way in which it approaches faith-based organizations and their place in the mix of public services: *seeing faith-based organizations as being in danger from over-regulation by government that will reduce their freedom and effectiveness.* This is especially seen as being the case when faith-based organizations accept government funding. Government is seen as more of a threat than as a potential partner. It was on this basis that the libertarian Cato Institute has opposed faith-based initiatives. A few months after President George W. Bush created his White House Office of Faith-Based and Community Initiatives, the Cato Institute published a seminal article whose title alone made clear its chief point: "Corrupting Charity: Why Government Should Not Fund Faith-Based Charities."[49] The same author, in an essay that appeared while Barack Obama was president, made clear he was against government funding whether a Republican or Democrat was president, declaring, "Government money never comes without strings," and, "There is no reason for government to be in bed with private charity."[50] Government is seen as toxic—inherently corrupting and unnecessary. Both Cato Institute essays make the point that faith-based charities do not need to partner with government; they can successfully pursue their charitable ends just as effectively, indeed better, without government.

Admittedly, there are many conservatives who do not accept this position of the strongly libertarian Cato Institute and who believe it is fully appropriate for government to help fund the programs of faith-based organizations. Many examples of this can be found, including that of President George W. Bush, persons who were associated with his Office of Faith-Based and Community Initiatives, and various studies coming out of the Heritage Foundation. But running through them is a certain wariness of government and a fear that with government's shekels will come government's shackles, as it has sometimes been put.

The Right's fears that faith-based organizations' partnerships with government will result in a loss of freedoms and autonomy are not without some basis. This chapter earlier documented how the Left's mindset can threaten the religious autonomy of faith-based organizations. The Right's wariness is well placed. But even here the Right's thinking is not without problems. If the position I have put forward thus far—that of both the Left and the Right lacking thought-out, defensible concepts with which to define and defend the rightful autonomy of faith-based organizations—is correct, the answer to the Right's fears would seem to be to develop and insist upon those concepts, not simply to avoid partnerships with government or to continue to rely on the pragmatic considerations just discussed. For faith-based organizations to accept government funds for certain of their programs, while relying on pragmatic claims of greater effectiveness or of reducing government's reach, is to put themselves in a vulnerable position; to refuse to accept government funds that are available and going to their secular counterparts would be to accept a second class status and would tend to marginalize themselves. Also, not accepting government funds can lead to a false sense of security. Government shackles *without* government's shekels is a danger as well as government shackles *with* government's shekels. Think of nondiscrimination laws that seek to require faith-based adoption agencies to place children with same-sex couples, even when contrary to their religiously formed consciences. The case mentioned in chapter 1 of employees let go by World Vision due to their no longer being in agreement with its statement of faith did not turn on World Vision accepting some government funding, but on the employees' claim that World Vision is not a religious organization. Even without government funding, World Vision could have found itself in court having to defend its hiring practices.

In short, the Right's wariness in regard to government regulation is well placed, but at least for some faith-based organizations the answer is not to avoid all government funds, but to develop and insist upon concepts and principles that defend their rightful religious autonomy. That is what this book seeks to do.

In summary, the Right's mindset towards faith-based organizations and their role in the world of services to the public has been shaped by an Enlightenment-inspired fear of government; a Burkean conservative respect for tradition and suspicion of radical change, a rejection of the strict separation, no-aid-to-religion line of Supreme Court reasoning in favor of an accommodationist position; and a rejection of government as a trustworthy agent of change. The Right's mindset that has been shaped by these forces leads it sometimes to fail to see or recognize the importance of faith-based organizations in the public life of the nation; to take a pragmatic defense of the role for faith-based organizations in the public realm; to support and defend the faith elements in faith-based programs, but often on inadequate bases; and to be suspicious of faith-based partnerships with government.

This chapter and the previous ones have put forward the very basic point that we as a people are now not responding well to the many questions surrounding the place of faith-based organizations in the public realm, resulting in threats to both religious freedom and religious pluralism, because we as the American polity—including the Left and the Right, Democrats and Republicans—do not have appropriate theoretical concepts and perspectives with which to properly frame and answer the questions. The remaining chapters seek to move us towards remedying that lack by laying out theoretical concepts and perspectives that place faith-based organizations in a context that describes their role in society, the basis of that role, and the nature and extent of the freedom or autonomy they possess as a right.

Chapter 5

Structural Pluralism in Christian Democratic Thought

A consistent, underlying theme of this book is that we as a polity are experiencing deep disagreements over faith-based public service organizations because we do not have an agreed upon set of theoretical concepts, beliefs, assumptions, and patterns of thought—a mindset—that governs our ways of looking at and understanding faith-based organizations and their place in the mix of public health, educational, and social services. We stand divided because our starting points are so different. The religious freedom of persons of all faiths and of none, the rightful autonomy of faith-based organizations, and the provision of services to those in need—all three—are thereby limited and in jeopardy.

All of us—the Left and the Right, no-aid strict separationists and conservative accommodationists—need to go back to square one and think through basic assumptions, concepts, and ways of thinking. If one has taken a wrong turn in a road, the quickest way to get on is to turn around, go back to the beginning, and seek a different road. This chapter does this by presenting the ideas and concepts of structural pluralism, a theoretical concept that has played a large role in Christian Democratic thinking in Europe. I am convinced the framework it provides for understanding faith-based organizations and their place in the mix of public services offers a way to protect the religious autonomy of faith-based organizations and the religious freedom rights of all persons, religious and irreligious alike.

This chapter first considers the ways in which the neutrality, equal treatment line of reasoning that has been gaining acceptance in the Supreme Court leads, more broadly, to an understanding of church-state separation and religious freedom that forms a legal foundation for the constitutionality of the structural pluralist approach to the place of faith-based organizations in the public policy mix. I then present the theory of structural pluralism, its underlying concepts, and how, in the European Christian Democratic tradition, it developed and shaped thinking about pluralism and faith-based organizations in the public policy realm. The last two sections consider the ongoing impact of structural pluralist, Christian Democratic thinking in many of today's European liberal democracies and several factors that suggest the time may be right for it to take root and flourish in the United States.

RELIGIOUS FREEDOM IN THE CONTEXT OF CHURCH-STATE SEPARATION

In the world of religious faith and belief an amazing diversity of religious belief systems give meaning and direction to Americans in a host of different ways, as do various secularly based belief systems. Some are rooted in faith traditions going back thousands of years; others arise and disappear like spring flowers. Some hold to a personal God who actively intervenes in human affairs and guides the lives of individuals; others hold to a God who is an impersonal spirit or force that one discovers within one's self. Some are religious in a traditional sense; others reject the existence of the supernatural altogether, yet possess a system of beliefs that guides them in much the same way that religious faith does for others. To say the United States is marked by religious pluralism understates the case.

A second understatement is that Americans disagree on what is meant by church-state separation and how the First Amendment should be interpreted in order to achieve religious freedom for all. Supreme Court decisions dealing with church-state issues are often decided by 5-to-4 votes, followed by conflicting media comments, with some advocacy groups applauding the decision and others condemning it, only to be followed by further litigation.

In light of differences of opinion over how to attain religious freedom for all in a society deeply divided by religious differences, this section presents an understanding of religious freedom and the means to attain it that has significant support among some legal scholars and Supreme Court justices, but is far from accepted doctrine among the media and academic elites and has not penetrated deeply into popular culture. Yet it is important for a structural pluralist understanding of societal diversity and religion's place in it.

It is important to recall that chapter 3 considered three competing standards the Supreme Court and its justices have used in interpreting the religious freedom language of the First Amendment as applied to today's religious freedom and church-state separation issues: the no-aid-to-religion, strict separation; the neutrality, equal treatment; and the accommodationist standards.

The first two in particular are competing with each other as criteria by which to interpret the First Amendment and define religious freedom today. As also seen in chapter 3, although the no-aid standard advanced the cause of religious freedom in response to the issues being debated in the late eighteenth and early nineteenth centuries, it has serious shortcomings in answering the church-state issues under debate in the twenty-first century. As I maintained there, it does not provide a guide to what governmental regulations of faith-based organizations are appropriate and inappropriate, and it puts faith-based organizations at a government-created disadvantage when it funds secular educational and human service programs but refuses to fund similar or parallel faith-based programs or offers funds to them only on the condition that they secularize their programs. The accommodationist standard has the same problem as the no-aid standard, only it would put secular organizations and views, not faith-based ones, at a government-created disadvantage. Chapter 4 argued that both the Left, in supporting the no-aid strict separation standard, and the Right, in supporting an accommodationist, generalized encouragement of religion, are deficient.

This leads directly to the neutrality line of reasoning that the Supreme Court has been relying upon more frequently in recent years. I believe this principle, when given a more exact definition and formulated as a standard that can be applied in a wide variety of situations, leads to the fullest religious freedom for persons and organizations of all faiths and of none. This standard is what has been called substantive religious neutrality. In the midst of a colorful diversity of belief systems, substantive neutrality means that government and the public policies it pursues must not favor certain religious faiths or certain secular belief systems over others. As much as possible, government and its actions should not encourage its citizens to follow one religious or secular faith or another, nor should it discourage them from doing so. Its policies should neither advantage nor disadvantage one religious faith or secular belief system over another. Nor should it encourage or discourage either religious belief systems generally or secular belief systems generally.

Douglas Laycock is the legal scholar most closely associated with substantive neutrality. He states that it means "the Religion Clauses require government to minimize the extent to which it either encourages or discourages religious belief or disbelief, practice or nonpractice, observance or nonobservance."[1] He then goes on to argue that substantive neutrality means religion

> should proceed as unaffected by government as possible. Government should not interfere with our beliefs about religion either by coercion or by persuasion. Government is not to make it easier for citizens to accept any particular religion

or spirituality and religious faith more generally, nor make it harder for them to do so. Religion may flourish or wither; it may change or stay the same. What happens to religion is up to the people acting severally and voluntarily; it is not up to the people acting collectively through government.[2]

Substantive governmental neutrality on matters of religion—that is, a real, authentic governmental neutrality, with genuinely evenhanded incentives and disincentives in its treatment of religion—should be the goal of government, including government in its relationships with faith-based organizations.[3] Both the strict separation of church and state and the accommodation of religion ought not to be seen as goals or ends to be pursued for their own sake; rather the substantive neutrality of government towards religion and religious organizations, and comparable secular systems of belief, should be the goal or end pursued. It is the standard against which proposed governmental actions should be evaluated. Sometimes and under some circumstances strict separation may help reach the goal of substantive neutrality, other times it may not. The same can be said for accommodation.

Substantive neutrality is closely related to the equal treatment, neutrality standard of First Amendment interpretation that has been gaining acceptance on the Supreme Court. Both insist that equal treatment of religious and secular organizations that are conducting similar or parallel programs is a surer path to a genuine government neutrality—a neutrality that favors neither religious or secular beliefs—than is a rigid no-aid-to-religion standard. The neutrality, equal treatment line of reasoning and the fact that it has been gaining acceptance by the Supreme Court in recent years demonstrates that substantive neutrality has legitimate constitutional merit. This means that structural pluralism and how it treats faith-based organizations has a base in American constitutional interpretations.

I need to clarify what I mean by a term I use here and elsewhere in this book, namely, secular belief system or secular systems of belief. They deserve respect and a freedom on par with religion and religious belief systems, but I have not explained what exactly I mean by them. Surely not all nonreligious, secular beliefs can be included, from beliefs concerning the superiority of one sports team over another to beliefs about the best year for a vintage wine. A secular belief system, as I use the term in this book, is a combination of attitudes and beliefs that, while excluding the existence of a supernatural force and thus are purely naturalistic, nontheistic in nature, functions in much the same way as does religion in the lives of theistic believers. A secular belief system incorporates beliefs about life, human beings and their nature, and the goals, purposes, and meaning of life (or, sometimes, the absence of any goals, purposes or meaning). These beliefs will vary in the extent to which they are explicitly, self-consciously thought out and held versus being implicitly and unself-consciously held. But they are there. It is these sorts of beliefs, not every belief or value to which one holds, that structural pluralism says deserve equal treatment or respect as religiously based beliefs.

In summary, a true, genuine—that is, substantive—government neutrality on matters of religion has as its goal neither the favoring nor disfavoring, the encouragement nor discouragement, of any particular religion, religion as a whole, or secular belief systems that are competing with religious belief systems. It avoids making it easier or harder for anyone to follow his or her religious beliefs or practices, or to follow their secular counterparts. Substantive neutrality is achieved by the government's equal treatment of competing or parallel organizations and belief systems, whether religious or secular in nature. Since religious congregations in their core religious and worship activities, celebrations, and rituals have no secular counterparts engaged in similar or parallel activities, they never should be subsidized or favored by government policies outside of public services that are available to all organizations alike. Substantive neutrality is the key to understanding and applying the religious freedom language of the First Amendment and is basic to structural pluralism's acceptance as being in keeping with the First Amendment and religious liberty for all. Its importance to a structural pluralist understanding of faith-based organizations in the mix of public services and their relationship with government will be seen as this chapter unpacks structural pluralist thinking and the following chapter notes its practical applications.

STRUCTURAL PLURALISM AND CHRISTIAN DEMOCRACY

We are now ready to consider structural pluralism that has played a large role in Christian Democratic thinking in Europe. While not absent from American thinking, it has had a limited influence in shaping political thinking in the United States. In this section I consider first how it arose in the nineteenth century in response to events in Europe and then the basic theories and concepts that constitute structural pluralism in both the Catholic and Protestant traditions.

Origins in Nineteenth-Century Events and Political Currents

Structural pluralism and the role it has played in Christian Democratic thinking have their origins in late eighteenth- and nineteenth-century events and political currents. As noted in chapter 3, Enlightenment liberalism challenged the authority of existing religious, class, and economic authorities with an emphasis on individual freedom. Meanwhile, as the nineteenth century and industrialization progressed, social democratic, or socialist, critiques of prevailing conditions increased. Social democrats advocated a wider franchise for the working classes and the use of the state to control the industrialized units of production. Such efforts—especially in their more radical, socialist forms—were seen by their opponents as a collectivism that would create an all-powerful state that itself would threaten personal freedoms. Kenneth Grasso has referred to "efforts by German Catholic thinkers to forge an alternative to the individualism and libertarianism of nineteenth-century liberalism and the collectivist statism of its socialist adversaries."[4] At the same time in the Netherlands, Abraham Kuyper—a nineteenth-century Dutch theologian, founder of the Dutch Protestant Christian Democratic party, and prime minister—was forging a Protestant response to the challenge posed by Enlightenment liberalism that bore many similarities to the Catholic response. Thus Christian Democracy and the social teachings that underlie it can best be seen as a third way marked by neither the collectivism of socialist thought and its near-relatives nor the libertarianism of those who fear any interference with individuals' freedom to act as they wish.

What must be stressed at the outset is that structural pluralism sees the distinctions and concepts presented here not as artificial constructs that are products of abstract thinking, but as accurate understandings of the way human society in fact is and is intended to be. They are a reflection of the created order, of the inherent, innate nature of human beings and of human society as they intrinsically are. They can be identified by observations of and reflection on human relationships. Christian faith enters in the sense that what one learns from biblical teachings and historic patterns of Christian thought over the centuries guide, support, and reinforce one's observations. Christian Democracy insists that its theoretical understanding of structural pluralism rests on the world of social relationships as it truly is, guided by and confirmed by the witness of the Bible and hundreds of years of Christian reflection.

Personalism

A key concept serving as an underpinning of structural pluralism is what has been termed personalism. Two key concepts or ideas together contribute to personalism, which at times has also been called Christianized individualism.[5] The starting point of personalism is to see human beings in all of their multiple aspects: material, spiritual, social, emotional, and moral. Pluralists see the liberal Enlightenment understanding of human beings as focusing overly much on their material or physical aspect. R. E. M. Irving, in describing the political theory of the Christian Democratic parties has written, "The essence of personalism is its strong emphasis on the importance of the development of *all* dimensions of human personality, social as well as individual and spiritual as well as material."[6] All facets of human beings, in Christian Democratic thinking, are important. The French Catholic theorist, Jacques Maritain, reacted against liberal individualism as being a purely material concept that saw individuals as only a "fragment of a species."[7] Abraham Kuyper, the Dutch theologian and political activist, condemned the individualism of the French Revolution and its liberalism for reducing human beings to the material, "earthly things," creating "a sphere of lower pressures in which money was the standard of value, and everything was sacrificed for money."[8] Historian Dirk Jellema reflected this perspective when he wrote that Kuyper believed "Christianity, in contrast [to the French Revolution and the Enlightenment], means that people must be treated as *persons* rather than as 'machines of flesh.'"[9]

The second facet of personalism places due weight on the social nature of human beings. We engage in the distinctive activities of human beings—creating culture, making artifacts, worshipping, providing for our families, finding our identity and purpose—not as solitary individuals, but in conjunction with other human beings. The Second Vatican Council's document, *Gaudium et Spes*, makes this point clearly:

> The fact that human beings are social by nature indicates that the betterment of the person and the improvement of society depend on each other. Insofar as humanity by its very nature stands completely in need of life in society, it is and it ought to be the beginning, the subject and the object of every social organization. Life in society is not something accessory to humanity: through their dealings with others, through mutual service, and through fraternal and sororal dialogue, men and women develop all their talents and become able to rise to their destiny.[10]

Similarly, Dutch scholar Kees van Kersbergen has, in reference to personalism, explained that under it persons "should be grouped in a plural social structure, in which room is left for the free, though socially responsible, development of groups of all shapes and sizes."[11] Human beings are social creatures and thus part of their nature as persons is their need to live in community with other human beings.

In summary, personalism places an emphasis—in contrast to classical, Enlightenment liberalism—on the whole person in all of his or her God-given facets and on persons as social beings, necessarily and inherently integrated into broader human communities and societies. The British scholar, David

Hanley, has stated it well: "Personalism sees society as composed not of individuals (as in the liberal paradigm), but persons. The person is an outgoing, fundamentally sociable being, whose destiny is realised . . . through insertion into different types of community, be it neighbourhood, church, family or nation."[12]

The Pluralism of Structural Pluralism

Structural pluralist thought builds upon personalism to insist on the unavoidable existence and crucial importance in all human societies of a diversity of social institutions and structures. Human beings do not exist purely as autonomous, discreet individuals nor as individuals united only by belonging to a national political community. All human societies are marked by a multiplicity of intermediate social structures that lie between individuals and the national political community: families, religious congregations, neighborhood groups, social clubs, nonprofit social service organizations, universities, businesses, labor unions, athletic leagues, and a host of other such social structures. These are not the result of rational individuals voluntarily choosing to form themselves into social entities, nor are they simply a pragmatic means to achieve certain goals. Rather, they are of the very essence of human society, an intrinsic, essential characteristic of society as intended and created by God. This is the pluralism of structural pluralism.

The types and exact nature of the social institutions vary, of course, from one society and culture to another. Western culture is marked by a high proportion of formal associations with established rules and processes; some other cultures are marked by informal kinship and tribal groupings with unwritten norms and processes. In some cultures, "family" is largely defined in terms of nuclear families of father, mother, and unmarried children; in other cultures, "family" is defined in terms of extended families that encompass what the former cultures would consider distant relatives, if they would see them as relatives at all. In some cultures families are patriarchal; in others they are matriarchal. But in all societies in all times and places there have been patterns of organization and behavior that have linked persons together into social structures. This means all societies consist of more than individuals and the national state; there are a host of intermediate structures lying between the individual on the one hand and the nation and the state on the other.[13] They emerge out of the inherent, inborn, God-created nature of human beings. Therefore, the national community is truly a community of communities.

As its name indicates, structural pluralism is a pluralism of social structures and associations, not the cultural pluralism of ethnic, racial, religious, or regional groups in a society. This latter type of pluralism is often celebrated in Americans' praise of diversity or in multicultural days on college campuses. Structural pluralism, in contrast, argues that even a society that is completely homogenous in terms of linguistic groups, race, ethnicity, religion, and regions would still be marked by structural pluralism. It is the latter type of pluralism— not cultural pluralism—with which we are concerned here. But structural pluralism and cultural pluralism overlap in that different subnational cultural, ethnic, racial, regional, or religious groups often lead to structural social institutions based on the differing identities of cultural pluralism. There are a host of social entities in the United States based on its rich cultural diversity, all the way from religious congregations and associations of congregations based on differing beliefs and traditions, to religious-ethnic associations such as the Ancient Order of Hiberians, to racial/ethnic advocacy organizations such as the American Indian Movement and the NAACP. Structural pluralism insists a host of social structures would exist and play a vital role even in the absence of cultural diversity, since they are an intrinsic, necessary aspect of human society. The existence of many cultural differences in a society, as is the case in the United States, simply means there will be even more social structures and associations, since many are based on such diversity.

The structural pluralism of societies and its importance has been noted by many scholars, including a number of American scholars, even those who strictly speaking cannot be considered part of the structural pluralist tradition. The conservative sociologist Robert Nisbet (1913–1996) is one. He has written: "For man does not, cannot, live alone. His freedom is a social, not biologically derived, process. We are forced to consider . . . the indispensible role of the small social groups in society. It is the intimacy and security of each of these groups that provide the psychological context of individuality and the reinforcement of personal integrity."[14] He also quotes John Dewey as insisting, "Individuals who are not bound together in associations, whether domestic, economic, religious, political, artistic, or educational are monstrosities."[15] That American society is marked by a host of social structures is also clearly testified to by the Communitarian Platform, first promulgated in 1991 and signed by many noted American intellectuals such as Robert Bellah, Emitai Etzioni, William Galston, Mary Ann Glendon, and Barbara Dafoe Whitehead. It begins with these words:

> American men, women, and children are members of many communities— families; neighborhoods; innumerable social, religious, ethnic, work place, and professional associations; and the body politic itself. Neither human existence nor individual liberty can be sustained for long outside the interdependent and overlapping communities to which all of us belong.[16]

The mere existence of these intermediate social structures is undeniable, but structural pluralism goes on to insist on two key additional points. One is that the social structures found in every society receive their right to exist and their powers not from the state nor from autonomous individuals freely entering into contractual arrangements, but from God—or, for the more secularly minded, from the necessary, inherent nature of human society. They are seen as a part of God's intention for human society. Thus, just as individuals in democratic thinking possess certain inalienable human rights given them by their Creator—that is, by God—which no government has a right to violate or take away, so also in structural pluralist thinking the social structures of civil society possess a certain autonomy as a right given them by God that no government has a right to violate or take away. Families, religious congregations, social service agencies, service clubs, fraternal organizations, and the wide variety of other social structures and associations all possess—as a right—a certain autonomy or freedom of action. The early twentieth-century British pluralist thinker and Anglican cleric, John N. Figgis, made this point clearly:

> Now the State did not create the family, nor did it create the Churches; nor even in any real sense can it be said to have created the club or the trade unions; nor in the Middle Ages the guild or the religious order, hardly even the universities or the colleges within the universities: they have all arisen out of the natural associative instincts of mankind, and should all be treated by the supreme authority as having a life original and guaranteed.[17]

A second key idea insisted upon by structural pluralists is the vital, indispensable nature of social structures for a healthy, free society. They are a part of God's intention for human society, and therefore without them, a society would collapse, or at best would remain in a weakened position marked by disorder, the psychologically wounded, economic failure, and ripe for takeover by a freedom-denying, totalitarian government. This may appear counterintuitive for some, since it is often assumed that families, religious organizations, small town life marked by informal groups, and other such social structures inhibit freedom by forging ties that limit, direct, and constrict. Nevertheless, structural pluralism insists the opposite is the case. Nisbet has made a compelling case for this conclusion. He has written: "Neither personal freedom nor personal achievement can ever be separated from the contexts of community. . . . This is not to deny the role of the individual, nor the reality of personal differences. . . . It is merely to insist on the fundamental fact that the perspectives and incentives of the free creative mind arise out of communities of purpose."[18] Nisbet goes on to argue that the free market is dependent upon the existence of intermediate social structures:

"But there has never been a time when a successful economic system has rested upon purely individualistic drives or upon the impersonal relationships so prized by the rationalists. There are always, in fact, associations and incentives nourished by the non-economic processes of kinship, religion, and various other forms of social relationships."[19] Earlier in the same work Nisbet also argued that intermediate social structures serve as a bulwark against totalitarianism and that the first goal of totalitarian regimes such as the Nazi regime in Germany and the Stalinist regime in the Soviet Union was to destroy existing social structures such as labor unions, churches, families, and other subnational community entities, with the attachments and loyalties they command. Doing so rendered persons isolated, atomistic individuals, ripe for being regimented into a single national community ready to do the bidding of the state. He has written:

> What gives historical identity to the totalitarian State is not the absolution of one man or of a clique or a class; rather, it is the absolute extension of the structure of the administrative State into the social and psychological realm previously occupied by a plurality of associations. Totalitarianism involves the demolishment of autonomous social ties in a population . . . What is central is simply the absolute substitution of the State for all the diversified associations of which society is normally composed.[20]

In summary, structural pluralism emphasizes the existence of a plurality of social structures in society—structures whose place in society, their right to exist, and their powers are God-intended and inherent, and whose role in society is essential to a healthy, free, diverse society in which individuals are able to flourish.

At this point structural pluralism may appear to be a prescription for anarchy, or at the very least a libertarian, *laissez faire* approach to public policy issues. If the innumerable social structures of society possess an inherent autonomy as a right, what role is then left to the state? The nature and extent of the autonomy possessed by society's social structures needs to be specified, which will both authenticate it and place restrictions on it. In doing so, a significant role for the state to play in relation to them will be specified. Under structural pluralism, social structures possess an autonomy that is real, but it is a limited or quasi-autonomy, not an absolute autonomy. Structural pluralism does not lead to anarchy or to the minimalist state of libertarianism any more than it leads to the all-encompassing state found in collectivist regimes. It is indeed a third way. We will first consider what Roman Catholic social thought has said about the nature and extent of the autonomy of social structures, then what continental neo-Calvinist thought has said. Together they have had enormous influence on Christian Democratic thinking.

Subsidiarity in Roman Catholic Social Thought

The word "subsidiarity" comes from the Latin "subsidium," meaning relief, assistance, or reinforcement, as in the case of a reserve military unit that comes to the aid of another unit that is hard-pressed in battle. At the heart of the concept of subsidiarity is the thought that the state or other higher, larger social structures in society ought to offer help or relief to other social structures, such as the family or neighborhood, when they are hard-pressed and in trouble—but not to usurp their functions or completely take over for them.

This principle emerged out of the observation that we earlier saw Grasso making, that nineteenth-century German Catholic thinkers attempted to develop an alternative both to an individualistic libertarianism and to a state-dominated collectivism.[21] In nineteenth-century Europe, Catholic thinking was being challenged by the anticlerical heirs of the French Revolution and their emphasis on the rational, autonomous individual making his or her own way in a world stripped of authoritarian government and religious authority. At the same time it was also being increasingly challenged by those looking to the sovereign state and its collective actions as the answer to the emerging problems being spun off by rapid industrialization. But Catholic thinking also increasingly saw that simply clinging to the old order of class privilege and rigid social and political categories was unacceptable.

Subsidiarity in Roman Catholic social thought therefore developed as a third way that did not merely steer a middle course between classic liberalism and socialism, but was genuinely rooted in a Christian view of human beings and human society. It was first developed by Pope Leo XIII in his 1891 encyclical, *Rerum Novarum*. He did not use the term "subsidiarity," yet for the first time in an official papal document the basic idea was articulated and rooted in the innate social, associative nature of human beings:

> Although private societies exist within the State and are, as it were, so many parts of it, still it is not within the authority of the State universally and per se to forbid them to exist as such. For man is permitted by a right of nature to form private societies; the State, on the other hand, has been instituted to protect and not to destroy natural right, and if it should forbid its citizens to enter into associations, it would clearly do something contradictory to itself because both the State itself and private associations are begotten of one and the same principle, namely, that men are by nature inclined to associate.[22]

The classic articulation of the fully developed concept of subsidiarity is found in Pope Pius XI's encyclical, *Quadragesimo Anno,* issued in 1931, on the fortieth anniversary of *Rerum Novarum.* Its often-quoted formulation is as follows:

Just as it is gravely wrong to take from individuals what they can accomplish by their own initiative and industry and give it to the community, so also it is an injustice and at the same time a grave evil and disturbance of right order to assign to a greater and higher association what lesser and subordinate organizations can do. For every social activity ought of its very nature to furnish help to the members of the body social, and never destroy and absorb them.

The supreme authority of the State ought, therefore, to let subordinate groups handle matters and concerns of lesser importance, which would otherwise dissipate its efforts greatly. Thereby the State will more freely, powerfully, and effectively do all those things that belong to it alone because it alone can do them: directing, watching, urging, restraining, as occasion requires and necessity demands. Therefore, those in power should be sure that the more perfectly a graduated order is kept among the various associations, in observance of the principle of "subsidiary function," the stronger social authority and effectiveness will be the happier and more prosperous the condition of the State.[23]

There are three interrelated ideas, or assertions, present in the concept of subsidiarity. One—as discussed in the prior section—is that society is made up of social structures with as much right to exist and an autonomy that is theirs as a right. It is not a gift from the state, a gift that could be withdrawn at the pleasure of the state. Second, these social structures are in a hierarchical order, with lower-level, less inclusive structures and higher-level, more inclusive structures. Third, societal tasks should be performed at the lowest level that can appropriately perform them, and higher, more inclusive structures should only help lower, less inclusive structures to perform those tasks they cannot perform alone. Even then, the higher structures ought not to take over and replace the lower structures, but only provide what help the lower structures need to enable them to fulfill their appropriate responsibilities. Jonathan Chaplin has put it succinctly: "The general principle is that the state has a duty to offer lesser communities such help as is needed in order for the latter to realize their distinctive ends."[24] The principle is even broader than this, with higher structures—and not only the state—having an obligation to help lower level structures when they need help. Thus, the family should help the individual when in need, the local congregation or neighborhood when a family is in need, the whole community when a neighborhood or congregation is in need, higher units of government when lower units of government face challenges they are unable to meet, and the national government when regional governments need help.

Subsidiarity is thereby both a limiting and an empowering principle. It has a robust, but limited view of the role of the state in society. It insists that higher units indeed have a responsibility to come to the aid of lower units when they are in need. Thus it forms the basis for local and even national governments to come to the help of private, nonprofit social service, health, and educational organizations when they are overwhelmed by needs beyond their capacity to meet. Think of social service organizations in New Orleans and the Louisiana Gulf Coast following Hurricanes Katrina and Rita in 2005, or a relief and development agency in Africa overwhelmed by the HIV/AIDS pandemic. However, subsidiarity is also a principle that limits the role of higher structures. Their role is to help the lower structures to fulfill their rightful functions, not to take over for them and surely not to intrude into their activities when there is no need to do so. Van Kersbergen has put it well when he referred to "the duty of the state to act as a subsidizer in case of inadequate lower social organs. State intervention is limited to the extent that it must not absorb the smaller social units, but should help those to such an extent that they can again take over themselves."[25] The state's role is one of enabling, complementing, and coordinating, but not overwhelming. This means that the role of higher level social institutions, and especially that of government, is extensive (they should stand ready to come to the aid of all lower social institutions when they are in need), but not intensive (the aid given should be limited and not take over or usurp the work of the lower institutions).[26]

Two additional observations are needed to understand subsidiarity fully. One is that subsidiary is not merely a theory seeking to promote in pragmatic fashion the most efficient accomplishment of societal goals, nor is it simply an antidote to overcentralization of political power. Grasso has made this point well: "Subsidiarity embodies far more than a simple recognition of the dangers of overcentralization. Likewise, far from being a mere prudential expedient, subsidiarity is rooted in a principled commitment both to the centrality of freedom in human social life and to what might be termed institutional pluralism, the idea that human flourishing requires a wide range of institutions and communities."[27] Subsidiarity needs to be seen in the context of the Catholic understanding of persons and society as created by God and as one aspect of a broader social doctrine that includes such key elements as solidarity, the common good, and social justice. Van Kersbergen and Bertjan Verbeek have made clear that subsidiarity is not a stand-alone principle, but that "in Catholic social doctrine subsidiarity is intrinsically linked to other fundamental principles, such as personalism, solidarity, pluralism and distributive justice."[28]

A second aspect of subsidiarity that must be emphasized is that it results in a conception of intermediary social structures that respects their rightful autonomy. Rightly understood subsidiarity, as Kersbergen and Verbeek have put it, "stresses the relative autonomy of social organizations in the context of a plural society."[29] This autonomy is rooted in social structures' God-given nature as necessary, inherent aspects of human society. They are not creatures of the state, nor constructs of individual human choice or social engineering. Thus their existence and the role they play in society are theirs as a right.

One final note: an aspect of subsidiarity that some have questioned is its emphasis on hierarchy. Chaplin has raised a vital question when he suggests that whatever the merits of thinking in terms of hierarchy,

> it creates evident difficulties when applied to the social world. While it is essential to acknowledge that human beings function within a *diversity* of communities, it is problematic to view these as ranked within a *hierarchy*. When we attempt to picture the multitude of communities, institutions, and groups which populate a modern, differentiated society in terms of an idea of graded hierarchy, numerous questions arise. . . . It appears difficult to find a satisfactory single criterion according to which a complete ranking could be achieved—which suggests that the very idea of a ranking may be misplaced.[30]

Can one properly say, for instance, that the family is a lesser institution than a municipal government? It certainly is less inclusive, but one could also argue that the family is more foundational, and thus in a very real sense more important and superior to a city or other regional government. Similarly, a local congregation or even a national denomination can in some ways be considered more important, playing a more vital role in their members' lives, than do other social structures that subsidiarity would seem to rank higher. The question this raises is by what criterion does subsidiarity rank the various social structures of society into lower and higher, lesser and greater, subordinate and higher categories? Grasso, while not giving up on hierarchical thinking completely, acknowledges that Chaplin raises some legitimate questions and the "problematic character of the idea of a top-to-bottom ranking."[31]

It is, however, important to recognize that the presence or absence of hierarchy in thinking about the communities and social structures of any society does not affect the point vital for our purposes, namely, that both the state and intermediate social institutions are vital parts of society, neither one receives its authority and powers from the other, and both have important roles to play in the public life of the nation.

Sphere Sovereignty in Dutch Neo-Calvinist Thought

The rise of neo-Calvinist pluralist thought in the Netherlands in the latter half of the nineteenth century and the part it played in conjunction with Catholic social thought in successfully resisting Enlightenment liberal thought is a story not well known in the United States, but one that is important in understanding the origins of Christian Democracy. It is a clear instance of structural pluralist thinking arising in response to Enlightenment liberalism.

In the early decades of the nineteenth century, Dutch liberals fought against the old order marked by a semi-established Reformed church (the *Hervormde Kerk*) and ingrained privileges for the aristocratic classes. The liberals' goal was to create through mass education a citizenry not bound to religious, occupational, and regional loyalties, but marked by a commitment to the Dutch nation as a whole and to values that were common and non-sectarian. Dutch scholar Siep Stuurman described the liberals' goal in these words: "Through education and propagation of (Liberal) 'culture' among all classes the circle of citizens could be broadened and the basis of the state as well. On this course a homogeneous Dutch nation would come into being, and would naturally take on a liberal coloration."[32] Opposition to this vision came largely from a group of traditional, or orthodox, Calvinists led by the charismatic preacher, theologian, journalist, and political leader, Abraham Kuyper (1837–1920).[33] The passage by the liberals of a new school law in 1878—that was seen as nearly putting confessional schools of both the Calvinist and Catholic traditions out of business—led to massive protests and, in turn, to an alliance between the orthodox Calvinist groups and the Catholics. This alliance became a major political force and won a majority in the lower house of the Dutch parliament in 1888. Over the next forty years it won support for religiously based schools of various types in addition to public schools, all sharing equally in government funding.

Most importantly for our purposes here, underlying these successful efforts from the Protestant side was the concept of sphere sovereignty developed and advanced by Kuyper. Johan van der Vyver, a noted human rights expert and professor of international law and human rights at the Emory University School of Law, has summarized sphere sovereignty in this manner:

> Individuals—as we all know—have several group-related affiliations and participate in all kinds of social institutions. Each one of those social structures have, and may be identified by, a certain leading function . . . The doctrine of sphere sovereignty recognizes the existence and importance of such group entities in human society, but is equally adamant in its condemnation of all endeavors to afford to group interests a pertinence that would exceed the confines of its structural leading or qualifying function. . . The doctrine of sphere sovereignty thus requires of every social entity to focus its activities on its characteristic function, and—negatively stated—not to indulge in, or obstruct the exercise of, functions that essentially belong to social entities of a different type.[34]

There are three aspects to sphere sovereignty as Van der Vyver here describes it. One is that persons do not live their lives as discreet, autonomous individuals, but are woven into a host of social structures and groupings: families, churches, neighborhood groups, voluntary associations, nonprofit social service agencies, and more. Other structural pluralist thinkers have emphasized this same point. Second, Van der Vyver stresses that under sphere sovereignty each of these social entities possesses a distinctive function. Here one can think of the family, for example, as providing for persons' need for mutual love and affection and for the raising, nurture, and training of children. One can think of religious communities meeting the human need for spiritual understanding and practice. There are faith-based social service organizations that function to offer help to those in need and to enable persons to meet faith-mandated requirements to do so. And there are sports leagues to meet the need for recreation, exercise, and human companionship. Third, sphere sovereignty insists that one social entity ought not to attempt to take over the functions of other social entities. Each is "sovereign" in its own sphere of activities and is not to be dominated by other social structures. It is not the task of religious communities to take over and attempt to raise children; that is the function of the family. The function of sports leagues is not to engage in worship. Arie Oostlander, an official in the Dutch Christian Democratic party and a Christian Democratic member of the European Parliament from the Netherlands from 1998 to 2004, summarized this concept of sphere sovereignty in these words: "Every sphere of life has its own objective, its own character, its own autonomy and its own rights. Precisely this is what is meant by the idea of a 'pluralist society.'"[35] In fact, one can argue that it is the very definition of totalitarianism if one of these social structures, or spheres, would take over from all the others and perform all of their functions. This is certainly the case when, as earlier we saw Nisbet stressed, the state undercuts and takes over from other social institutions such as the family, labor unions, churches, schools, and other such entities.

It is important to note the overall picture that emerges from this description of sphere sovereignty and to note two qualifications. The overall picture that is crucial for our purposes was described well by Kuyper at Princeton University when in 1898 he was invited to give the Stone Foundation lectures that year:

> In a Calvinistic sense we understand hereby, that the family, the business, science, art and so forth are all social spheres, which do not owe their existence to the state, and which do not derive the law of their life from the superiority of the state, but obey a high authority within their own bosom; an authority which rules, by the grace of God, just as the sovereignty of the State does. . .
>
> [T]hese different developments in social life have *nothing above themselves but God*, and that the State cannot intrude here, and has nothing to command in their domain.[36]

In Kuyper's view—which as we have seen earlier is central to structural pluralist thought—the various social entities that make up society have not been established by the state, nor do they exist at the sufferance of the state. Instead, they owe their existence and have been given their functions to perform in society directly by God, just as government has. One is not over or superior to the other. The concept of sphere sovereignty is thereby distinguishable from both a government-dominated collectivist perspective and a classical liberal, individualist perspective. It differs from the latter by emphasizing the fact that human beings live not as discrete individuals but as members of a multitude of social entities. It is within the contours of these social entities that we live our lives and find purpose and meaning. It differs from a government-dominated, collectivist perspective in that it makes clear that the social entities within which we live our lives have an existence and functions to perform that are independent from the state. The state is limited to its own sphere and is not to intrude into the spheres of other social entities.

There are, however, two important observations or qualifications remaining to be made. Without them sphere sovereignty would be left incomplete. First, the functions to be performed by the various social structures, or spheres, to some degree overlap. They ought not to be thought of as exclusive functions. Families, for example, sometimes engage in religious worship or provide material help to neighbors in need. And religious congregations can meet persons' need for sociability and companionship. Nevertheless, sphere sovereignty insists that one can distinguish the primary, principal, or foremost function that is the mark of each of the various social spheres.

A second qualification or observation is that the sovereignty possessed by social structures even in their own spheres is not an absolute sovereignty; it is a quasi or qualified sovereignty. The government or the state is especially important here. In his Princeton lectures, Kuyper switched from a marine to a horticultural metaphor to stress that the state has a limited role to play: "The State may never become an octopus, which stifles the whole of life. It must occupy its own place, on its own root, among all the other trees of the forest, and thus it has to honor and maintain every form of life which grows independently in its own sacred autonomy." But he immediately asked: "Does this mean that the government has no right *whatever* of interference in these autonomous spheres of life? Not at all."[37] He then went on to say that government may intervene to maintain the boundary lines between the various spheres, to defend weak persons who might be victims of the abuse of power by those who are stronger, and to tax all to maintain the state. Kuyper saw the state as having a certain overarching or coordinating role in regard to the other social spheres in order to promote a just order in which one structural sphere did not interfere with the proper functioning of another sphere, or did not oppress or otherwise abuse its power in its dealings with those within it. He made this clear in an 1891 address to the Christian Social Congress:

Government exists to administer his [God's] justice on earth, and to uphold that justice. The tasks of family and society therefore lie outside government's jurisdiction. With those it is not to meddle. But as soon as there is any clash among the different spheres of life, where one sphere trespasses on or violates the domain which by divine ordinance belongs to the other, then it is the God-given duty of government to uphold justice before arbitrariness, and to withstand, by the justice of God, the physical superiority of the stronger.[38]

Kuyper saw the state as having the duty to promote and protect public justice. He was no libertarian. If a family would abuse or neglect its children, the state would have a duty to intervene; if one religious community would seek to oppress another, the state has a right to intervene to preserve religious freedom. Lew Daly has accurately summarized Kuyper's thinking on justice and the role of the state in this way: "The role of the state is to provide the 'justice'—the ordering power—that protects the distinct social spheres but has no authority within them."[39] Chaplin has also emphasized the real, but limited role of the state: "The defining purpose of the state—*its* particular sphere sovereignty—thus involves adjudicating conflicts of sphere sovereignty among all other social structures."[40]

One final comment on Kuyper and his thinking: he was no theocrat. Some might suppose that Kuyper's call for religiously based involvements in public life might harbor a theocratic agenda. Nothing could be further from the truth. As theologian John Bolt has written: "Kuyper was as rigorous an opponent of theocracy as he was a proponent of self-consciously Christian involvement in political life."[41] Instead, he insisted that nonbelievers and those of other faiths should have the same freedom of belief and expression that he argues his own faith—that of orthodox Calvinism—deserved. His sphere sovereignty led him not only to oppose the state's interference with the church, but also the church's interference with the state. In 1879 he wrote: "We do not desire that Reformed [Calvinist] Churches receive the power to dictate to the civil authorities how they must apply the Word of God to the political arena. . . In a pluralistic society, not only do we not desire such a theocracy but rather we oppose it with all our might."[42]

Common Ground between Catholics and Protestants

One mark of the Christian Democratic movement in Europe has been—especially since World War II—the high level of cooperation and even union between Catholic and Protestant political parties. In Germany when, following the Nazi era, political life was reconstituted, Catholics and Protestants together formed the Christian Democratic Union (the Christian Social Union in Bavaria), the largest political party in Germany for most of the years since 1945. In the Netherlands, there had been for years Catholic and Protestant parties that often cooperated in forming coalition governments, and in 1980 two Protestant parties and the Catholic party formally united to form one Christian Democratic party: the Christian Democratic Appeal (CDA). Since 1980, except for an eight year period (1994–2002) the CDA has been a member of every government. When the European Union began to emerge in the post–World War II years, the Christian Democratic parties of various countries formed the European Union of Christian Democrats, which in 1976 became the European People's Party.[43] In short, European Christian Democrats from Catholic and Protestant backgrounds and from differing nations have increasingly been finding common ground and working together. This is more than an accident of history or a proving of the old adage that "politics makes strange bedfellows." Instead, structural pluralist thinking binds together Christian Democrats of different countries, whether Catholic or Protestant. Irving has written that European Christian Democrats "are committed to certain common ideas and principles which amount to a solid corpus of Christian Democratic theory."[44] This section explores these commonalities that continue to play an influential role down to today.

Bolt discusses the Dutch Protestant, Abraham Kuyper, and Pope Leo XIII and considers what they had in common. He reports that both favored some government involvement in social and economic matters in order to promote justice or to protect the public interest, both favored the right of labor to organize, and both advanced limited property rights. [45] Pope Leo XIII, as we saw earlier, released his famous encyclical, *Rerum Novarum*, on May 15, 1891. Six months later, on November 9, 1891, Kuyper gave a major address to a neo-Calvinist social congress. It is still in print and read today. In it he acknowledged the similarities between the two Christian traditions: "We must admit, to our shame, that the Roman Catholics are far ahead of us in their study of the social problem. Indeed, very far ahead. The action of the Roman Catholics should spur us to show more dynamism. The encyclical *Rerum Novarum* of Leo XIII states the principles which are common to all Christians, and which we share with our Roman Catholic compatriots."[46] Van der Vyver notes that in *Rerum Novarum* Leo's definition of the relationship between the state and trade unions "seemingly come[s] close to the notion of internal sphere sovereignty."[47] What both Kuyper in 1891 and Van der Vyver today note is that subsidiarity and sphere sovereignty contain the principle that the intermediary social structures lying between the individual and the national government possess an inherent right to a certain autonomy, a right to be what they are and to follow their calling as they perceive it. Catholic scholar Jeanne Heffernan Schindler commented in 2008 on the "striking convergences" between Catholics and Neo-Calvinists who both contributed essays to a volume she edited.[48]

More specifically, there are four points of convergence between Catholic and Protestant thought that have contributed to Christian Democratic, structural pluralist thought. The first is that both were attempts to respond to the individualism of Enlightenment thinking and, as the nineteenth century progressed, to social democracy, especially in its more radical socialist forms. Pope Leo XIII, Abraham Kuyper, and other Christian Democratic thinkers of both Catholic and Protestant traditions saw themselves as staking out a third way that was differentiated from both the individualism and the *laissez faire* commitments of classical liberalism on the one hand, and the collectivist tendencies of social democracy on the other hand. In both of their thinking, one emphasized too much the sovereign individual, the other the sovereign state. As Irving has written, "Christian Democrats have made some attempt to reconcile liberal democracy and industrial society with traditional Christian teaching; to achieve class reconciliation rather than class conflict; and to find a middle way between liberalism and collectivism."[49]

Second, both Catholic and Protestant structural pluralist thought accepted the existence of a certain natural moral order in the universe that was neither accidental nor created by human thought or effort. Although more often assumed than explicitly defended, nevertheless thinkers from both traditions operated on the basis that there is a certain structure or order in the world that is God-intended. Thus both saw themselves as discoverers of patterns and structures that are an inherent part of the world and social relationships as God established them, not as creators of abstract theories that posited the existence of social structures and patterns that would operate to the benefit of humankind. Human beings could conform their actions and institutions to the natural moral order of the world, leading to human flourishing, or they could create institutions not in conformity to the natural order, leading to human misery and decline. What human beings cannot successfully do is to remake the natural, God-established and God-intended order. Instead, they ought to develop social institutions and structures that conform to and work with the natural, moral order. That is what both traditions saw themselves working to do.

Third, as seen earlier in this chapter, both Catholic and Protestant thought was committed to what was termed personalism, that is, to seeing human beings as multifaceted, social creatures. Irving has properly linked the concept of a natural moral order with personalism when he writes: "Personalism differs from liberalism . . . in its contention that the individual can only reach fulfillment within the 'natural social structures' of society, such as the family, the community or the place of work."[50]

Fourth, both the Catholic and Protestant wings of Christian Democracy see society made up of the "natural social structures" to which Irving referred and are equally committed to the idea that these social structures—families, religious congregations, informal groupings, and formal associations—possess a rightful, but limited autonomy that they receive, not from a sovereign state, but directly from the natural order of things, that is, from God. This is crucial and is a theme to which all Christian Democrats return again and again. Grasso, for example, quotes Johannes Messner as writing that "society is a unity composed of member communities relatively independent, or autonomous, since they have their own social ends, their own common good, and consequently their own functions."[51] Pope John XXIII wrote in the encyclical, *In Pacem Terris*:

> Men are by nature social, and consequently they have the right to meet together and to form associations with their fellows. They have the right to confer on such associations the type of organization which they consider best calculated to achieve their objectives. They have also the right to exercise their own initiative and act on their own responsibility within these associations for the attainment of the desired results. . . [T]he founding of a great many such intermediate groups or societies for the pursuit of aims which it is not within the competence of the individual to achieve efficiently, is a matter of great urgency. Such groups and societies must be considered absolutely essential for the safeguarding of man's personal freedom and dignity, while leaving intact a sense of responsibility.[52]

On the Protestant side, this idea was so central to Kuyper's thinking that it gave birth to his term, "sphere sovereignty," that is, that the various social structures were to be sovereign in their own spheres. As seen earlier, this sovereignty was not so much a sovereignty that said they could do whatever they wished, but rather an insistence that social structures do not receive what powers they have from a sovereign state that in its beneficence gives some out to certain associations and structures (and thus can also recall them at its will), but possess them as a right. Thus they possess a quasi-autonomy, yet one that is real and inalienable. Theologian H. Henry Meeter expressed this idea clearly and forcefully:

> As each of these spheres has been authorized and commissioned by God to carry on its specific task, it has therefore sovereign rights within its own domain. No outside influence, whether of State or Church or other social unit, may interfere with the proper pursuance of this task by the group itself, without thereby infringing upon the authority which God has delegated to that group. This is what is known as the sovereignty of the spheres of society.[53]

In short, the basic contentions of the structural pluralist position can be summarized under three headings: (1) intrinsic to the nature of human society are a host of communities, associations, and other social structures that (2) make human flourishing and a healthy, well-functioning society possible and (3) possess a certain autonomy or independence that is theirs as an inalienable right and that governments are bound to honor and respect. It is in the context of these social structures that human beings live their lives and are able to flourish as beings with religious, economic, emotional, reasoning, procreative, artistic, and other facets.

Faith-based human-service organizations are a part of the structural pluralism of society. As they help persons to live out their calling as religious beings and as they provide needed assistance to others, they take their part as an important feature of human society and play an important part of the world of public policies that provide services to the public. As such, they deserve an underlying respect and acceptance as a means for persons to live out the commands of their faith and for meeting human needs. Emerging out of this respect and acceptance arises an acceptance of their right to an autonomy that tolerates differences in beliefs and practices. All persons are not expected to live out their faith in the same way or to meet the needs of those facing adversity in the same manner. Diversity is normal and to be accepted.

CONTEMPORARY STRUCTURAL PLURALISM

Although structural pluralism and its attendant theories of subsidiarity and sphere sovereignty emerged in the nineteenth century in reaction to Enlightenment liberalism and various forms of collectivistic social democracy and socialism, it nevertheless remains an active, influential force in the twenty-first century. The website of the Dutch Christian Democratic party, the Christian Democratic Appeal, introduces itself with these words: "The CDA is a modern Christian-democratic Party. For Christian-democracy the community is the essence of our society. The different communities are made up of the people who are responsible for all aspects of this world. The family, the school, the neighborhood, the association; they form the backbone of our society, of the Netherlands."[54] The concept of the nation as a "community of communities" is front and center.

Paul Misner has pointed out that in post–World War II Europe "in the Christian Democratic movements, with their political aspirations, the importance of subsidiarity, intermediate bodies, and social justice for humane democratic regime was stressed."[55] Misner's conclusion was vividly demonstrated in 1992, when the European People's Party—which is the Christian Democratic Party on the level of the European Union—placed subsidiarity central in its "Basic Programme," which is still in effect:

141. On the basis of these values, the Christian Democratic vision of society is based on the principle of subsidiarity.

142. The principle of subsidiarity means that power must be exercised at the level which corresponds to the requirements of solidarity, effectiveness and the participation of citizens, in other words where it is both most effective and closest to the individual. Tasks that can be performed at a lower level must not be transferred to a higher level. However, the principle of subsidiarity also means that the higher level must help the lower level in the performance of its tasks.

143. This principle is based on the premise that society can be constructed in freedom. The public authorities must therefore respect human rights and fundamental freedoms, recognize the relative autonomy of social groups and not take the place of private initiative unless the latter is weak or non-existent.[56]

Pope Leo XIII, Pope Pius XI, or Abraham Kuyper could not have stated it better! For our purposes it is especially important to note the emphasis on "the relative autonomy of social groups" in this statement.

Similarly, two European scholars, van Kersbergen and Verbeek, have written: "With the conclusion of the Treaty of European Union at Maastrict in December 1991 a new word has entered the fashionable language of Eurospeak: Subsidiarity . . . Indeed, subsidiarity appeared as the guiding principle to delineating the competences of Brussels versus other administrative authorities, such as national states and regions."[57] They later go on to explain that the worldview underlying subsidiarity is "one that stresses the relative autonomy of social organizations of a plural society."[58] They also linked subsidiarity in Christian Democratic theory with the Protestant theory of sphere sovereignty when they wrote: "The political theory inspired by the religious inclination of the reformed churches—at least in the Netherlands—has a comparable principle [to subsidiarity], which is called 'sovereignty in one's own circle.'"[59]

Helmut Anheier and Wolfgang Seibel have reported in Germany: "The principle of subsidiarity of public welfare became the most influential ideological counterweight to state-centered ideas of welfare provision."[60] Several German laws explicitly provide that if nongovernmental associations are providing certain services, government agencies are not to step in to provide those services.[61] Also, due to the continuing influence of the principle of subsidiarity, a large measure of autonomy or self-determination is allowed in Germany not only to churches, but also to faith-based human service organizations. Gerhard Robbers, one of the foremost German scholars on religious autonomy, has written:

A church's right of self-determination is not restricted to a narrowly-drawn field of specifically "ecclesiastical" activities. The idea of freedom of religious practice extends to preserve the right of self-determination in other areas that are also based or founded upon religious objectives, such as the running of hospitals, kindergartens, retirement homes, private schools and universities.[62]

In short, structural pluralism and its applied concepts are not some artifacts left over from the nineteenth century, to be taken down occasionally from museum shelves and examined as an historic curiosity. Instead, they continue to shape Christian Democratic thinking and have a continuing, active impact on public policy in Europe today.[63]

STRUCTURAL PLURALISM AND THE AMERICAN POLITY

Structural pluralism, which continues to play a major role in Europe, has had a limited impact in the United States to date. There are historical reasons for this. Organized religion in nineteenth-century America did not face the same challenges it did in most continental European countries.[64] In Europe structural pluralism was a "third way" Catholic and Protestant thinkers developed in response to an often anticlerical liberalism and a secular socialist collectivism, both of which mounted serious, sustained challenges. In the United States, as seen in chapter 3, the Second Great Awakening with its popularizing of Protestant Christianity resulted in an overwhelming Christian consensus and a lack of vigorous secular challenges. The United States never experienced a strong anticlerical challenge. When free, universal education was adopted in the nineteenth century, consensual Protestant elements were incorporated into the schools: readings from the Protestant King James Version of the Bible, prayers, and observances of Christian holidays. Therefore, nineteenth-century American religious leaders did not have the same need to find a "third way" to defend their place and that of their religious institutions in a society, as had been the case with European religious leaders. They were in such a dominant position in society that they never had to develop a system of thought that explicated and defended their place in the social-political order. The populist, anti-intellectual tendencies of nineteenth-century American Christianity were also no doubt a contributing factor to their failure to do so.

But the latter part of the twentieth century saw the emergence of what has been called a culture war, a "war" that has continued into the twenty-first century. As seen in chapter 3, organized religion is facing sharp challenges from a growing secularization trend in American society. The major religious divide in the United States today is between traditional religionists from various religious traditions and those with a secularized understanding of life and the world. No-aid, strict separationist interpretations of the Constitution have resulted in Supreme Court decisions that have held unconstitutional many religious recognitions and practices that had been common at an earlier time. Similar to Europe in the nineteenth century, American Christianity is facing clear secular challenges in the social and political arenas. This means structural pluralism and the ways it has become embodied in Christian Democratic thought have a relevance for the United States today that was not as clear or recognizable in earlier time periods.

The possibility of structural pluralist thought taking root in a twenty-first-century United States is increased not only because of its potential to help resolve the emerging religious-secular tensions in American society, but also because four key features of the American setting suggest it may indeed be congenial to structural pluralist thought. Together, these features suggest that structural pluralist, Christian Democratic thought is not something totally foreign to American ways of thinking, but instead is congruent with certain key aspects of the American experience and American thinking.

The first of these is that *the Supreme Court's principle of freedom of association and its equal treatment, neutrality standard for applying constitutional religious freedom protections offer a legal basis for structural pluralism.* As seen earlier in chapter 3, freedom of association means associations have a constitutional right to define who they are and to insist that only persons in support of who they are may be members. Clearly, this cannot be an absolute right, but with proper safeguards it can form the basis for structural pluralism's insistence on the rightful autonomy of organizations—on the right of persons to associate together and to determine and act upon the identity and beliefs that brought them together. In addition, the Supreme Court's equal treatment, neutrality standard for interpreting the First Amendment's religious freedom language—which has been gaining acceptance in the Court in recent years—fits wells with structural pluralist concepts and intentions. This standard—as seen earlier in this chapter—is compatible with the substantive neutrality interpretation of the First Amendment's religious freedom protections, which, in turn, supports the constitutionality of a structural pluralist approach to faith-based organizations in the public realm. This means as the Supreme Court has moved away from a strict separation, no-aid standard and towards a neutrality standard, it has created the constitutional grounds for a structural pluralist understanding of church-state relations.

A second feature of the American context that increases the likelihood of structural pluralism taking root consists of *a renewed communitarian emphasis in American thought that has challenged classical liberalism.* As noted earlier in this chapter, American scholars such as Robert Nisbet, Robert Bellah, Emitai Etzioni, and Mary Ann Glendon are part of a group of thinkers who have stressed the communitarian nature of society. They have reacted

against an overly individualistic liberalism and have reemphasized the importance of groups, formal and informal, in human society. One result of this has
been a renewed emphasis on the importance of civil society for democratic
society.[65] Many observers have pointed to the host of formal and informal
groups and associations that play a vital role in the lives of individuals—and
in achieving stable democracy.

The growth in communitarian understandings of society and political
relationships—including the recognition of the importance of civil society—
suggest there may be fertile ground for structural pluralism in the United
States. These understandings emphasize—as does structural pluralism—the
existence of and the essential role played by a myriad of informal groups and
formal associations and organizations in the flourishing of individuals and
society. They also see them as being, in an important sense, prior to the individual and deserving of respect and protection. Those who have developed
civil society as a key aspect of democratic societies and communitarians more
generally demonstrate that a basic tenet of structural pluralism is far from
foreign to American thinking.

A third factor that suggests structural pluralism may find acceptance in
the United States is *the continued strength of faith-based organizations and
of religion more generally.* Chapter 2 documented the vitality and strength
of public-serving, faith-based organizations and of the nonprofit sector more
generally. Many observers and surveys have commented on the continued strength of religion in the United States, especially when compared to
religion in many other Western democracies.[66] The continuing strength of
religion can cut two ways: the secularly minded may see religion as a more
significant threat than they would if it were weak; the traditionally religious
can use their numbers and strength to insist that they have certain rights and
a role in society that need to be more fully recognized. If, however, the religious among us use their strength to support the sort of genuine pluralism
for which structural pluralism calls, the fears of their more secularly minded
fellow citizens may well be reduced. Then the strength of traditional religion
in the United States would be a reason why structural pluralist thought may
indeed find acceptance.

A fourth aspect of American society that suggests structural pluralism may
find wide acceptance is *a strong tradition of pluralism and tolerance.* The
United States has a tradition of religious tolerance going back to colonial
times. And today it celebrates cultural diversity and sees tolerance and the
acceptance of a diversity of ethnic, racial, and belief traditions as a strength,
not a weakness. Admittedly, what we have espoused in theory we often have
not lived up to in practice, as at various points in American history there has
been intolerance towards Catholics, Mormons, certain immigrant groups,

African-Americans, atheists, gays, and others. Nevertheless, Americans remain committed to accepting societal diversity and the tolerance that makes it possible for differing groups to live together in peace. Since structural pluralism at its core offers a basis for accepting a pluralism in society in which citizens are mutually tolerant of their differences in belief and practice, the American tradition of pluralism and tolerance may make the acceptance and growth of structural pluralism more likely. What structural pluralism calls for is to take this tradition of American pluralism and tolerance and to apply it in some new and unaccustomed ways. Such shifts in thought are never easily achieved; yet, the existence of a tradition of pluralism and tolerance makes the shift for which structural pluralism calls more likely.

In conclusion, this chapter has outlined the basic contours of structural pluralism, suggesting it has the potential to answer rightly many questions surrounding the place of faith-based organizations in the public realm in a way that protects the religious freedom rights of those of all faiths and of none. Of necessity it has had an abstract character; now it is time to see how in concrete terms it would respond to the contentious questions concerning faith-based organizations now being debated. That is what the next chapter does.

Chapter 6

Faith-Based Organizations in a Pluralistic Public Square

Applications

In this chapter I apply structural pluralism's theories and concepts to the issues and controversies that surround the place of faith-based organizations in the provision of public services. I thereby demonstrate structural pluralism's ability to serve as a basis for developing concrete answers to those issues and controversies, answers that protect both the religious autonomy of faith-based organizations and a robust religious freedom for all. This chapter first considers three very basic perspectives on faith-based organizations to which structural pluralism leads. To a large degree they determine the way one views faith-based organizations and their place in the provision of public services. Next I consider how a structural pluralist point of view would respond to four specific questions or issues that currently are sources of bitter disagreement and debate.

THREE BASIC PERSPECTIVES

A Respect for Religion and Its Role in the Public Policy World

American society has a certain ambivalence towards religion in the public life of the nation. As a matter of private belief and devotion, religion is widely respected and admired. Few dare run for public office without a religious affiliation of one type or another. When a national tragedy strikes, such as the 2011 wounding of Congresswoman Gabrielle Giffords and the killing of six others in Tucson, Arizona, responses of officials from President Barack Obama on down are filled with religious references. And this is expected. But as seen earlier in chapter 3, an ambivalence arises from the fact that when it comes to public policy issues and debates, Americans—especially the academic and media elite—tend to view religion as not having a legitimate public role to play. Religion is personal, private, and when introduced into public policies and debates it carries with it a dangerous divisiveness and substitutes unthinking faith for rational discourse.

In contrast, structural pluralism and its embodiment in Christian Democratic thinking insist that religious points of view and associations are to be respected and allowed at the public policy table, just as secular points of view and associations are. Religion is welcomed as a legitimate party with something useful to contribute in the public policy world, both as a participant in public policy debates and as an organized provider of health, educational, and other human services to the public.

This attitude of structural pluralism is rooted in the response of Catholic and Protestant thinkers to classical liberal and socialist attempts to delegitimize and ignore the relevance of religion for public affairs. Structural pluralism emerged from a self-conscious effort to defend a role in public life for religiously based ideas and religious organizations, rooted in particularistic religious traditions, not in some generic, vague, lowest-common-denominator religion. In the very act of developing concepts and theories relevant to public life—such as personalism, subsidiarity, and sphere sovereignty—structural pluralism demonstrated the political relevance of religion. Also, its concept of personalism served as a theoretical basis to insist that persons should not be required to lay aside their religious dimension when entering public life. Human beings are complex beings, with many facets: social, political, economic, emotional . . . and religious. To say persons should participate in public life while segregating out their religious dimension is to say they should participate as partial, incomplete persons. As a result, in countries where structural pluralist thought gained significant influence, a public role for religion came to be taken as right and appropriate. Religious leaders and associations are seen as part of the diversity and pluralism that is a natural, healthy feature of a free, democratic society. Religious intolerance is avoided, not by reading religion out of the public square, but by welcoming all religions on equal terms into the public square. Religious individuals and the faith communities in which they are embedded are given their due, and this means religiously rooted beliefs and values are one of the legitimate ways in which individuals express who they are as citizens and contributors to public policy discussions and debates. Religious leaders and associations are seen as having a right, and perhaps even an obligation, to participate in the public affairs of the nation.

For instance, Germany is one country where Christian Democratic thinking has had a significant influence. Gerhard Robbers of the Trier University law faculty has written of the accepted role of the German churches in the public realm: "It is part of the special position of the Churches that they have a special public mandate. This public mandate . . . has its foundations in the religious freedoms of the Churches. This accordingly allows them to have a say and a right to information in the matters and affairs of public life."[1] Many Germans—following the disastrous Nazi era when many churches and church leaders did not speak up forcefully against Hitler and his regime—see a separation of church and state that gives religion and religious leaders no voice in public affairs as a dangerous doctrine.[2] One searches in vain the church-state decisions of the German Constitutional Court for any references to the dangers of divisiveness posed by religion, such as is often found in American Supreme Court church-state opinions.[3] The very acceptance of "Christian" in the Christian Democratic name signifies the acceptance of the legitimacy of religion in the political realm. Countries influenced by Christian Democratic thinking indeed have a quite different attitude towards the legitimacy of religion as a force in the public life of the nation than do many in the United States.

A concluding qualification is that under structural pluralist thinking, some religious and secular belief systems are excluded from the respect and the-soon-to-be-discussed religious freedom rights this chapter advocates. Although this section has spoken of *all* religions, faith communities, and secular belief systems, an important qualification must be introduced. Excluded are systems of belief, whether religious or secular, that themselves do not respect other religious and secular belief systems or human beings as willing, choosing, free individuals. At the heart of structural pluralism is personalism. Personalism involves a respect for human beings as possessing many facets and inalienable rights. These are to be respected and honored. Belief systems must accept and respect human beings in this light if they are to be part of the structural pluralism and the free, pluralistic, democratic society being advanced here.

Therefore, excluded from the pluralism and diversity that structural pluralism defends are religious and secular belief systems that teach violence towards the political system, other religions, or individuals whom they are seeking to recruit for their communities or who are seeking to leave their communities. So also would be sects or cults that engage in brain-washing its converts and potential converts by making them psychologically dependent on that sect and its leaders. Obviously, a group that believes in human sacrifice would be excluded, as would a cult that practices prostitution or physical or sexual child abuse as part of its rituals or life styles. This means a white supremacist group—whether religiously or secularly based—is not deserving of the rights other faith communities and secular belief systems are accorded under structural pluralism. The same can be said for violent, intolerant Islamist groups and certain fringe cults.

There will, of course, be borderline cases where persons may disagree on whether to place a particular group on the acceptable or unacceptable side of the line. But this is nothing new. When it comes to individual rights, it also is sometimes difficult whether to judge a person's beliefs or practice are constitutionally, legally protected or not. Where does freedom of speech end and libel or incitement to violence start? That is why we have courts to decide difficult cases. What is important is that the basic principles and values we as a society are seeking to uphold are clear and are themselves rooted in a true respect for pluralism and diversity, as well as the equal treatment of all legitimate players entering the public square. And that is what structural pluralism and the Christian Democratic tradition seek to do.

Faith-Based Organizations Possess Religious Freedom and Autonomy Rights

Structural pluralism has an expansive understanding of religious freedom rights, one that includes the religious communities and associations in which persons take part. A basic tenet of structural pluralist thought is that communities and associations do not exist at the sufferance of the state, nor is their role in society assigned them by the state. If government impairs the freedom of religious groups to act as their faith dictates, the government is trespassing where it has no right to be, as much as if the government would attempt to restrict how an individual practices his or her faith. Both subsidiarity in Catholic social thought and sphere sovereignty in Dutch Protestant thought—indeed, Christian Democratic thought generally—emphasize the existence of social structures and associations with a right to exist and a role in society that is given them by God. They thereby possess a certain autonomy that is theirs as a right.

Americans are used to thinking in terms of individual religious freedom rights. We are rightly proud of the First Amendment and its ringing words: "Congress shall make no law respecting an establishment of religion, or prohibiting the free exercise thereof." But Americans typically think of these protections as applying only to individuals; to use them to refer to religious freedom rights of organizations sounds a bit strange to American ears. What this attitude misses is that individuals' freedom of religion is rendered meaningless—or at the least seriously compromised—if the communities or associations in which we live our lives and practice our various faiths do not have their religious freedom rights protected. To speak of individual religious freedom rights without there being organizational religious freedom rights makes no sense. Persons typically exercise and practice freedom of religion not as isolated individuals, but as members of faith communities and faith-based associations. To deny religious freedom to the community is to deny religious freedom to the individual. If a locality would block a group of Muslims from building a mosque, resulting in their having no focal point for their faith, no place to worship, and no classrooms in which to teach their beliefs, the religious freedom of this faith community would be violated, but the freedom of its individual members to live out their faith would also be violated.

Structural pluralism's emphasis on the autonomy of society's social structures reflects the fact that group religious rights and individual religious rights are bound together. Supreme Court Justice William Brennan once made this point in a concurring opinion in a religious liberty case that involved a church-sponsored entity:

> For many individuals, religious activity derives meaning in large measure from participation in a larger religious community. Such a community represents an ongoing tradition of shared beliefs, an organic entity not reducible to a mere aggregation of individuals. . . [F]urtherance of the autonomy of religious organizations often furthers individual religious freedom as well.[4]

There are, of course, limits to the religious autonomy of faith-based organizations and their right to act as they please. Structural pluralism advocates a limited or quasi-autonomy for associations and communities, not an absolute autonomy. There can and will be disputes in specific, concrete situations over exactly when a group has crossed the line of legally protected actions, but this is no different than in the case of individual religious freedoms. The important point is that one can speak of and insist upon religious organizations having religious freedom rights that work to protect their autonomy from illegitimate government restrictions.

Other democracies, where Christian Democratic thinking has played a larger role than it has in the United States, offer concrete examples of the application of this second perspective. The Dutch constitution, for example, reflects this understanding of religious freedom when it provides: "Everyone shall have the right to manifest freely his religion or belief, either individually or *in community with others*, without prejudice to his responsibility under the law."[5] The constitution, in good structural pluralist fashion, explicitly guarantees religious freedom rights to all Dutch citizens both as individuals and as members of communities. This makes good sense from the structural pluralist point of view.

Substantive Religious Neutrality as the Key to Freedom of Religion

A third basic perspective to which structural pluralist thought leads is that religious freedom for all is most fully assured by way of governmental neutrality towards the many religious and secular systems of belief in their numerous manifestations and between religion as a whole and secular belief systems as a whole. Therefore, structural pluralism supports the substantive neutrality standard discussed in the prior chapter as a surer guide to religious freedom for all than either the accommodationist position or the no-aid standard.

This aspect of structural pluralist thinking emerges out of its belief in the legitimate place of religion and religious groups in the public life of the nation and its deep commitment to a true pluralism. Based on these commitments, structural pluralism believes that the substantive neutrality conception of religious freedom leads to greater religious freedom for all than does either strict church-state separation, no-aid-to-religion as an end to be pursued in its own right, or an accommodationist stance that favors government support for generalized religious beliefs and practices. As seen in prior chapters, the no-aid standard erects a wall between church and state, relegating religion to one side of the wall while allowing secular systems of belief onto the other side of the wall where government subsidies and other types of favoritism are allowed. The accommodationist stance makes the same error, but in the opposite direction: it allows government favoritism toward religiously rooted practices and points of view of a broad, generic nature over secularly rooted ones. This stance is also less than evenhanded and neutral.

Under structural pluralism religious organizations are not accorded a favored position in public life, but they do have a right to a voice in the public arena, the ability to share equally in any governmental funds their secular counterparts are receiving, and a right to a genuine measure of independence from government control. Equal treatment—neither favored nor disfavored treatment—is the key. And this is what substantive neutrality seeks to achieve.

One can readily find examples of substantive neutrality thinking in countries where structural pluralist thinking has had a greater impact than it has in the United States. Australia is one such country. There an official with the Department of Education, Employment, and Youth Affairs has explained that "in terms of funding [of schools], we take a no favoritism approach; we look at a school regardless of its religious affiliation, its curriculum, or its philosophy."[6] Robbers reflected this same neutrality, equal treatment mindset when he wrote that "it is generally acknowledged [in Germany] that, given a comprehensive support by the State of social activities, the religious communities may not be excluded from such support and so discriminated against."[7] Similarly, Sophie van Bijsterveld, a key Dutch legal scholar and a Christian Democratic member of the upper house of the Dutch parliament, has written:

> It [Article I of the Constitution] guarantees equal treatment in equal circumstance to all persons. . . It is clear that under the Constitution public-authorities in the Netherlands shall be neutral with respect to the various religions and non-religious denominations. . . [I]t is clear that once authorities subsidize or support certain activities, religious counterparts cannot be excluded for that reason. Article I forbids this.[8]

Note that in the mindset of all three of these persons to fund or otherwise recognize or assist secular organizations or programs without funding, recognizing, or assisting their faith-based counterparts would be inequitable and discriminatory. This is central to structural pluralist, Christian Democratic thought.

SPECIFIC ISSUES: GOVERNMENT FUNDS AND RELIGIOUS HIRING RIGHTS

Nowhere are there sharper and more bitter legal and policy disagreements than over the right of faith-based organizations, when receiving government funds, to take religion into account in their hiring decisions. One side describes faith-based hiring as "discrimination" and an exercise in bigotry; the other side sees it as essential if faith-based groups are to retain and live out their religiously based missions.

Structural Pluralism's Answer

Structural pluralism says clearly and forcefully that faith-based organizations must have the right to make hiring and firing decisions on a religious basis.[9] If a condition for accepting government funding is to lose this right, such a condition would violate faith-based organizations' basic religious freedom rights and their rightful autonomy. Government would be meddling where it has no right to be. Some faith-based organizations will think it important to consider religion in their hiring; others will not. Yet others will believe faith-based hiring is important for some positions, and not for others. The question is not one of whether the "some," the "others," or the "yet others" are right; it is one of who is to decide for the organization. Structural pluralism, with its strong sense of autonomy that belongs to faith-based organizations as a right, says it is faith-based organizations, not the government, that has this right. That is what pluralism, diversity, and organizational autonomy are all about.

More specifically, the structural pluralist perspective formulates its response to the question of religiously based hiring rights on all three of its just-discussed, underlying perspectives. Taking a stand on these beliefs and commitments, structural pluralist thinking insists faith-based providers receiving government funding must have the right to engage in religion-based hiring—if they believe religion-based hiring, whether for some or for all of their employees, is important to who they are and the living-out of their mission. It recognizes that religious faith for many faith-based organizations has a clear public facet to it and is at the heart of what they do. This is a theme that emerged in chapter 2 already, where I documented the large number of faith-based organizations, their important, if not irreplaceable, contribution in the three specific service areas examined, and the importance of religion in who they are and how they define themselves. The mission of many faith-based organizations, as they define it, is tied up with their religious tradition and the faith community out of which they come. To those many faith-based organizations who see their religious identity as being at the heart of who they are and what they do, faith-based hiring is best described as mission-critical hiring, that is, hiring that is based in a desire to protect and advance the mission to which the organization is committed.

This point was made by Justice William Brennan in his concurring opinion in a religious hiring case: "Determining that certain activities are in furtherance of an organization's religious mission, and that only those committed to that mission should conduct them, is thus a means by which a religious community defines itself."[10] This opinion was given in a case in which government funds were not involved, but its basic point is not changed by the presence of government funding. Douglas Laycock made the same point in testimony before a congressional subcommittee:

> Nothing—nothing—is more important to religious identity than the ability to hire employees who actually support the religious mission and will faithfully execute it, and if you want to take that away you are saying the groups—the religious groups that participate in these [government funded] programs—have to secularize themselves in a very dramatic way. It uses the coercive power of the purse to force religious social service providers to become much more secular than they were.[11]

If Laycock and Brennan are correct—and what they are saying is hard to deny—a ban on faith-based hiring would mean that many faith-based organizations either would have to give up or modify their religious mission as they had defined it or would have to give up government funding that their secular counterparts are receiving. Both clash directly with structural pluralist thinking and with the substantive neutrality concept of religious freedom. For government to pressure a faith-based organization to give up or modify its religious mission on pain of losing funding would be a major violation of its religious freedom rights and of governmental religious neutrality. The government's power of the purse would be used to pressure and coerce. It is worth quoting Laycock at length:

> An offer of funding conditioned on forfeiting the right to employ adherents of the faith would force the religious organization either to abandon its religious exercise in order to fund its program, or to forfeit potential funding in order to maintain its religious exercise. Such conditional offers of funding would convert the faith-based initiative from a program that protects religious liberty by prohibiting discrimination between religious and secular providers, into a program that attacks religious liberty by bribing or coercing religious providers into surrendering their religious identity. Opponents of the faith-based initiative, who would exclude religious providers from participating in government-funded programs in the first place, can get their way indirectly if they can require all the religious providers to secularize their workforces as a condition of participation.[12]

Significant, negative public policy consequences would flow from insisting that all faith-based organizations accepting government funding may no longer hire based on applicants' commitment to their religious mission. To the extent such a requirement would result in the secularization of faith-based organizations, pluralism in programming would be lost and a gray sameness would replace the current diversity of religious and secular programs. To the extent faith-based organizations would give up government funding rather than giving up their religious missions, the number and size of faith-based organizations would be reduced. With government already cutting back many of its services to the needy, this would shrink even further the all-too-small safety net on which many persons in need depend.

Although often under attack, to date the United States' policy has largely protected the right of faith-based organizations to take religion into account in their hiring practices, whether or not they accept government funding for some or all of their programs. The strong religious exemption language in the 1964 Civil Rights Act, as amended and strengthened in 1972, as well as the freedom of association doctrine the Supreme Court has defined have helped achieve this result. Also, the number and strength of faith-based organizations have probably helped them defend their religious hiring rights. What structural pluralism offers is support for a policy based in a principled understanding of the nature of faith-based human service organizations and their place in the network of public services.

In summary, structural pluralism, as it has been incorporated into Christian Democratic thought—with its respect for religion having a legitimate place in the public policy domain, its commitment to the right of faith-based organizations to define who they are and what they wish to accomplish, and its support for a governmental religious neutrality that neither favors nor disfavors faith-based or secularly based service providers—insists that religious freedom for all means that faith-based organizations that win government grants or contracts in fair competition on a level playing field must be accorded the right to remain who they are. And this includes religious hiring rights. Religious liberty, governmental neutrality on matters of religion, and a diversity of public services demand no less.

Objections to the Structural Pluralist Position

The challenge to the right of faith-based organizations receiving government funds to hire based on religious considerations has largely come from the political left. Indeed, it has been the primary argument the Left has used against the faith-based initiatives of both the Bush and Obama administrations. It is important to look carefully at this challenge, the objections it raises, and three assumptions underlying it.

Those who argue that faith-based organizations receiving government funds may no longer take religion into account in their staffing decisions begin with a very basic assumption: that religion is largely a matter of private, personal belief, with no genuine relevance to the provision of human services. This assumption has led a cadre of advocacy groups, some members of Congress, and many of the media and academic opinion leaders to insist that when a faith-based organization considers the religious beliefs of its current and potential employees, it is engaging in irrational, indefensible discrimination. After all, religion is a purely private matter with no relevance to the work of a health, educational, or social service agency. And when such an organization is receiving government funds, its "discriminatory" employment practices become unconstitutional and illegal. As it is sometimes put, for a faith-based provider being funded by the government to put out a sign that says "No Catholics need apply" or "Only Christians need apply" is the sort of discrimination our nation fought for years to overcome, and now to allow it would be to roll back civil rights protections that had been obtained by years of effort.

Barry Lynn of the Americans United for Separation of Church and State advocacy group typifies this assumption and conclusion. He has termed faith-based hiring by faith-based organizations as "taxpayer-subsidized job discrimination" that "would roll back nondiscrimination rules dating back to Franklin Delano Roosevelt's administration."[13] Similarly, the *New York Times* editorialized against an Obama administration executive order because it "fails to draw a firm line barring employment discrimination on the basis of religion" and asserts the common-sense-sounding principle: "Public money should not be used to underwrite discrimination."[14] Representative Bobby Scott (D-VA) termed religion-based hiring as "bigotry based on religion."[15] These statements consistently charge "religious discrimination" without defending the proposition that this is invidious, unsupportable discrimination, not the making of a distinction defendable on rational, reasoned grounds. Their assumption seems to be that a religious organization using religion as a hiring criterion is so obviously engaging in invidious discrimination that no defense of this conclusion is even needed.

This thinking can be seen in a letter the strict separationist alliance, the Coalition Against Religious Discrimination (CARD), sent to a Senate committee in 2008 that was considering substance abuse legislation. The letter argued against allowing "religious organizations to take governmental funds *and* use those funds to discriminate in hiring a qualified individual based on nothing more than his or her religion or religious beliefs."[16] Similarly, Lynn has stated: "If government pays for a social work position, every qualified applicant should be considered for the job regardless of their views on religion."[17] Both statements are highly revealing of a certain mindset. Both refer to religious organizations not hiring "qualified" persons based on applicants' religious beliefs. They simply assume that a person's "religion or religious beliefs" always and necessarily have nothing to do with him or her being "qualified" for a position at a faith-based organization. But this only makes sense if one begins with the unexamined assumption that religion is a purely personal, private matter with no consequences or implications in the world of public services and policies. But as we have seen at various points in this book, that position is demonstrably, factually inaccurate, somewhat comparable to assuming that pigs indeed do fly. To insist to faith-based human service organizations that their faith commitments have nothing to do with the services they are providing, even when they insist that they do, is to do profound violence to their autonomy and religious freedom rights. It is not up to government and its courts and laws to make the determination whether or not religion is a *bona fide* job qualification. To argue otherwise is to give to government the right to determine what are and are not genuine religious beliefs and how they are to be lived in society.

A second assumption that feeds into the denial of faith-based organizations' religious hiring rights is that "discriminating" on the basis of religion by a religious organization is no different than discriminating on the basis of religion by nonreligious organizations. Those making this assumption simply accept the position that the right of faith-based organizations to hire based on religion involves the same issue as that of the successful and rightfully applauded efforts to outlaw generally employment discrimination based on race, ethnicity, gender, religion, and disabilities. But this cannot be. Even the original Civil Rights Act of 1964 that made hiring on the basis of religion illegal, recognized that it is not "discrimination" for a religious organization to make hiring decisions based on religion and carved out a clear exception for religious organizations.[18] This provision was further strengthened by amendments in 1972 and found constitutional by a unanimous Supreme Court in 1986.[19]

Everyone recognizes that what is inappropriate discrimination in some settings is appropriate "discrimination" in other settings. No one raises a complaint when a hospital "discriminates" on the basis of medical education and experience in hiring its medical staff, or when an environmental advocacy group "discriminates" in hiring on the basis of persons' views and past activities on environmental issues, or when a political party committee "discriminates" in hiring staff on the basis of persons' political memberships and views. But all would object if a hospital would discriminate in hiring on the basis of race, an environmental group on the basis of gender, or a political party committee on the basis of ethnicity. What distinguishes the first set of examples from the second? In the first set, the characteristics on which the employing agency was "discriminating" were clearly relevant to the ability of the person hired to fill the job and contribute to the mission of the organization; in the second set, the characteristics were clearly irrelevant to the ability of the person hired to fill the job and contribute to the mission of the organization. The issue thus becomes, when a religiously based organization is hiring a person, whether religion is a relevant or irrelevant characteristic of job applicants. And a second question asks whether it is up to the government or the faith-based organization itself to decide the first question. Those opposed to granting faith-based organizations receiving the proverbial dime of government funding the ability to make hiring decisions based on religion—blinded by their own hidden assumption of the private, personal, and therefore irrelevant nature of religion—link the right of a religious organization to make hiring decisions based on religion with hiring decisions based on factors irrelevant to the organization and the position being filled. And since the issue is so clear to those critics, they insist it is the government and the courts that have the right to make this call, even when a faith-based organization insists that religion is relevant to the position being filled and the mission of the organization.

A third assumption made by those opposed to granting faith-based organizations the right to hire in accordance with their religious mission is that the strict wall of separation, no-aid-to-religion concept is rightly *the* bedrock principle for interpreting the meaning of religious freedom. They typically assume this is the only acceptable principle and ignore the competing neutrality or equal treatment line of reasoning the Supreme Court has increasingly relied upon in recent years. They thereby close their eyes to the substantive neutrality principle that comports well with structural pluralism. They see no difference among government funding a religious congregation in its core religious rituals and celebrations, funding a religious congregation's temporal, this-world services to the general public, and funding an independent nonprofit, faith-based organization that is providing certain human services to the public. All are lumped together and labeled "aid to religion." Those who see the no-aid principle as inviolable are either blind to the government-sponsored disadvantages to which faith-based organizations would be put if it were always followed or believe that the no-aid principle trumps those disadvantages, no matter how severe they may be.

Those who emphasize the strict separation, no-aid-to-religion standard as controlling can cite the basis on which government funding of faith-based programs has often been justified, namely that the government is only funding purely secular services, even though the provider is faith-based. If the persons being hired will be carrying out purely secular services, to introduce religious hiring criteria into their hiring becomes an exercise in bigotry and irrational discrimination. Since the religious and secular programs and activities of a faith-based organization must be sorted out into separate compartments to meet the constitutionally mandated no-aid-to-religion standard, why should the religious beliefs and practices of employees of those in the secular compartment make any difference?

There are two answers that structural pluralism makes to this position. The first is that the secular and religious facets of the programs run by many faith-based organizations are not, cannot, and ought not to be segregated into hermetically sealed compartments. The next section discusses this at greater length and argues that certain religious elements can be allowed into government-subsidized programs without violating freedom of religion standards. But here a second answer can be noted, one that rests on the fact that an organization is more than its individual programs. Every organization has a certain culture, ethos, or spirit that is molded and communicated in a host of subtle and sometimes not-so-subtle ways. The location and physical layout of an office, posters or art on the walls, the formality or informality of its staff meetings, unwritten and unarticulated expectations, the words used by staff members as they greet each other in the morning or say good-bye in

the evening—all these and more go to create a certain culture in any organization. This is also true of faith-based organizations, where religious references
and practices contribute to the nature of their organizational culture, ethos, or
spirit. For a faith-based organization to decide that even staff members running programs with no overt, explicit religious content can and should contribute to this organizational culture in a way that supports and strengthens its
religious mission should be its right.

A final note is that the political right, as seen earlier in chapter 4, has been
strong in its support of the religious hiring rights of faith-based organizations.
The fact that religious hiring rights of faith-based organizations receiving
government funds are still largely intact can no doubt in part be credited to
the political right. But many conservatives—in accommodationist fashion—
have a tendency to support religious hiring rights based on their acceptance
of governmental encouragement or support of generalized religion, not on the
basis of substantive neutrality and a genuine pluralism. Their support for religious hiring rights of faith-based organizations receiving government funding
thereby is based on an acceptance of the legitimacy of government's generalized support of religion. Structural pluralist thinking, on the other hand, bases
its defense of religious hiring rights on the advocacy of a genuine pluralism
among faith-based and secular human service providers.

SPECIFIC ISSUES: RELIGIOUS ELEMENTS
IN GOVERNMENT-SUBSIDIZED SERVICES

A second area of current disagreement and controversy concerns the extent
to which religious elements should be allowed to be integrated into a human
service program of a faith-based provider that the government is helping to
fund. Structural pluralism can help frame the issue appropriately and point
in the direction of answers that respect all faith traditions. Others have noted
that faith-based organizations can be arrayed along a continuum in terms
of the extent to which religious ingredients are present in an organization
and integrated into its programs.[20] They range from what can be termed
"faith-permeated" organizations where the entire organization and all of its
programs are marked by explicit religious references, activities, and rituals.
At the other extreme are organizations that are faith-based in nature, but
their religious elements are largely in the background and unseen, serving
as a source of motivation for their board members, staff, volunteers, and
financial supporters and as an implicit contributor to the general culture or
ethos of the organization. Yet other faith-based organizations and their programs fall at various points between these extremes. This raises the question

of how many and what sorts of religious elements may be present in human service programs the government is helping to fund. Freedom of religion surely means that no one should be subjected to unwanted religious rituals and messages, but governmental religious neutrality means a faith-based organization ought not to be forced to choose between totally secularizing or forgoing government funds that similar, parallel human service organizations are receiving. Is there a way to protect the faith commitments of faith-based organizations receiving government funds without violating persons' right to be free of unwanted religious activities and messages? Structural pluralism says there is.

Structural Pluralism's Answer

The basic position to which structural pluralism leads is that faith-based organizations, even when the government helps fund one or more of their programs, must not be forced to secularize these programs totally, as long as no one is forced to take part in these programs or in religious devotions, rituals, and other explicitly religious activities. This position to which structural pluralism leads is more nuanced—with some important, but fine distinctions—than is the position to which it leads on faith-based hiring discussed in the previous section.

An underlying perspective to which a structural pluralist approach leads is that the autonomy of faith-based organizations *as* faith-based organizations should be protected within the bounds set by the demands of freedom of religion for all. They should be viewed as having an inherent right to be who they are, as possessing a certain identity and pursuing a certain mission that should, if at all possible, not be interfered with by governmental rules and regulations. Government should act as a true partner that respects and allows a large degree of freedom to its partner, not attempt to turn its partner into a secular clone of itself. As Ram Cnaan of the University of Pennsylvania has written, "Marginalizing the uniqueness of faith-based organizations and forcing them to act secularly is the cookie-cutter type of mistake."[21]

A second underlying perspective structural pluralism brings to the table is that government ought only to use tax-payer dollars to subsidize programs and services that have a clear and direct this-world, temporal benefit to their beneficiaries, not a spiritual or next-world benefit. Government ought never to fund religious services, devotional exercises, or celebrations of any religion's core, distinguishing truths, or beliefs. These may have spiritual benefits for their participants and may even have some indirect this-world benefit—as they, for instance, might inspire one to struggle to overcome challenges life has thrown on his or her path. But, along with Madison and Jefferson, we as a society have decided long ago that financial support for purely spiritual, other-worldly activities is none of the government's business. Freedom of religion means one is free to worship as one sees fit and to support one's faith and the community in which it is rooted with financial gifts—and not to be forced to support, financially or otherwise, a faith other than one's own. Applying this second perspective in specific, concrete situations—and squaring it with the first perspective—requires distinctions that are as nuanced as they are crucial.

In applying these perspectives to the contentious question of what, if any, religious elements may be included in programs the government is helping to fund, the first conclusion is that the freedom of choice by beneficiaries of such programs should be protected as fully as possible. It is important that persons not be subjected to unwanted religious messages, especially when they involve attempts at proselytization or the celebration of religious rituals that could make unbelievers feel they are outsiders. Structural pluralism sees giving recipients of government-subsidized services the opportunity to opt out of a faith-based program entirely or out of the religious aspects of a program as a better guarantee of freedom of religion than forcing all persons in faith-based programs to receive services scrubbed clean of every and all religious features, even if many recipients would prefer and would be helped by such features. Allowing choice protects both the recipient of services from exposure to unwanted religious features and faith-based programs from undue pressure to remove all religious features from their programs.

Freedom of choice can usually best be achieved by allowing beneficiaries of a government-subsidized faith-based program to choose to receive those services either from a secular program or from the program of a different faith tradition. Voucher programs achieve this by making certificates available to those eligible for a certain service, which they can then take to a program of their choice providing that service. And since government funds are reaching faith-based programs indirectly, by the choice of the program participants, the Supreme Court has ruled the programs may integrate religious elements into them without running into First Amendment problems. But in many human services areas there are practical, logistical problems to creating voucher programs.

Whether or not it is practical to establish a program using vouchers, the goal should be to optimize the beneficiaries' opportunity to choose the provider most in tune with their beliefs and background. This includes the simple expedient of informing beneficiaries of the right to switch from one provider to one more in tune with them. President Obama's Advisory Council on Faith-Based and Neighborhood Partnerships was right in 2010 to recommend that beneficiaries of a faith-based program subsidized by the government should receive notice that they may opt for a similar but secular program.[22] Persons in a secular program should also have the right to opt into a faith-based program whenever a similar program of a faith-based nature is available—and they should be informed of that fact. Whenever possible, the choice should go both ways: those in faith-based programs should be able to and should be told they can move into a secular program and those in a secular program should be able to and should be told they can move into a faith-based program. A fully pluralistic approach says the default position ought not to be secularly based programs and the right to choose need only be assured in the case of faith-based programs.

But sometimes it is impossible or impractical for someone to switch from one program to another. Especially in small towns and rural areas, there may be no other agencies offering the same services, and even in large cities transportation, child care, schedules, or convenience of location may dictate that one attend a faith-based program that one would prefer not to attend.[23] In such circumstances freedom of choice indicates that a person should be able to opt out of all or most of the religious elements in the program. This means a faith-based program receiving government subsidies should still be able to conduct religious or devotional services or rituals, but they should be separated from the government-subsidized facets of the program in time or location and funded with private donations. Also, such religious activities should be voluntary for program participants. This already is standard practice. The language normally used in legislation and regulation bars government subsidies from funding "inherently religious activities such as worship, religious instruction, and proselytization."[24] President Obama's Advisory Council on Faith-Based and Neighborhood Partnerships recommended that the language be changed from "inherently religious activities" to "explicitly religious activities" and a November 17, 2010, executive order of President Obama did so.[25] This executive order continues to cite as examples of "explicitly religious activities" "worship, religious instruction, or proselytization." The concepts of choice on the part of program participants and of no government funding for religious activities without direct temporal, this-world benefits support this position.

But the words "worship, religious instruction, or proselytization" have an ambiguity that leaves some questions unresolved. In the course of my research over the years I have observed many faith-based human service programs and activities. When doing so I have observed in some faith-based programs explicitly religious devotional activities, most commonly Bible studies or group prayer sessions. These activities were almost always conducted separately from other program classes or activities and were voluntary for program participants, whether or not the other program activities were government-subsidized. And they should be. For many faith-based organizations, however, that is not the crucial issue. Their faith-based nature comes out in a different way. I have found a large number of faith-based programs that contain religious facets one would normally not describe as "worship, religious instruction, or proselytization," yet are more than a background, unseen motivation for staff or prayers offered in private. For instance, in a study of welfare-to-work programs in Los Angeles, Chicago, Dallas, and Philadelphia, I found that a majority of the faith-based programs reported they made use of religious values to encourage the recipients of their services to change their attitudes.[26] In my experience the most commonly found religious features consist of pictures or posters with a religious theme in program facilities (e.g., "God made you and has a plan for your life"), references in private, one-on-one counseling sessions to God and the resources a church may be able to provide, and general religious references in group or class settings designed to encourage and support program participants. Many faith-based human service providers see such religiously rooted values, beliefs, and references lying near the heart of who they are. Yet they fall far short of "explicitly religious activities (including activities that involve overt religious content such as worship, religious instruction, and proselytization)" as the Obama executive order puts it.[27]

Structural pluralism leads to the conclusion that religious elements in government-subsidized programs such as these are fully permissible. In the case of religious pictures, posters, and symbols, they are passive items that, while they help label a program as being faith-based and may contribute to a certain ethos or atmosphere, their passive nature and their potential— especially in the case of the posters seeking to encourage or build self-esteem—to have a direct, this-world purpose in line with many programs' goals indicates their acceptability. In fact, the Obama 2010 executive order—even though his advisory council was divided on this issue and could not make a recommendation—explicitly allowed for religious art of this nature.[28]

To forbid references to religious ideas or themes in private, one-on-one counseling sessions where both the counselor and the person receiving counseling believe such references to be appropriate and helpful would be to force them into a secularized mold against their will—nearly the definition of the violation of freedom of religion. To require faith-based organizations and their staffs, volunteers, and clients to eschew religiously oriented counseling ideas and themes, while allowing secular organizations and their staff, volunteers, and clients to engage in a wide variety of secular themes and treatment modalities, is to put religion at a government-created disadvantage and to favor secular perspectives and beliefs over faith-based ones. And given the one-on-one nature of the situation, no one is being exposed to religious ideas or values against his or her will. It is not hard to imagine that persons suffering the debilitating effects of long-term unemployment, or who have experienced the trauma of sexual or physical abuse, or who are facing death from a serious injury or disease, or who have just been released from prison and are seeking to turn their lives around and integrate into a society that often rejects them, may find solace and help in religion. To forbid such religiously based words of solace and hope in one-on-one counseling sessions, when the beneficiary is there by choice, would be to do violence to the concepts of freedom of religion and freedom of choice.

This leaves the question of the appropriateness in government-funded group or class settings of using references to religious ideals and themes that fall far short of "worship, religious instruction, and proselytization." I have observed classes at faith-based programs that sought to encourage and support program participants by referring to a loving God who has a plan for them, is forgiving of past mistakes, and sees them as being of great worth. Structural pluralism says that it is acceptable in government-funded programs to use references such as these as a means to encourage, comfort, and lift up the beneficiaries of a program in an effort to help them to overcome the challenges they are facing. This conclusion is supported by the fact that persons are in such classes by choice and could opt out of the program in favor of a secular program and that such religious references fall far short of proselytizing or worship. Also, many faith-based programs see such references as expressions of who they are and vital to why they believe they can help those in need. In such a situation, any possible feeling of passing discomfort by an occasional client in such a program is clearly outweighed by the importance of protecting the autonomy and religious freedom rights of the faith-based organization. Again, in doing so the religious diversity and pluralism of the public square are protected.

A concluding observation is helpful in understanding the position to which structural pluralism leads as I have outlined it here. It is that secular human service programs, whether governmental or nonprofit in nature, engage in similar or parallel efforts to those of faith-based programs in meeting their recipients' needs. They may have pictures or posters on their walls with nonreligious sayings or quotations seeking to encourage and build up self-esteem. In private counseling sessions the counselor's own life experiences or various therapeutic approaches and techniques will be used to meet their clients' needs, and in classes examples of others who have overcome the same challenges the class members are facing will be used to encourage and motivate. The substantive neutrality principle supported by structural pluralism says that whether a program is seeking to use certain religious themes or parallel secular themes to achieve certain goals ought not to make a difference in whether or not government money can help fund those efforts. If even the sort of broad, general religious themes discussed here cannot be used in government subsidized programs, even while similar secularly based themes are allowed, it would mean a clear violation of governmental religious neutrality—and for no good public policy or freedom of religion purposes. Faith-based organizations would face the choice of completely secularizing their services and removing all religious elements that they believe important, or forgoing money that similar, competing programs are receiving. The thumb of government would be firmly on the secular side of scales in the divide between religiously based and secularly based human services.

Objections to the Structural Pluralist Position

The differences between the structural pluralist position on integrating religious elements into government-subsidized faith-based programs outlined above and that of those who have objections to that position are more subtle and muted than is the case concerning faith-based hiring rights. There is agreement that overt, explicit "worship, religious instruction, and proselytization" ought not to be supported by government funds, and when offered by a faith-based provider they should be offered at separate times or locations than the government-funded activities. Also, participation must be voluntary. There also is agreement that faith-based organizations whose religious commitments are present only in the religiously rooted motivations or staff and supporters are no barrier to government funding. Where problems begin to arise is in a gray area that is less than overt "worship, religious instruction, and proselytization" and more than unseen and unspoken religiously rooted motivations. Here one finds faith-based organizations for whom religious symbols, posters, or art are important statements of who they are, who wish to be able to discuss religious perspectives in one-on-one counseling sessions or make referrals to religious congregations when they feel doing so would be helpful to a client, and who believe certain gentle religious references and assurances can be a source of comfort, reassurance, or motivation to the persons they are seeking to help.

Some persons—usually on the political left—object to these "gray area" religious elements being integrated into faith-based programs that have received some government funding. Two of the twenty-five members of President Obama's Advisory Council on Faith-Based and Neighborhood Partnerships recommended no government-funded services could be offered in rooms where religious pictures or symbols were present, and another seven felt they should be allowed only if it were impractical to remove or cover them.[29] Some also raise questions concerning religious references in one-on-one counseling sessions and gentle religious references in class settings. The key problem is uncertainty and confusion over in what settings what religious references are and are not permissible, as different persons interpret "worship, religious instruction, and proselytization" either narrowly or broadly.

There are two presuppositions often held by those who interpret these terms to include almost all religious references, thus putting themselves clearly at odds with the much narrower interpretations structural pluralists would make. We have encountered them before. One is the persistent idea that religion is properly a private, personal affair, one of private devotions, personal commitments, and worship and celebrations carried out in religious congregations. It has no appropriate role in the public realm of health care, education, and social services. Thus removing all religious elements from a faith-based program will do no real harm to that program since religion is something having to do with one's personal, private life and is not integral to human service programs anyway. A second presupposition is a commitment to the wall of separation, no-aid-to-religion principle as *the* bedrock principle for interpreting the religious freedom language of the First Amendment. Many of those holding to this second presupposition can still support government subsidization of faith-based human service programs. They do so on the condition that all religious elements have been carefully separated out from the nonreligious elements, the religious elements are then isolated in aspects of the program separate from the nonreligious elements, and government subsidies then only go to help fund the nonreligious elements. One thereby can have government money flowing to faith-based human service programs without government money funding religion. These presuppositions lead those holding them to insist that all religious elements be removed from faith-based programs the government helps subsidize.

But many on the political left, and surely those on the political right, take a permissive attitude towards religious elements that are less than "worship, religious instruction, and proselytization." They have problems, however, in articulating what is and is not permissible. The Left seems to take the attitude that some limited religious elements are probably a violation of church-state separation, but they are too minor to bother with. The Right sees them as conforming to its support for government favoring or supporting religion of a broad, general nature. In either case faith-based organizations, government regulators, and the courts are left with little guidance on what is and is not permissible. The principles and guidelines of structural pluralism outlined above do not, of course, lead to clear, unambiguous answers either. But there are principles and there are guidelines to be followed, which—while often not leading to clear, automatic answers in all situations—do give guidance.

Nevertheless, one comes away from a consideration of issues surrounding the integration of religious elements into government-funded faith-based programs with the conclusion that the answers given by structural pluralists and most of the political left—and the political right—end up closer to each other here than they do in the other three specific policy areas being considered in this chapter.

SPECIFIC ISSUES: NONDISCRIMINATION AND HIRING AND MEMBERSHIP STANDARDS

All religions hold to certain ethical or behavioral standards. From the five pillars of Islam, with such prescribed norms such as daily prayers and alms giving, to Sikhs with the proscription on the cutting of hair, to Orthodox Judaism with required Sabbath-keeping norms, to traditional Christianity with its proscription of sexual relations outside of male-female marriage, all religions possess ethical commitments rooted deep in their understandings of God and his expectations of human beings. If religious pluralism and freedom of religion mean anything, they mean that to the fullest extent possible faith communities must be free to follow the dictates of their faith and live out its norms. We all cringe at the thought of persons or organizations being forced into actions contrary to their religious beliefs. Such actions have more in common with Nazi totalitarianism than a free society.

Nevertheless, in the case of faith-based organizations active in the public realm many questions have arisen concerning how many and what types of religiously rooted practices can and should be tolerated. May a Catholic hospital refuse to perform abortions or provide birth control services? May a university student club rooted in a particular religious tradition and with official school recognition limit its membership or its officers to members of that religious tradition? The gay rights movement in particular has raised new issues. May an evangelical Protestant adoption agency refuse to place children with same-sex couples? May a Christian faith-based agency refuse to hire someone actively involved in a same-sex relationship? Most of us would instinctively believe that a faith-based organization that somehow believes only whites are blessed by God and thus refuses to hire any person of color is beyond the pale and cannot use its religious nature to obtain exemption from laws that prohibit hiring decisions based on race or color. If this is the case, how can one object to laws forbidding hiring policies that reject hiring persons in same-sex relationships? Yet if autonomy, diversity, and pluralism—all concepts appealing in the abstract—mean anything, it seems they must protect religious communities from being penalized for their religiously rooted practices or forced into practices their faith finds reprehensible. Such questions arise even in the absence of government funding. Nondiscrimination laws—existing and proposed—can clash with religiously rooted beliefs whether or not government funding is involved. This section considers nondiscrimination regulations and their application to faith-based organizations in their hiring and membership standards; the next section considers attempts to require faith-based organizations to provide certain services that run counter to their religious beliefs.

The issue of nondiscrimination in the hiring and membership policies of faith-based organizations has arisen, first, in regard to state and federal Employment Non-discrimination Acts (ENDAs) that propose to add—and in some jurisdictions already have added—sexual orientation to the previously protected categories of race, religion, sex, and national origin. The Roman Catholic, evangelical Protestant, and Orthodox Jewish traditions in particular have strong beliefs concerning the immorality, indeed the sinfulness, of homosexual behavior. Meanwhile, those advocating such legislation see it as simply extending legal protection to a group long subject to discrimination. Second, the nondiscrimination issue has arisen in connection with a number of faith-based student organizations or clubs on college and university campuses—usually in the evangelical Protestant tradition—that have run into problems when they have insisted that their leaders need to agree to a statement of faith that includes certain basic religious beliefs and an acceptance of their faith's behavioral standards, including limiting sexual intimacy to one man and one woman within marriage. Student chapters of InterVarsity Christian Fellowship, for instance, have faced challenges to their right to meet on campus and have access to additional advantages other student organizations enjoy at such institutions as Rutgers University, the University of North Carolina, the University of Wisconsin, and Tufts University.[30] This is the same issue raised by the earlier-discussed case of the Christian Legal Society's student chapter at the Hastings College of Law. When a faith-based student organization insists on certain religious and behavioral standards for its members or leaders, is it engaging in invidious discrimination or is it exercising its legitimate right to religious autonomy and freedom?

Structural Pluralism's Answer

A structural pluralist approach to questions of nondiscrimination regulations as applied to faith-based organizations in their hiring and membership standards begins by insisting on the three basic perspectives discussed in the first section of this chapter: that religion and faith-based organizations have a public role to play in society that ought to be respected, that these faith-based organizations possess certain religious freedom rights that protect their religious autonomy, and the substantive neutrality interpretation of the First Amendment is the surest guarantee of religious freedom for all.

An additional fact to recognize at the outset is that many religious traditions see same-sex behavior and relationships as a moral evil—a sin—that they clearly and strongly condemn. What is a lifestyle choice based on their sexual orientation to some—who they are, as it is often put—is a grave moral sin to others. A 2010 letter to the members of Congress by the United States Conference of Catholic Bishops sent in reaction to an ENDA proposal under consideration at that time stated their church teaches "that all sexual acts outside of marriage between one man and one woman are morally wrong."[31] This letter went on to urge, if the bill were to be passed, a very strong exemption for religious organizations be added so that the law "could not be used to punish as discrimination what the Catholic Church teaches."[32] Similarly, the National Association of Evangelicals officially declared in 2004:

> The Scriptures declare that God created us male and female. Furthermore, the biblical record shows that sexual union was established exclusively within the context of a male-female relationship (Genesis 2:24), and was formalized in the institution of marriage. . . Everywhere in Scripture the sexual relationship between man and woman within the bonds of marriage is viewed as something natural and beautiful. Homosexual activity, like adulterous relationships, is clearly condemned in the Scriptures.[33]

The point here is not whether or not the Catholic and evangelical Protestant traditions are right or wrong in the positions they have taken; rather it is whether or not faith communities such as these have the right to hold to and follow their beliefs that homosexual behavior is morally wrong. And no one can claim that this is an idiosyncratic position recently arrived at with little thought. Even those who disagree with this position must agree it is a reasoned position that traditional branches of Christianity, Judaism, and Islam have held for thousands of years and is deeply rooted in their understandings of the God-created nature of human beings. Nor is this position a simple matter of "gay-bashing," as both the Catholic Bishops' letter and the National Association of Evangelicals' document explicitly state their problem is not with persons who have a homosexual orientation or inclination but with homosexual practices or lifestyles.[34] The behavior, not the inclination or orientation is the issue. But it is cold comfort to most in the gay rights movement to be told that their orientation is all right, but do not act on it. The clash between the gay rights movement and traditional religion could not be clearer.

How would one, with the principles and perspectives of structural pluralism as a guide, seek to deal with the public policy question of employment rights of persons in active lesbian, gay, bisexual, and transgender (LGBT) relationships as they apply to faith-based organizations? Given the long history of discriminatory and even hateful treatments of gays in American society, this question poses especially sensitive and painful issues. For LGBT persons—who have long been objects of derision and suffered from a loss of opportunities in education, housing, and employment—being included in the protections of civil rights laws that now protect persons from discrimination based on race, religion, gender, and national origin is understandably an important goal. But to require a faith-based organization whose religious tradition holds homosexual behavior and lifestyles to be moral evils nevertheless to hire such persons would violate their religious-freedom rights. The question thereby comes down to whether government policy should support the employment rights of persons in active LGBT relationships or should it support the religious freedom rights of faith-based organizations. Is there a way to protect the employment rights of LGBT persons, while not violating the religious-freedom rights of faith-based organizations?

The most reasonable answer in keeping with structural pluralist thought supports ENDA-type legislation that seeks to assure LGBT persons are not denied employment due to their sexual orientation or practices, but with strong exemptions for religious congregations and other religious organizations, including faith-based organizations. The existence of state and federal ENDAs would assure LGBT persons that under most situations their employment rights would be protected. But if such laws would attempt to force a Catholic Charities homeless shelter, an evangelical Protestant domestic violence program, or an Orthodox Jewish child care center to employ active LGBT persons, it would be a major violation of their religious freedom rights and their autonomy as religious organizations. The state would be telling them they must employ persons whose behavior is at odds with their moral teachings, thereby being put in a position of condemning certain behaviors with one hand and endorsing them with the other. This would be as destructive of their religious character as they have defined it as forcing them to hire persons not in agreement with their religious mission. The points made in the earlier section of this chapter that supported faith-based organizations receiving government funds being able to make hiring decisions based on religion for positions they judge to be critical for carrying out their mission are relevant here. This is the path taken by the 1964 Civil Rights Act, as amended in 1972, which forbids discrimination based on religion in hiring, but goes on to carve out an exemption for religious organizations.

In a pluralistic society we must learn to live together with our differences. Religious organizations need to recognize the wrongs done to LGBT persons and be willing to accept nondiscrimination laws in situations where their religious autonomy and beliefs are protected; LGBT persons need to recognize that their behavior and lifestyles are morally objectionable to many religious traditions and not seek to impose their beliefs onto them. In weighing the competing rights, one must weigh the clear and inescapable violation of the religious-freedom rights of faith-based organizations on one side of the scales with the inability of LGBT persons to seek employment among the faith-based organizations whose religious traditions hold intimate same-sex relationships to be immoral on the other side of the scales. Since the vast majority of employment opportunities would not be affected by a religious exemption, it is clear that LGBT persons would be giving up much less in what I am proposing here than would faith-based organizations if ENDAs would be enacted with no exemption for them.

A caveat that springs from the parallel that is often drawn by gay rights activists between racially discriminatory hiring practices and discriminatory hiring practices towards LGBT persons is in order. ENDA proposals are not simple extensions of earlier-enacted nondiscrimination legislation, merely expanding legal protections to an additional category of persons by extending the trajectory of earlier legislation. Earlier nondiscrimination legislation sought to protect certain categories of persons: African-Americans, other racial and ethnic minorities, women, the handicapped, and others. ENDA proposals, on the other hand, seek to protect persons who have been objects of discrimination based on their actions, behavior, or lifestyle choices. This is an important distinction because when an entire category of persons is subjected to discrimination that action says that those persons, no matter who they are or what they do, are not worthy of employment. But when persons are subjected to differential treatment because of their actions or behavior that is saying, in the eyes of those engaging in differential treatment, it is the action or form of behavior that is seen as being morally objectionable.

Thus any ENDA legislation passed with strong religious exemption language should make clear it is designed to protect faith-based organizations' right not to hire persons engaged in certain behaviors they consider morally wrong and not to protect a right not to hire a category of persons because of who they are. The law should suspect that a faith-based organization is discriminating against a category of persons and not against persons engaged in certain behavior if either of two conditions is present. One is if an organization refuses to hire anyone with a LGBT orientation or inclination, even if they are celibate. The second one is if an organization is careful to exclude from its employment any sexually active LGBT persons, but hires heterosexuals who are sexually active outside of a marriage relationship, and hires other persons who are acting in violation of other moral norms of their religious tradition. The latter, in the Christian tradition, would include racial bigots, slum lords, or other persons who act in slanderous, hateful ways. If a faith-based organization, accepts as employees "sinners" such as unrepentant heterosexual adulterers and fornicators and unloving, hateful persons who prey on others, but refuses to hire persons in LGBT relationships, one can fairly conclude that their refusal to hire the latter has more to do with bias, fear, or prejudice than a broader policy of not employing persons whose lives are in violation of religious norms their faith tradition holds dear.

A second area of current controversy concerns on-campus student religious groups who wish to limit their membership or leaders to persons of their own faith tradition and to those who live in keeping with their faith's behavioral standards, including sexual intimacy standards. This issue gained national prominence in 2010 in the Supreme Court case mentioned in chapter 1 that involved the Christian Legal Society student organization at the Hastings College of Law in California. In a 5-to-4 vote the Court majority held that the law school was within its rights when it required all recognized student campus organizations, including religiously based ones, to admit all students to membership and leadership positions, regardless of their religious beliefs and personal behavior.[35]

Structural pluralism says that faith-based student groups on campuses should have the ability to limit their membership and surely their leaders to persons who are in agreement with the groups' faith and behavioral standards. It says the Supreme Court got it wrong in the above decision. From a structural pluralist perspective it makes no sense to say a religious organization may not "discriminate" on religious grounds. Justice Samuel Alito made the needed point in his dissenting opinion when he quoted from one of the *amicus* briefs filed in this case: "This point was well put by a coalition of Muslim, Christian, Jewish, and Sikh groups: 'Of course there is a strong interest in prohibiting religious discrimination where religion is irrelevant. But it is fundamentally confused to apply a rule against religious discrimination to a religious association.'"[36] It indeed makes no more sense to disallow a religious organization to "discriminate" on religious grounds than to disallow a university to "discriminate" in hiring faculty on academic grounds, or a pro-choice organization to "discriminate" in choosing its leadership on persons' views on abortion. The identity of all three organizations, the very reason for their being in existence, is bound up with religious views, academic qualities, or views on abortion. This is an instance of the nondiscrimination principle being applied in a setting where it just does not fit. As a result, the student-formed organizations of religious minorities are left vulnerable to take over from students in the religious or secular majority. Quoting from the same *amicus* brief from which Alito quoted: "Hasting has changed the prohibition on religious discrimination from protection for religious minorities into an instrument for excluding and victimizing those minorities."[37]

In reaching this decision the Supreme Court concluded other values trumped its own legal doctrine of freedom of association discussed earlier in chapter 3. The Court recognized a right to expressive association, but the majority ruled that in this case the law school's policy of requiring all student organizations to accept "all comers" was "reasonable and viewpoint neutral."[38] The Court's recognition of a freedom of association, or expressive association, demonstrates this doctrine's continued viability in Supreme Court jurisprudence; the Court's failure sees it as controlling in this situation demonstrates this doctrine's limited strength.

This results in three major problems. One is that the autonomy of an independent, student-organized faith-based group is put at risk. On pain of losing benefits all other student organizations enjoy, the student group is told it may not insist on religious commitments that are at the heart of its identity—that which sets it off from other student organizations. Second, the principle of governmental religious neutrality is thereby violated. If a faith-based organization gives up its right to hold to faith-based standards, it will receive public benefits; if it does not, it loses those benefits. This point was confirmed in embarrassingly clear terms by the Court's majority opinion when Justice Ruth Bader Ginsburg wrote that the Christian Legal Society student group "faces only indirect pressure to modify its membership policies; CLS may exclude any person for any reason if it foregoes the benefits of official recognition."[39] For there to be a government-created "indirect pressure" on a student organization to modify its religious or religiously based moral standards for its members or leaders is to violate governmental religious neutrality. In principle this is no different than imposing a tax on a religiously based student organization that secular student organizations do not have to pay. Third, it results in a loss, not a gain in diversity and pluralism in the public square. This last result is rooted in the structural pluralist recognition that the recognition and preservation of diversity and pluralism of individuals is rooted in their ability to collectively develop, express, and contend for their ideas. This point was made clearly and forcefully in an *amicus* brief filed by Gays and Lesbians for Individual Liberty when it stated:

> Freedom of association protects the interests and advances the rights of minority groups in two fundamental ways, both recognized repeatedly by this Court. First, it enables disfavored groups to pursue their *distinctive ends*—including the goal of civil rights—by giving them a collective voice and equipping them for "[e]ffective advocacy of both public and private points of view." . . . Second,

associational freedom enables minority voices to cultivate and maintain their *distinctive identity*, thereby preserving political and cultural diversity."[40]

The key point is that the effect of all organizations—and in this case of all student organizations on college or university campuses—being required to accept as members and officers any and all persons who walk in the door would be to reduce, not promote, pluralism and diversity. Taken to its final conclusion all student organizations would look the same, with the same mixture of religions, political views, and opinions on issues of the day—which means that majority religions, political views, and opinions on issues of the day would dominate in all of them. Whereas a policy that allows groups to insist upon members and officers that subscribe to the distinguishing identities of the various campus groups will protect the right of minorities to organize and meet and will result in a colorful diversity of groups based on differing religions, viewpoints, and opinions—the very goal that universities are presumably committed to protect.

Objections to the Structural Pluralist Position

Most of the opposition to the positions to which the prior section has argued structural pluralist thinking leads comes from the LGBT lobby and others on the Left. Crucial to most of their arguments—whether self-consciously or unself-consciously held—is the assumption that faith-based human service organizations are not religious in the same sense that a church, synagogue, or mosque is. We are again back to the mindset, influenced by Enlightenment thinking, that limits religion to the private sphere, leading it to view only religious congregations, seminaries, and other institutions directly involved in the core religious teachings and rituals of a faith community as being religious. When a faith community seeks to provide food to the hungry, offers help to persons just released from prison, provides development assistance to poverty stricken villages overseas, makes health care available to those in need, or in other ways works to meet the needs of hurting persons, it is seen as engaging in secular activities much as any other humanitarian organization might.

This mindset was fully on display in the case mentioned in chapter 1 that involved World Vision, an international relief and development agency in the evangelical Protestant tradition. It had fired several employees because they could no longer sign a statement of faith World Vision requires of all its employees. They brought suit on the basis that World Vision is not a religious but a humanitarian organization. Therefore, they argued, the religious exemption that federal law provides to religious employers being able to make hiring decisions based on religion did not apply to World Vision. In a split 2-to-1

decision, the U.S. Court of Appeals held that World Vision is indeed a religious organization, and thus the religious exemption on hiring applied, since
"it 1) is organized for a self-identified religious purpose . . . 2) is engaged in
activity consistent with, and in furtherance of, those religious purposes, and
3) holds itself out to the public as religious."[41] It was up to the organization,
not to government, to declare whether or not it was religious in nature. The
dissenting judge argued that in spite of what World Vision holds itself out to
be, it in fact is not a religious organization. She wrote: "World Vision does
not require or urge aid recipients to participate in religious worship or instruction, although it does 'offer those opportunities.' World Vision also does not
ordain ministers, and it is not affiliated with any particular church. . . Finally,
the plaintiffs performed completely secular job duties."[42] She concluded: "In
short, World Vision is nothing like a church, but resembles in its primary
activities a wide range of charitable organizations."[43] Her mindset could not
conceive of an organization that did not look or act as a church nevertheless
being a deeply religious organization as it claimed it was.

The same set of assumptions that informed the dissenting judge's opinion
can be seen elsewhere. For example, it is clearly present in a conclusion
reached in a 2002 study authorized by the American Civil Liberties Union:
"When, however, religiously affiliated organizations move into secular
pursuits—such as providing medical care or social services to the public or
running a business—they should no longer be insulated from secular laws.
In the public world, they should play by public rules."[44] One can perhaps
agree with the ACLU in regard to running a business, but "providing medical care or social services" are profoundly religious activities for many faith
traditions. The Christian tradition, for instance, insists that in doing so one
is providing care to Jesus Christ himself and failing to do so condemns one
to hell.[45] In spite of this the dissenting judge and the ACLU—and many
others on the left—start out seeing religion as something having to do only
with the private sphere of religious congregations, worship, devotional
activities, religious rituals and celebrations, and narrowly defined religious
instruction. We are back to the venerable but false idea that religion is a
purely private matter.

Beginning with this mindset, when faced with the issue of faith-based organizations being able to make hiring decisions based on LGBT persons' sexual
lifestyles, it is easy to see organizations that are not churches, synagogues,
or mosques but are providing human services as not really being religious
in any integral sense. Persons taking the position that faith-based service
organizations are not really religious in nature would naturally also see their
attempts to "discriminate" against LGBT persons in their hiring practices as
just one more case of persons being held down and limited by who they are.

One's religious beliefs are appropriately controlling in one's personal, private life, but if one, or an organization, tries to take them into the public realm of education, health care, and other human services, one is dragging into the public realm what should be left at home or limited to Sunday morning in church. Therefore, Catholic, evangelical Protestant, and Orthodox Jewish human service organizations that see homosexual lifestyles as morally wrong and running counter to beliefs held for thousands of years are dismissed as though acting on irrational prejudices when they refuse to hire a practicing homosexual. And forcing them by law not to do so will really do no harm to their religious scruples. After all, they can worship and celebrate their faiths' beliefs every weekend as they see fit, either including or excluding homosexuals as they please.

This type of an assumption can be seen in an essay by Richael Faithful when she wrote of "discrimination" by faith-based organizations against persons in LGBT lifestyles: "The goal to eliminate discrimination does not in itself offend religious views. It may offend privacy interests of those who are uncomfortable with LGBT people, yet privacy interests are not synonymous to religiosity, particularly within a constitutional context."[46] She makes the amazing judgment that eliminating hiring "discrimination" against LGBT persons does not "offend religious views," and goes on to assume that it is merely a matter of religious folks feeling "uncomfortable" around LGBT folks. One can only understand such a position—which runs completely counter to what Orthodox Judaism and the major Christian traditions in the United States have repeatedly declared—if Faithful is operating out of the Enlightenment-inspired idea that religion is personal and private, dealing only with narrowly defined religious rituals and celebrations. But blind to her own assumptions, Faithful is able to conclude: "Uncomfortable co-existence is sometimes a fact of life that privileged groups must endure for the sake of progress, for which conservative Christians and other religious people are no exception."[47] Since opposition to hiring LGBT persons in sexual relationships by faith-based human service organizations is not rooted in religious views, but is only a matter of feeling uncomfortable around persons who are different, there is no problem in civil rights laws that would force faith-based organizations to hire persons regardless of their sexual lifestyles. But if the never-say-die assumption that religion is purely personal and private with no legitimate role in the public realm is false—as this book as repeatedly argued and documented is the case—expanding nondiscrimination laws to LGBT persons in active relationships without an exemption for faith-based organizations would be an exercise in the denial of religious freedom.

Those who argue that on-campus, faith-based student clubs should not be able to have faith requirements or behavioral standards for their members or leaders also may begin with the underlying assumption that since religion and moral standards rooted in religion are a purely private matter, they have no rational relevance for student organizations on university campuses. And those student organizations that do insist on such standards are therefore engaging in the same sort of discrimination as would student organizations that exclude persons based on race or ethnicity. The nondiscrimination mentality—which indeed is applicable in many situations—is applied unthinkingly to student religious organizations with no consideration of the different situation they pose. Religion is then seen as dealing with certain personal, private beliefs and practices that lead to biases and prejudices against those of other beliefs and to persons in unmarried or LBGT relationships. Religion is not seen as a rational system of belief with defensible, thought-out ethical standards. With this mindset in control, it is easy to conclude that all student organizations, religious and nonreligious alike, should be held to the same nondiscrimination standards.

However, the relevance of religion to a religious student organization would appear to be so obvious that one suspects there may be something else in play. Douglas Laycock once wisely noted, "Too many Americans react to claims of religious or sexual liberty on the basis of what they think of the religious belief or sexual practice at issue."[48] This may be the key explanation for why some religious student organizations on university campuses have run into challenges based on their membership standards. Most such student groups that have been challenged have been in the evangelical Protestant tradition, a tradition that has received high negative rating in surveys among university faculties.[49] This may lead those opposed to what these groups believe and stand for to search for ways to keep them off campus or from receiving on-campus recognition and benefits all other student groups receive.

Laycock's observation may also help explain why many on the political right oppose expanding nondiscrimination laws to cover LGBT persons. Their advocacy of a religious exemption is often only a fall-back position in case the enactment of ENDA appears inevitable. They would prefer no ENDA expansion at all. There are both principled and tactical reasons for this. Tactically, they fear that the LGBT lobby, once they achieve the expansion of ENDA even with a strong religious exemption, will come back and seek to narrow that exemption or to use the ENDA expansion as a springboard to restrict faith-based organizations in other ways. Such fears are not entirely groundless as "hate speech" laws have been used in some other countries to limit criticisms of LGBT lifestyles and there have been suggestions the nonprofit 501(c)(3) status of faith-based organizations that resist some goals of the gay rights agenda should be revoked.[50] The principled reason for the Right's frequent opposition to ENDAs is rooted in conservative attempts to defend traditional morality, which is seen as crucial to a stable, successful society. ENDAs are then seen as attempts legally to sanction what their traditional morality sees as an immoral lifestyle that has the effect of undercutting the health and stability of society.

But a true pluralism insists on principle, as Kevin Hasson has expressed it, that "we can, and should, respect others' duty to follow their consciences even as we insist that they're mistaken."[51] If one calls on structural pluralism and the freedom it accords faith-based and secular organizations and movements only when one agrees with their goals, one has truly not accepted structural pluralism but is only using it for tactical advantages. Also, accepting the legitimate demands of a group one believes is wrong in what they are doing is often, from a tactical point of view, a good way to undercut their demands for even more extreme, less defensible, demands. Resisting every and all calls for greater equality by LGBT activists can inadvertently increase popular support for those demands; accepting limited, legitimate demands can, by eliminating the most egregiously inequitable situations, undercut demands for more extreme, less legitimate demands.

SPECIFIC ISSUES: REQUIRING FAITH-BASED ORGANIZATIONS TO PROVIDE SERVICES THEY FIND RELIGIOUSLY OBJECTIONABLE

A final area where questions have arisen over faith-based organizations and their right to religious autonomy concerns the degree to which they are free not to provide certain services they find religiously objectionable. Three types of issues have been especially prominent. One concerns faith-based hospitals and whether or not they can be forced to provide abortions and birth control services they find objectionable on religious grounds. This controversy has involved a number of Catholic hospitals, since the Catholic tradition has, of course, long opposed abortion and artificial birth control as being morally repugnant. The *Los Angeles Times* has reported, "In city and county meetings and in state hearing rooms, the activists are seeking to make public funding [of Catholic hospitals] . . . contingent on a full menu of reproductive services, including abortion."[52] A second area of controversy is whether or not a faith-based organization can be required by law to include provisions in its employees' insurance policies that it finds morally objectionable. This issue has arisen both in regard to providing birth control services in Catholic Charities' health insurance policies and including same-sex partners on employees' insurance policies. In 1996 Catholic Charities of San Francisco ran into problems when the Board of Supervisors required organizations contracting with the county to provide the same benefits to domestic partners they do to spouses. In 2004 Catholic Charities of Sacramento lost a court case in which it sought exemption from a California law that required all prescription drug coverage in health insurance plans to include birth control coverage.[53]

A third controversy involves proposals and attempts to require faith-based organizations to provide services to same-sex couples even when doing so would violate their religious beliefs. There have, for example, been attempts to require faith-based adoption agencies to place children for adoption and foster care with same-sex couples. In 2011 Congressman Pete Stark (D-CA) introduced H.R. 1681, which would require all adoption agencies that receive some federal government funding to place children with same-sex couples on the same basis as they do with mother-father families. Catholic Charities in both Boston and Washington, D.C., ended adoption and foster care services when they would have been forced by local laws to place children with same-sex couples.[54] This is hardly a purely Catholic issue, as the largest faith-based adoption agency in the United States, which is in the evangelical Protestant tradition, also has a policy based on its religious beliefs not to place children with same sex couples.[55] Another example: a Methodist pavilion had its tax-exempt status revoked by New Jersey when it decided not to rent its facility for use by a lesbian couple to solemnize their union.[56] Also, the Orthodox Jewish Yeshiva University, under threat of a court order, changed its policy to allow same-sex couples to live in its married student housing.[57] A National Public Radio reporter summarized that "same-sex couples are beginning to challenge policies of religious organizations that exclude them, claiming that a religious group's view that homosexual marriage is a sin cannot be used to violate their right to equal treatment."[58] As same-sex marriages become available in more states, conflicts such as these are likely to increase in number.

All three types of issues raise the question of whether or not faith-based organizations should be forced to act contrary to their religious beliefs, if otherwise certain persons would not be able to receive services from faith-based organizations that others are able to receive, or if persons would not be able to receive certain services from a faith-based provider that they would be able to receive from most other providers. When the answer to this question is no, some charge discrimination that violates the equal protection of the law.

Structural Pluralism's Answer

As is the case with faith-based organizations and hiring and membership standards, two underlying tenets of structural pluralism shape its response to the question of the right of faith-based human service organizations not to provide certain services they find religiously objectionable. One is the basic concept of religious autonomy, leading to religious freedom rights that all faith-based organizations possess. As emphasized at many points in this book, this autonomy is theirs not at the sufferance of the government but is an inherent right. To tell a faith-based, religious organization that by its actions it must condone, support, or affirm behavior that it condemns in its theology and its words is to do violence to its autonomy and its right to the free exercise of its religious faith. It must also be recalled that individual religious freedom is closely tied to organizational religious freedom. To force a faith-based adoption agency, hospital, health clinic, or pavilion to offer services it finds morally objectionable means there are persons associated with these entities that would be required to act contrary to their religious beliefs. This fact is sometimes forgotten. Ever since the Supreme Court's 1973 Roe v. Wade decision, which established abortion as a constitutionally protected right in most cases, conscience clauses that protect health professionals from having to participate in abortions have generally been in force.[59] There is a long and tangled history of conscience clauses as applied to health professionals and abortion and abortion-related services. Congress has added conscience clause protections of varying strength in annual appropriation measures. Presidential executive orders have over the years also added to the situation, strengthening or weakening conscientious protections. But one fact in this history stands out: it has been easier to protect the religious conscience rights of individual health care providers than that of health care organizations. These efforts to provide strong, explicit conscience protections to individual health care workers in regard to abortion are commendable, but a structural pluralist approach insists such protections should apply in more areas of conscientious concern than abortion and that they should apply to organizations as well as to individuals.

As noted in several places earlier in this chapter dealing with other issue areas, it is also important that the fundamental right of a faith-based organization to decide if it is and in what sense it is a religious or religiously based organization must be protected. This is the second basic tenet to which an approach based on structural pluralism insists. If the state possesses the ability to decide which organizations are religious and which ones are not, any notion of religious freedom is seriously diminished. For an organization to insist it is a faith-based organization acting on the basis of its religious faith and possessing religious freedom rights to be told by the government that it is a secular organization and thus possesses no religious freedom rights is to make a mockery of its religious autonomy.

These basic principles mean, in the structural pluralist point of view, that faith-based service organizations must be free not to provide services their faith traditions believe to be morally repugnant.[60] Thus, in all of the examples and cases cited above the structural pluralist viewpoint says the faith-based organization should be free not to provide the service in question—whether it is an evangelical Protestant adoption agency not placing children with same-sex couples (whether married or not), an Orthodox Jewish university being able to exclude same-sex couples from its married student housing, a Catholic faith-based organization not providing contraceptive coverage in its health-care plans, or a Catholic hospital not providing abortions or contraceptive services. Respect for religion and sincerely held religious views and for the autonomy and religious freedom rights of faith-based organizations demand no less.

This means that some persons will have to go elsewhere to find certain services that they desire. But it is hard to argue against the point made by Laycock when he wrote that "the right to one's own moral integrity should generally trump the inconvenience of having to get the same service from another provider nearby."[61] Usually the inconvenience will be minor, as when a same-sex couple who may legally marry in their state may not be able to be married in a church-related pavilion that was their first choice or an employee may need to obtain supplemental health insurance to cover procedures her faith-based employer considers morally objectionable. But one must also recognize that at times more than the inconvenience of going to "another provider nearby" may be at stake. There may sometimes be a potential for persons to suffer adverse consequences, as when a same-sex couple needs to search for off-campus housing even though it would have been cheaper and more convenient to stay in on-campus housing of a faith-based college or, more seriously, a woman whose medical condition indicates future pregnancies may pose health risks may need to be transferred to a different hospital to obtain the tubal ligation she desires.[62] Is there a way, or is it even necessary, to balance the autonomy and religious freedom rights of faith-based organizations with the ability of persons to obtain desired or needed services from faith-based organizations even when those faith-based organizations find those services morally objectionable?

The basic answer of structural pluralism is that religious autonomy rights trump the desires and needs of those wanting the services the faith-based organizations find morally objectionable. One can paraphrase Martin Luther's famous statement before the imperial Diet of Worms, in 1521, "It is neither right nor safe to act against conscience," by stating, "It is neither right nor safe to force faith-based organizations to act against conscience." A genuine, deeply respected pluralism in society means we need to live together with our deepest differences, even when doing so means some will be inconvenienced and some may even be disadvantaged in more serious ways.

To force a faith-based organization, for example, to place a child for adoption with a same-sex couple is to force it to condone by its actions behavior it sincerely and based on long-held and theologically developed ideas believes is morally repugnant—and to force individuals in that organization to act contrary to their religiously based beliefs. The same-sex couple can go to a state agency, a secular adoption agency, or a faith-based adoption agency that does not take a stand on the morality of a LGBT lifestyle. That couple may be inconvenienced and they will be made more aware of the fact that there are others who find their behavior morally objectionable, but those are relatively minor issues—that is, relative to forcing a faith-based organization and its employees to go counter to deeply held beliefs. A genuine respect for pluralism and diversity says that the law ought neither to forbid same-sex couples from adopting children nor force faith-based adoption agencies to go against their genuine beliefs concerning the morality of LGBT lifestyles.

One additional caveat that seeks to balance the rights of faith-based organizations whose religious beliefs require them not to provide certain services and those of persons desiring those services from those same faith-based organizations is to require faith-based organizations claiming the right not to provide certain services based on their religious beliefs to suggest to persons seeking those services alternative providers of them. This is common courtesy and fits with a recognition by faith-based organizations that we indeed are a pluralistic society where some will not agree with their moral standards. Just as the gay rights lobby ought not to force its beliefs onto those faith-based organizations that reject some of its goals, so also faith-based organizations ought not to try to force their beliefs onto the gay community nor hinder its members in finding elsewhere the services they desire. The same principle holds in the case of other services persons are seeking from faith-based organizations that have religious scruples against providing them.

Objections to the Structural Pluralist Position

Understanding the most frequently made objections to protecting the right of faith-based service organizations to refuse to provide services they believe morally objectionable begins with the basic view we have met many times before, namely, that religion is limited to the world of private devotional activities and religious congregations with their celebrations and worship services. Thus, when faith-based organizations provide human services to the public they have entered the secular realm and become like other secular agencies. Recall the revealing statement from the ACLU's reproductive health study quoted earlier: "When, however, religiously affiliated organizations move into secular pursuits—such as providing medical care or social services to the public or running a business—they should no longer be insulated from secular laws. In the public world, they should play by public rules."[63] If one accepts this viewpoint, the claims of a faith-based organization that certain services it is being required to offer are morally, religiously objectionable suddenly become a matter of either bigotry or a clinging to unreasonable traditions. How can a secular organization providing secular services possess religiously based scruples to providing certain services?

Once one accepts the notion that faith-based organizations providing services to the public are indistinguishable from secular nonprofit organizations or even government agencies providing similar services, nondiscrimination thinking takes over. Religious autonomy and religious freedom arguments that structural pluralism sees as being crucial disappear. Then if everyone is not treated the same and if instead faith-based organizations are allowed to make distinctions based on the desired services or the persons requesting the services, the resulting pluralism is seen as the result of irrational, invidious distinctions. This is especially the case in regard to same-sex couples, where faith-based organizations based on their moral scruples may refuse a same-sex couple the very same service they are willing to provide a male-female couple. Think of a college that refuses a same-sex couple housing in their married student housing facilities, even though they may be legally married under some states' laws. Or think of a church or church-related recreation center that often is used as a site for weddings, but refuses its use for a same-sex commitment ceremony or wedding. Those who are inconvenienced may feel not simply inconvenienced; they may feel they are objects of discrimination and made to feel second class citizens. Much of the gay-rights lobby's insistence that they not have to look elsewhere for certain services probably has more to do their feelings of being made to feel second class citizens than any severe inconvenience they face.

But the other side of this same coin means faith-based organizations that believe certain actions or lifestyles are deeply immoral are being asked to affirm those actions and lifestyles. For them, the distinctions they are making and therefore their actions are not matters of arbitrary discrimination or merely upholding long-held traditions, but they are matters of religiously rooted beliefs, usually beliefs held for hundreds, if not thousands, of years and supported by thought-out understandings of God's revealed will, human nature, and human relationships. One is free to disagree with their religiously rooted beliefs, but it is wrong to dismiss them as not genuine religiously based beliefs or as possessing an inconsequential nature for those who hold to them.

For the courts or other government agencies to decree that a faith-based organization that insists it is clearly and deeply religious in nature is in fact a secular organization engaged in secular activities is almost the definition of religious discrimination. Or to declare that potential feelings of second-class citizenship must trump sincerely held religious beliefs is wrong. We are back to the question of who has the right to determine what is and is not religion. If it is the government's right to do so, everyone's religious freedom is dependent on the government of the day and its conceptualization of religion. Everyone's religious freedom would thereby be put at risk.

The political right has been steadfast in insisting that no faith-based organization—and usually no for-profit business as well—should be forced to provide services it believes morally objectionable. It also often even resists legal provisions that an entity refusing to provide a certain service be required to refer persons to other providers who are willing to supply that service. These positions are in line with the Right's frequent advocacy of governmental policies that support by law religion and religiously based values, as well as traditional values more broadly. But such positions are in conflict with a genuine pluralism, just as are the positions held by those liberals who would force faith-based entities to provide services in violation of their religious beliefs. Both involve an unwillingness to accept a pluralism in our society that tolerates even those whom one is convinced is wrong. But if we are unwilling to tolerate and learn to live with those with whom we disagree, we are not really tolerant at all.

That point is an appropriate one to make at the close of this book. This book has not been a plea for the rightness or wrongness of the points of view held by certain religious traditions and their faith-based human service organizations. A structural pluralist approach to the issues of religious pluralism and diversity—even though it itself is rooted in a Christian understanding of the world, human society, and religion—argues first and foremost for making a public space for diversity in our society and in its public policies. This requires a tolerance on the part of the religious and irreligious, the political left and the political right, that leads to forbearance in the public realm that makes allowance for views other than their own.

Notes

PREFACE

1. I take this phrase from the delightfully entitled book by Kevin Seamus Hasson, *The Right to Be Wrong: Ending the Culture War over Religions in America* (San Francisco, CA: Encounter Books, 2005).

CHAPTER 1. THE ISSUE THAT WILL NOT GO AWAY

1. The case is Sylvia Spencer, Ted Youngberg, and Vicki Hulse v. World Vision, United States Court of Appeals for the Ninth Circuit, August 23, 2010 (No. 08-35532). For a summary of the court case and its background, see Kevin J. Jones, "Federal Court Rejects Case Charging World Vision with Religious Discrimination," EWTN News (January 27, 2011). Available at www.ewtnnews.com/catholic-news .US.php?id=2521 (accessed February 10, 2011).

2. See Patricia Wen, "Catholic Charities Stuns State, Ends Adoptions," *Boston Globe* (March 11, 2006).

3. See Christian Legal Society v. Martinez, 561 U.S. ____ (2010) (No. 08-1371 slip opinion) and Adam Liptak, "Rights and Religion Clash in Court Case," *New York Times* (December 8, 2009), A24.

4. Quoted in Liptak, "Rights and Religion Clash."

5. Christian Legal Society v. Martinez, opinion of the Court, 31.

6. Ibid., dissenting opinion, 37.

7. On the parachurch phenomenon see Wesley K. Willmer and J. David Schmidt, *The Prospering Parachurch* (San Francisco, CA: Jossey-Bass, 1998).

8. Mark E. Chapko, "Constitutional Protections for Church Autonomy: A Practitioner's View," in Gerhard Robbers, ed., *Church Autonomy: A Comparative Survey* (Frankfurt am Main, DEU: Peter Lang, 2001), 96.

9. Ibid., 97.

10. Gerhard Robbers, "Foreword," in Robbers, ed., *Church Autonomy*, 5.

11. See Robert Bellah, *The Broken Covenant: American Civil Religion in Time of Trial* (New York, NY: Seabury, 1975), 94.

12. For three such cases, see *Report on Enforcement of Laws Protecting Religious Freedom, Fiscal Years 2001–2006* (U. S. Department of Justice, Civil Rights Division), 11. Available at www.justice.gov/crt/spec_topics/religiousdiscrimination/report/report.pdf.

13. On the Amish buggies, see Foundation against Intolerance of Religious Minorities "Amish Buggies, Traffic Law Clash" (April 8, 2001). Available at www.firmstand.org/news/amish.html. Accessed February 11, 2011. On Native American use of peyote see the Supreme Court case, Employment Division v. Smith, 494 U.S. 872 (1990).

14. Words used to describe certain entities can be confusing. Usually nongovernment, nonprofit organizations that provide services—whether health, education, or social services—are referred to as private organizations to distinguish them from government agencies, which are referred to as public agencies. But this does not distinguish them from private, for-profit entities. And to refer to government agencies as "public" agencies and nongovernmental agencies as "private" agencies, even when they serve a public purpose by providing services to the general public—although commonly used—is really not accurate. For example, what we call a public rest room is not a government-owned and operated rest room, but a rest room that is available to the public. Similarly, a nongovernmental organization providing health, educational, or social services to the public can appropriately be considered a public organization. Since an underlying theme of this book is that nongovernmental organizations that are providing certain services to the general public are in some important aspects public organizations and part of the network of public services, I will normally refer to such organizations as nongovernmental, independent, or nonprofit organizations and, when they are religiously based, as faith-based organizations, not private organizations. For a good discussion of the terminological issues surrounding the nongovernmental, nonprofit sector, see Peter Frumkin, *On Being Nonprofit: A Conceptual and Policy Primer* (Cambridge, MA: Harvard University Press, 2002), 10–16.

15. On the Clinton and Bush administrations' efforts, see Amy E. Black, Douglas L. Koopman, and David K. Ryden, *Of Little Faith: the Politics of George W. Bush's Faith-Based Initiatives* (Washington, DC: Georgetown University Press, 2004).

16. Ben Smith and Byron Tau, "Obama's Stimulus Pours Millions into Faith-Based Groups," *Politico* (December 3, 2010). Available at www.politico.com/news/stories/1210/45897.html.

17. See Pew Forum on Religion & Public Life "U.S. Religious Landscape Survey." Available at http://religions.pewforum.org/reports.

18. W. Cole Durham, Jr., "The Right to Autonomy in Religious Affairs: A Comparative View," in Robbers, ed., *Church Autonomy*, 653.

19. The Coalition Against Religious Discrimination, "Letter to the Honorable George W. Bush," (January 30, 2001) [a photocopy of the letter in the possession of the author].

20. Quoted in Americans for Separation of Church and State, "The 'Faith-Based' Initiative: Church, Social Services and Your Tax Dollars." Available at www.au.org/resources/brochures/the-faith-based-initiative (accessed June 20, 2011).

21. "Faith-Based Discrimination," *New York Times* (October 14, 2009).

22. Quoted in Jones, "Federal Court Rejects Case."

23. United States Court of Appeals for the Ninth Circuit, Sylvia Spencer, Ted Youngberg and Vicki Hulse v. World Vision, No. 08-35532. Amicus brief for Christian Legal Society et al., 5.

24. Quoted in Daniel J. Wakin, "Charity Reopens Bible, and Questions Follow," *New York Times* (February 2, 2004), B1.

25. See President's Advisory Council on Faith-Based and Neighborhood Partnerships, "A New Era of Partnerships: Report of Recommendations to the President" (March 2010), 131–33.

26. Ibid., 129–30.

27. Maureen K. Bailey, "Contraceptive Insurance Mandates and *Catholic Charities v. Superior Court of Sacramento*: Towards a New Understanding of Women's Health," *Texas Review of Law and Politics* 9 (2000), 367–88.

CHAPTER 2. FAITH-BASED ORGANIZATIONS AND THE NETWORK OF HUMAN SERVICES

1. James Madison, "Memorial and Remonstrance against Religious Assessments" (1785), para. 3.

2. Lester M. Salamon, *The Resilient Sector: The State of Nonprofit America* (Washington, DC: Brookings, 2003), 1–2. This is not a recent phenomenon. For a collection of essays that describe the prominent role nonprofit organizations have played throughout American history, starting in the colonial era, see David C. Hammack, ed., *Making the Nonprofit Sector in the United States: A Reader* (Bloomington, IN: Indiana University Press, 1998).

3. Lester M. Salamon, *America's Nonprofit Sector: A Primer*, 2nd ed. (New York, NY: Foundation Center, 1999), 22.

4. Ibid., 9. Elsewhere Salamon has put the proportion of the total workforce in the United States working in the nonprofit sector at 7.8 percent, higher than in all but four of the twenty-two countries for which he presents data. See Lester M. Salamon, "The New Governance and the Tools of Public Action: An Introduction," in Lester M. Salamon, ed., *The Tools of Government: A Guide to the New Governance* (New York, NY: Oxford University Press, 2002), 7.

5. Salamon, *America's Nonprofit Sector*, 2.

6. Ibid., 149.

7. Michael O'Neill, *The Third America: The Emergence of the Nonprofit Sector in the United States* (San Francisco, CA: Jossey-Bass, 1989), 20.

8. Steven Rathgeb Smith, "Comparative Case Studies of Faith-Based and Secular Service Agencies: An Overview and Synthesis of Key Findings," in Steven

Rathgeb Smith, John P. Bartkowski, and Susan Grettenberger, eds., *Comparative Views on the Role and Effect of Faith in Social Services* (Albany, NY: Roundtable on Religion and Social Welfare Policy, Rockefeller Institute of Government, 2006), 1.

9. See Kirsten A. Gronbjerg and Steven Rathgeb Smith, "Nonprofit Organizations and Public Policies in the Delivery of Human Services," in Charles T. Clotfelter and Thomas Ehrlich, eds., *Philanthropy and the Nonprofit Sector in a Changing America* (Bloomington, IN: Indiana University Press, 1999), 164.

10. See Ram A. Cnaan and Stephanie C. Boddie, "Philadelphia Census of Congregations and their Involvement in Social Service Delivery," *Social Service Review* 75 (2001), 568 and 570.

11. Ibid., 573.

12. See Edwin I. Hernandez and Neil Carlson, *Gatherings of Hope: How Religious Congregations Contribute to the Quality of Life in Kent County* (Grand Rapids, MI: Center for Social Research, Calvin College, 2008), 53.

13. Ibid., 61 and 65.

14. Heidi Rolland Unruh and Ronald J. Sider, *Saving Souls, Serving Society: Understanding the Faith Factor in Church-Based Social Ministry* (New York, NY: Oxford University Press, 2006), 32.

15. David J. Wright, *Taking Stock: The Bush Faith-Based Initiative and What Lies Ahead* (Albany, NY: Roundtable on Religion and Social Welfare Policy, Nelson Rockefeller Institute of Government, 2009), 71. Available at www.rockinst.org/pdf/faith-based_social_services/2009-06-11-taking_stock_faith-based_office.pdf.

16. Carol J. De Vita and Fredrica D. Kamer, "The Role of Faith-Based and Community Organizations in Post-Hurricane Human Service Relief Efforts," (an Urban Institute report prepared for the U.S. Department of Health and Human Services, December, 2008), 19. Available at www.urban.org/url.cfm?ID=1001245. However, the researchers also found that the faith-based organizations offered services for a shorter time than did the secular nonprofit organizations.

17. Scott W. Allard, "Access and Stability: Comparing Faith-Based and Secular Nonprofit Service Providers," (a paper presented at the 2007 conference of the National Poverty Center, University of Michigan), 48.

18. Ibid., 13.

19. Stephen V. Monsma, *Putting Faith in Partnerships: Welfare-to-Work in Four Cities* (Ann Arbor, MI: University of Michigan Press, 2004), 59.

20. See Working Group on Human Needs and Faith-Based and Community Initiatives, "Finding Common Ground: 29 Recommendations of the Working Group on Human Needs and Faith-Based and Community Initiatives," (Washington, DC: Search for Common Ground, January, 2002). Available at www.sfcg.org/programmes/us/report.pdf. The wide differences in faith-based organizations providing human services and several attempts at categorizing them is also discussed in Jason D. Scott, "The Scope and Scale of Faith-Based Social Services: A Review of the Research Literature Focusing on the Activities of Faith-Based Organizations in the Delivery of Social Services," 2nd ed. (Albany, NY: Roundtable on Religion and Social Welfare Policy, Rockefeller Institute of Government, June, 2003), 1–5.

21. On both nonprofit and governmental relief and development efforts, see J. Bruce Nichols, *The Uneasy Alliance: Religion, Refugee Work, and U.S. Foreign Policy* (New York, NY: Oxford University Press, 1988) and Rachel M. McCleary, *Global Compassion: Private Voluntary Organizations and U.S. Foreign Policy since 1939* (New York, NY: Oxford University Press, 2009).

22. McCleary, *Global Compassion*, 4.

23. Ibid., 16.

24. Ibid., 20. The 33 percent of the PVOs that were faith-based accounted for 46 percent of total PVO revenues.

25. Ibid., 25.

26. Ibid., 29.

27. McCleary, *Global Compassion*, 24.

28. Nicholas D. Kristof, "Learning from the Sins of Sodom," *New York Times* (February 28, 2010), wk11.

29. USAID, *2009 VOLAG Report of Voluntary Agencies*, 158–59. Available at http://www.usaid.gov/our_work/cross-cutting_programs/private_voluntary_cooperation/volag2009.pdf.

30. Email to the author from Lisa Story, a paralegal in World Vision's Legal Department (June 7, 2010).

31. On the budget, see Catholic Relief Services, "2009 Annual Report," 34. Available at http://crs.org/about/finance/pdf/AR_2009.pdf. On the number of employees, interview with Joan Rosenhauer, Vice President for Operations, Catholic Relief Services (May 25, 2010).

32. See www.crs.org/where.

33. Catholic Relief Services, "2009 Annual Report," 34.

34. Compiled by the author from USAID, *2009 VOLAG Report of Voluntary Agencies*. I included in the category of government assistance USAID's category of "Other government and international organizations." This annual reports gives revenue and expenditure information for all PVOs registered with USAID. It should be noted that since World Vision is a member of AERDO, its almost $1 billion in revenue mentioned earlier is also included in the total revenue figures given here for AERDO members.

35. Interview with Chad Hayward, AERDO executive director (May 18, 2010). It should be noted that AERDO recently changed its name to Accord. See www.accordnetwork.org.

36. Compiled by the author from USAID, *2009 VOLAG Report of Voluntary Agencies*. This was a lower percentage than that of all PVOs registered with USAID, which in 2009 came to 25 percent of their revenues (about $6.5 billion). Nevertheless, the evangelical members of AERDO received significant amounts of money and in-kind contributions from USAID and other government agencies.

37. See American Jewish World Service, "Annual Report 2009," 38. Available at http://secure.ajws.rog/pdf/2009_annual_Report.pdf.

38. See www.mercyusa.org/mission.cfm.

39. USAID, *2009 VOLAG Report of Voluntary Agencies*, 148–49.

40. Gloria Steele, "Testimony before the Subcommittee on State, Foreign Operations, and Related Programs, Committee on Appropriations, U. S. House of Representatives (March 23, 2010). Available at www.usaid.gov/press/speeches/2010/ty100323.html (accessed August 3, 2010).

41. "Collaboration with a Community-Based Organization Is Key to a Successful ITN Distribution Campaign in Liberia." Available at www.fightingmalaria.gov/news/voices/liberia_itn.html (accessed August 3, 2010).

42. Kristof, "Learning from the Sins of Sodom."

43. From the opinion of Judge Diarmuid O'Scannlain in Sylvia Spencer, Ted Youngberg, and Vicki Hulse v. World Vision, United States Court of Appeals for the Ninth Circuit, August 23, 2010 (No. 08-35532), 1402.

44. See www.worldvision.org/content.nsf/about/who-we-are (accessed August 3, 2010).

45. Interview with Steven McFarland, Chief Legal Counsel, World Vision (May 24, 2010).

46. "The Mission of Catholic Relief Services," available at http://crs.org/about/mission-statement/ (accessed August 3, 2010).

47. Interview with Joan Rosenhauer, Vice President for U.S. Operations, Catholic Relief Services (May 25, 2010).

48. See http://www.aerdo.net/standards_faith.php (accessed August 3, 2010).

49. See http://afsc.org/mission-and-values (accessed February 14, 2011).

50. Sharon Vandivere, Karin Malm, and Laura Radel, *Adoption USA: A Chartbook Based on the 2007 National Survey of Adoptive Parents* (Washington, DC: U.S. Department of Health and Human Services, Office of the Assistant Secretary for Planning and Evaluation, 2009), 1.

51. Ibid., 3.

52. Paul Placek, "National Adoption Data," in Thomas C. Atwood, Lee A. Allen, and Virginia C. Ravenel, eds., *Adoption Factbook IV* (Alexandria, VA: National Council for Adoptions, 2007), 22–23. Researchers in the area of adoption statistics warn that all numbers should be taken as estimates, not firm figures. There is no one central place where adoption statistics are gathered. Each state keeps its own records and those records are not always complete or do not use comparable categories, leaving the possibility of there being gaps as well as double counting. The numbers I have used in this section are as accurate as possible given the state of adoption record keeping. For an account of the challenges in collecting reliable, complete information on adoptions, see Placek, "National Adoption Data," 14–18 and National Adoption Information Clearing House, "How Many Children Were Adopted in 2000 and 2001?" in Atwood, Allen, and Ravenel, eds. *Adoption Factbook IV*, 97–99.

53. Placek, "National Adoption Data," 36

54. Ibid., 8.

55. Vandivere, Malm, and Radel, *Adoption USA*, 7 and Placek, "National Adoption Data," 13.

56. On September 30, 2008, there were 463,000 children and youths in foster care in the United States. See Child Welfare Information Gateway, "Foster Care

Statistics," U.S. Department of Health and Human Services, Administration for Children and Families, Administration on Children, Youth and Families, Children's Bureau, 3. Available at www.childwelfare.gov/pubs/factsheets./foster.pdf (accessed September 14, 2010).

57. Ibid., 4. Another 25 percent stay with relatives who act as foster care families.

58. Ibid., 6.

59. Ibid., 5. This number does not vary greatly from one year to the next. See Thomas Atwood, "Improving Child Protective Services," in Atwood, Allen and Ravenel, eds. *Adoption Factbook IV*, 322.

60. Compiled from Michigan Federation for Children and Families, "Fact Card, 2007." Available at http://michfed.org/wp-content/uploads/2008/09/2007factcard.pdf.

61. Ibid.

62. The Pew Commission on Children in Foster Care, "Fostering the Future: Safety, Permanence and Well-Being for Children in Foster Care." Available at http://pewfostercare.org/research/docs/FinalReport.pdf.

63. See William J. Doherty and others, *Why Marriage Matters: Twenty-One Conclusions from the Social Sciences* (Institute for American Values, 2002), 10–11. Also see Barbara Dafoe Whitehead, "Dan Quayle Was Right," *The Atlantic* (April 1993). Available at http://www.theatlantic.com/magazine/archive/1993/04/dan-quayle-was-right/7015/.

64. See http://adoption.state.gov/pdf/adoption_visa_issurance_2009.pdf.

65. Scott Simon, *Baby, We Were Meant for Each Other: In Praise of Adoption* (New York, NY: Random House, 2010), 21.

66. Michael Gerson, "International Adoption: From a Broken Bond to an Instant Bond," *Washington Post* (August 27, 2010), A21.

67. See Vandivere, Malm, and Radel, *Adoption USA*, 7. In addition, 70 percent of international adoptions are of children who have come from "congregate care facilities," that is, orphanages. Ibid.

68. Mary L. Gautier and Anna Campbell Buck, *Catholic Charities USA: 2009 Annual Survey* (Washington, DC: Center for Applied Research in the Apostolate, Georgetown University, 2010), 37.

69. See the "Press Room" tab on the website of Bethany Christian Services: www.bethany.org/A55798/bethanyWWW.nsf/0/EF897E12C6F4D0718525704D00 5C3491 (accessed August 4, 2010).

70. Email to author from Marc Andreas, Vice President of Marketing and Communications, Bethany Christian Services (August 12, 2010).

71. I arrived at the one-third number by adding the number of Catholic Charities domestic adoptions in 2009 (3,309) and the number of Bethany Christian Services domestic adoptions in 2009 (1,716) and dividing by the number of domestic adoptions processed by private, nongovernmental agencies. The result is a percentage of 30 percent. It should, however, be noted that the numbers on which this one-third estimate is based are not all from the same year. But since the numbers of adoptions

do not vary greatly from one year to the next, I am confident that the one-third estimate is accurate.

72. Interview with Chuck Johnson, president and CEO of the National Council for Adoption (May 25, 2010).

73. All God's Children International processes about two hundred international adoptions a year. See its website: www.allgodschildren.org/adoption (accessed September 4, 2010). Holt International processed in 2009 711 international adoptions. Email from Courtney N. Young, Policy and External Affairs, Holt International, November 11, 2010.

74. Gautier and Buck, *Catholic Charities USA*, 39.

75. Email to the author from Jeanean Merkel, Director of Communications, Lutheran Services in America (September 16, 2010).

76. One should note that the numbers of children in foster care for Catholic Charity agencies and Lutheran Services agencies come from different years. But there is no evidence that the numbers differ greatly from one year to the next.

77. Interview with Janet Reynolds Snyder, Executive Director, Michigan Federation for Children and Families (August 18, 2010).

78. More specifically, Holy Cross Children's Services reported 397 children in foster care from September 1, 2009 through August 31, 2010 (email to author from Sharon Berkobien, Chief Clinical Officer, Holy Cross Children's Services, September 15, 2010), Bethany Christian Services reported 944 children in foster care in 2009 (email to author from Marc Andreas, Vice-President for Marketing and Communications, Bethany Christian Services, September 14, 2010), combined Michigan Catholic Charities agencies totaled 2,122 children in foster care in 2008 (email to author from Mary Gautier, Senior Research Associate, Center for Applied Research in the Apostolate, Georgetown University, September 15, 2010), and Lutheran Social Services reported 1,380 children in foster care in 2009 (email to author from Barbara Lewis, Director of Communications, Lutheran Social Services of Michigan, September 14, 2010).

79. Interview with Chuck Johnson.

80. Gautier and Buck, *Catholic Charities USA*, 36.

81. See the "Quick Facts" tab on Bethany Christian Services website: www .bethany.org/A55798/bethanyWWW.nsf/0/3367CF236CEEA1178525704D00640FC E (accessed August 19, 2010).

82. Website of Lutheran Adoption Service of Michigan: www.lasadoption.org/ LSSM/Page.aspex?pid=415 (accessed September 4, 2010).

83. Electa Draper, "Adoption Initiative Halves Number of Kids Needing Families, *Denver Post* (March 5, 2010). Available at www.denverpost.com/news/ci_14516591 (accessed August 4, 2010).

84. Quoted in ibid.

85. For this quotation and additional information on One Church One Child, see the "About us" tab on its website: www.nationalococ.org/about.html (accessed October 28, 2010).

86. See http://www.bethany.org under the "About us" and Mission statement" tabs (accessed August 5, 2010).

87. Telephone interview with Bill Blacquiere, president and chief executive officer of Bethany Christian Services (August 20, 2010).

88. See www.christian-alliance-for-orphans.org/aboutus.

89. See www.lutheranservices.org/mission (accessed October 28. 2010).

90. Ibid.

91. Rev. Fred Kammer, S.J., "10 Ways Catholic Charities are Catholic," 2–4. Available at http://community.catholiccharitiesusa.org/NetCommunity/Document .Doc?id=388 (accessed August 5, 2010).

92. Ibid., 3.

93. Interview with Rev. Larry Snyder, head of Catholic Charities USA (May 27, 2010).

94. The Pew Center on the States, "Prison Count 2010," 1. Available at www.pewcenteronthestates.org/uploadedFiles/Prison_Count_2010.pdf?n=880 (accessed August 11, 2010).

95. U.S. Department of Justice, Office of Justice Programs, Bureau of Justice Statistics, "Prisoners at Yearend 2009—Advance Counts" (June 2010). Available at http://bjs.ojp.usdoj.gov/content/pub/pdf/py09ac.pdf (accessed August 11, 2010).

96. The Pew Center on the States, "Prison Count 2010," 1.

97. The Pew Center on the States, "One in 31: The Long Reach of American Corrections" (March 2009), Table A-2. Available at www.pewcenteronthestates.org/ uploadedFiles/PSPP_lin31_report_Final_WEB_3-26-09.pdf .

98. Solomon Moore, "Prison Spending Outpaces All but Medicaid," *New York Times,* (March 3, 2009).

99. See www.pewcenteronthestates.org/uploadfiles/www.pewcenteronthestates .org/Fact_Sheets_PSPP_lin31_factsheets_FINAL_WEB.pdf .

100. These numbers are from Re-Entry Policy Council, *Report of the Re-Entry Policy Council* (New York, NY: Council of State Governments, Re-entry Policy Council, n.d.), 3 and 9. Available at http://reentrypolicy.org/publications/1694;file.

101. U.S. Department of Justice, Office of Justice Programs, Bureau of Justice Statistics, "Reentry Trends in the United States."

102. Luke Mogelson, "Prison Break," *Washington Monthly* (November/December 2010), 1–2. Available at www.washingtonmonthly.com/features/2010/1011.mogelson .html.

103. Judith Greene and March Mauer, *Downscaling Prisons: Lessons from Four States* (Washington, DC: The Sentencing Project: Research and Advocacy for Reform, 2010), 27–28. Available at http://sentencingproject.org/doc/publications/ inc_DownscalingPrisons2010.pdf (accessed September 8, 2010). The 2008 Citizens Research Council report found that Michigan had in 2007 the eleventh highest incarceration rate per one hundred thousand population among the fifty states. See Citizens Research Council of Michigan, "Growth in Michigan's Corrections System: Historical and Comparative Perspectives," Report 350 (June 2008), 26–27. Available at www .crcmich.org/PUBLICAT/2000s/2008/rpt350.pdf (accessed February 15, 2011).

104. Michigan Department of Corrections, Office of Offender ReEntry, "MPRI: 2008 Progress Report," 10. The latter is available at www.michpri.com/uploads/ Reports/2008MPRIProgressReport.pdf (accessed September 11, 2010).

105. Quoted in Michigan Prisoner ReEntry Initiative, "MPRI: 2010 Progress Report: Making Strides in Public Safety," 1. Available at www.michigan.gov/documents/corrections/MPRI_2010_Progress_Report_343664_7.pdf (accessed February 15, 2011).

106. Department of Corrections, "MPRI Mission/Vision." Available at www.michigan.gov/corrections/0,1607,7-119-9741_33218---,00.html (accessed June 21, 2011). In 2011 Governor Rick Synder ended the MPRI program as such, but most of its elements have been retained by the Department of Corrections. Thus what I report in this section is still relevant.

107. Michigan Prisoner ReEntry Initiative, "MPRI: 2010 Progress Report," 12–13.

108. See Robert D. Putman, *Bowling Alone: The Collapse and Revival of American Community* (New York, NY: Simon and Schuster, 2000), 22–24.

109. Michigan Prisoner ReEntry Initiative, "Issues of Faith, Justice and Forgiveness: Working with Faith Based Organizations to Foster Diversity of Mission" (September 2008), 2. Available at http://docs.google.com/viewer?a=v&q=cache:-oKURZuIe8cJ:www.michpri.com/uploads/FaithJustice/Issue%2520Brief_Faith%2520and%2520Justice%2520Issues_v18_Sept08.doc+MPRI+issues+of+faith+justice+forgiveness&hl=en&gl=us&pid=bl&srcid=ADGEESidiuRgmYZ5JORh1D61QqQN45esbxwmIjeN4T5keeQZALaazbub8V9O1XRIyEGcQ32SyG9mpSWYQEtBPLJbo0-_JKTGwdamjHojfzdKyblwsc-bzvgAmBR_tDhMY4NWjcR1GWNr&sig=AHIEtbRZVfkh959RpvP-61dMesFpmwcP5A.

110. Michigan Prisoner ReEntry Initiative, "MPRI: 2010 Progress Report," 15.

111. U.S. Department of Justice, Office of Justice Programs, Bureau of Justice Statistics, "Prisoners at Yearend 2009—Advance Counts," 6.

112. Michigan Prisoner ReEntry Initiative, "MPRI: 2010 Progress Report," 15. Also see Gary Fields, "Lights Out at the Penitentiary," *Wall Street Journal* (September 5, 2009), A1.

113. Michigan Prisoner ReEntry Initiative, "MPRI: 2010 Progress Report," 15.

114. Speech by Patricia Caruso, Director, Michigan Department of Corrections, at a public meeting of Celebration Fellowship at the Church of the Servant, Grand Rapids, Michigan (October 11, 2010).

115. Interview with Robert Burroughs, Associate Director, Michigan Council on Crime and Delinquency (September 2, 2010).

116. See Stephanie Boddie, Robert M. Franklin, and Harold Dean Trulear, "Healing Communities and Restorative Justice: The Potential of Faith Communities in Preparing Neighborhoods for Prisoner Reentry" (a paper prepared for the Annie E. Casey Foundation Prisoner Re-entry Consultation, September 14, 2006.).

117. Interview with Jeffrey Padden, President, Public Policy Associates (September 3, 2010). Padden is a former chair of the Corrections Committee of the Michigan House of Representatives and his Public Policy Associates, a Lansing-based research firm, was a part of the public-private collaborative effort that resulted in MPRI. See the foreword to Michigan Prisoner ReEntry Initiative, "MPRI: 2010 Progress Report," 4–5.

118. Interview with Valerie Hart, September 17, 2010. Also see "Healing Communities in Michigan" at http://healingcommunitiesmi.org/Healing%20Communities%20in%20MI%20Fact%20Sheet.pdf.

119. See MPRI, "Issues of Faith, Justice and Forgiveness," 12.

120. Ibid.

121. Ibid., 16.

122. Ibid., 6. Italics added.

123. Boddie, Franklin, and Trulear, "Healing Communities," 23.

124. Ibid., 15.

125. Jamie Yoon and Jessica Nickel, *Reentry Partnerships: A Guide for States & Faith-Based and Community Organizations* (New York, NY: Council of State Governments Justice Center, 2008), 1 and 3.

126. Ibid., 51.

127. See www.drmm.org/mpri.htm (accessed February 15, 2011).

128. See www.drmm.org/whoweare.htm (accessed February 15, 2011).

129. See www.jvsdet.org (accessed November 3, 2010).

130. See www.jvsdet.org/homeless.htm (accessed November 3, 2010).

131. Interview with Clifford Washington, Coordination Manager, Michigan Prisoner ReEntry Program, Pine Rest Christian Mental Health Services (August 19, 2010).

132. www.pinerest.org/mission-vision.

133. www.pinerest.org/philosphy-care.

CHAPTER 3. THE SEEDBEDS OF ATTITUDES TOWARDS FAITH-BASED ORGANIZATIONS

1. Representative Bobby Scott in "Faith-Based Initiatives: Recommendations of the President's Advisory Council on Faith-Based and Community Partnerships and other Current Issues" (Hearing before the Subcommittee on the Constitution, Civil Rights, and Civil Liberties, Committee on the Judiciary, House of Representatives, November 18, 2010), 6. Available at http://judiciary.house.gov/hearings/printers/111th/111-156_62343.PDF (downloaded April 18, 2011).

2. Representative Jim Sensenbrenner in "Faith-Based Initiatives," 3.

3. I have struggled with what term to use in referring to what here and in chapter 4 I label a "mindset." What I have in mind is a broad mix of theoretical concepts, presuppositions, beliefs, values, assumptions, and patterns of thought that mark the manner in which persons react to and view phenomena and events. Thus what I am referring to as a mindset is something less than a worked out political or social theory, but something more than what one might call an unthinking gut reaction. It combines ideas and concepts that one has thought through, with leanings or assumptions towards which one's background and experience has—often unconsciously—predisposed one.

4. See the major work on the Enlightenment by Peter Gay, *The Enlightenment: An Interpretation* (New York, NY: Knopf, 1967).

5. Crane Brinton, *Ideas and Men: The Story of Western Thought* (New York, NY: Prentice Hall, 1950), 371.

6. Thomas Jefferson, "Letter to James Fishbank, September 27, 1809," in Norman Cousins, ed., *In God We Trust: The Religious Beliefs and Ideas of the American Founding Fathers* (New York, NY: Harper and Brothers, 1958), 138.

7. See John Witte, Jr., and Joel A. Nichols, *Religion and the American Constitutional Experiment*, 3rd ed. (Boulder, CO: Westview, 2011), 33–36. Witte and Nichols place civic republicans in a different category of founders from that of Enlightenment founders due to their strong emphasis on the need for a common religiously rooted ethic in the nation's public life. In this analysis I have placed them together since they tend to overlap, with a number of traits in common. For instance, the quotation by George Washington I cite later in this paragraph from his Farewell Address based his conclusion on "reason and experience," a typical Enlightenment stance, and in the just-cited Jefferson quotation he acknowledged that the "interests of society require the observation" of moral precepts common to all religions, a typical civic republican stance.

8. George Washington, "Farewell Address," para. 27. Available, among many other places, at www.earlyamerica.com/earlyamerica/milestones/farewell/text.html.

9. James Madison, "Memorial and Remonstrance against Religious Assessments," in Robert A. Rutland and William M. E. Rachel, eds., *The Papers of James Madison*, vol. 8 (Chicago, IL: University of Chicago Press, 1973), 299. The internal quotation is from the Virginia Declaration of Rights of 1776, Article 16.

10. Jefferson, "Letter to James Fishbank," 138.

11. Thomas E. Buckley, "The Political Theology of Thomas Jefferson," in Merrill D. Peterson and Robert C. Vaughn, eds., *The Virginia Statute for Religious Freedom* (Cambridge, UK: Cambridge University Press, 1988), 90.

12. Witte and Nichols, *Religion and the American Constitutional Experiment*, 31–32.

13. Washington, "Farewell Address," paras. 20 and 21.

14. *The Federalist*, (New York, NY: Modern Library, n.d.), 54.

15. See Barry Alan Shain, *The Myth of American Individualism* (Princeton, NJ: Princeton University Press, 1994), chapter 2.

16. Ibid., 65.

17. On the Second Great Awakening and its popularizing of Christianity, see Nathan O. Hatch, *The Democratization of American Christianity* (New Haven, CT: Yale University Press, 1989).

18. Ibid., 3.

19. Ibid., 220.

20. Robert N. Bellah, Richard Madsen, William M. Sullivan, Ann Swidler, and Steven M. Tipton, *Habits of the Heart: Individualism and Commitment in American Life* (New York, NY: Harper and Row, 1985), 221–22.

21. Witte and Nichols, *Religion and the American Constitutional Experiment*, 29.

22. Ibid.

23. Sidney E. Mead, *The Lively Experiment* (New York, NY: Harper and Row, 1963), 66.

24. Nathan O. Hatch, "The Democratization of Christianity and the Character of American Politics," in Mark A. Noll, ed., *Religion and American Politics* (New York, NY: Oxford University Press, 1990), 95.

25. Mark A. Noll, *The Scandal of the Evangelical Mind* (Grand Rapids, MI: Eerdmans, 1994), 92.

26. Richard T. Hughes and C. Leonard Allen, *Illusions of Innocence: Primitivism in American, 1630–1875* (Chicago, IL: University of Chicago Press, 1988), 143.

27. Noll, *The Scandal of the Evangelical Mind*, 24.

28. Stanley Fish, "Religion and the Liberal State Once Again," *New York Times Opinionator* (November 1, 2010). Available at http://opinionator.blogs.nytimes.com/2010/11/01/religion-and-the-liberal-state-once-again (accessed January 20, 2011).

29. Maureen Dowd, "Liberties," *New York Times* (December 10, 1999). Available at www.nytimes.com/1999/12/1/opinion/liberties.html?scp=5&sq=Bush%20Christ%20Political%20philosopher&st=cse (accessed January 20, 2011).

30. Ibid.

31. Ibid.

32. "For the Health of the Nation: An Evangelical Call to Civic Responsibility" (National Association of Evangelicals, 2004), 5. Scripture reference removed.

33. Ibid., 18.

34. "Forming Consciences for Faithful Citizenship: A Call to Political Responsibility from the Catholic Bishops of the United States" (United States Conference of Catholic Bishops, 2007), 4.

35. Ibid., 14–15. Scripture reference removed.

36. Alexis de Tocqueville, *Democracy in America*, vol. 2 (New York, NY: Vintage Classics, Random House, 1990), 106.

37. Everson v. Board of Education, 330 U.S. 1, at 16 (1947).

38. Ibid., 18.

39. Lemon v. Kurtzman, 403 U.S. 602, at 619 (1971).

40. Ibid., 625.

41. The cases are Engle v. Vitale 370 U.S. 421 (1961) and Abington School District v. Schempp, 374 U.S. 203 (1962).

42. Abington School District v. Schempp, 229.

43. The cases are Lee v. Weisman, 505 U.S. 577 (1992), Santa Fe Independent School District v. Doe, 530 U.S. 290 (2000), and Wallace v. Jaffree, 472 U.S. 38 (1985). But in the moment of silence case, it left the way open for its approval of a moment of silence if the context in which it was enacted did not signal that prayer was the preferred way for students to use that time.

44. See Edwards v. Aguillard, 482 U.S. 578 (1987) and Stone v. Graham, 449 U.S. 39 (1981).

45. The cases are Tilton v. Richardson, 403 U.S. 672 (1971), Hunt v. McNair, 413 U.S. 734 (1973), and Roemer V. Maryland Public Works Board, 426 U.S. 736 (1976).

46. The cases are Board of Education v. Allen, 392 U.S. 236 (1968) and Bowen v. Kendrick, 487 U.S. 589 (1988).

47. Mueller v. Allen, 463 U.S. 388, at 399 (1983). The internal quotation is from Widmar v. Vincent, 454 U.S. 263, at 274 (1981).

48. Zelman v. Simmons-Harris, 536 U.S. 639, at 649 (2002). Internal citations have been removed.

49. See Marsh v. Chambers, 463 U.S. 783 (1983) and Lynch v. Donnelly, 465 U.S. 688 (1984).

50. Lynch v. Donnelly, 716.

51. Everson v. Board of Education, 16.

52. Ibid., 18.

53. Widmar v. Vincent, 454 U.S. 261 (1981).

54. See Good News Club v. Milford Central School, 533 U.S. 98 (2001).

55. Rosenberger v. Rector, 515 U.S. 819, at 847 (1995).

56. Ibid., 839.

57. Ibid., 840.

58. Ibid., 863.

59. Ibid., 875.

60. Zelman v. Simmons-Harris, 662.

61. Jeffrey Rosen, "Is Nothing Secular?" *New York Times Magazine* (January 30, 2000).

62. Ibid.

63. From the dissenting opinion of Justice William Rehnquist in Wallace v. Jaffree, 106.

64. Ibid., at 113–14.

65. Ted G. Jelen and Clyde Wilcox, *Public Attitudes towards Church and State* (Armonk, NY: M. E. Sharpe, 1995), 78.

66. Ibid., 99. It should be noted that in the case of both the general public and the elites there was less support for the strict separation positions when the respondents were presented with specific issues such as prayer in Congress, manger scenes on city land, and prayer at high school sporting events. Ibid., 78, 100.

67. This is not fully accurate, since it was apparently first used by Rogers Williams in the seventeenth century already, when he referred to a wall between the garden of the church and the wilderness of government. See Mark DeWolfe Howe, *The Garden and the Wilderness: Religion and Government in American Constitutional History* (Chicago, IL: University of Chicago Press, 1965).

68. James Madison, "Memorial and Remonstrance against Religious Assessments," (1785), para. 3.

69. James Davison Hunter, *Culture Wars: The Struggle to Define America* (New York, NY: Basic Books, 1991), 76.

70. Hunter, *Culture Wars*.

71. The Pew Forum on Religion and Public Life, *U.S. Religious Landscape Survey, Religious Affiliation: Diverse and Dynamic* (February 2008), 11. Available at http://religions.pewforum.org/pdf/report-religious-landscape-study-full.pdf.

72. "The Rites of Americans," *Newsweek* (November 29, 1993), 80–82.

73. Calculated from Table 2.5 in Corwin E. Smidt, Kevin R. den Dulk, James M. Penning, Stephen V. Monsma, and Douglas L. Koopman, *Pews, Prayers and Participation* (Washington, DC: Georgetown University Press, 2008), 60–61.

74. The Pew Forum on Religion and Public Life, *U.S. Religious Landscape Survey*, 20.

75. Calculated from Table 2.5 in Smidt, et al., *Pews, Prayers & Participation*, 60–61.

76. For example, in a study of welfare-to-work programs in Los Angeles, Chicago, Dallas, and Philadelphia, I found that of the faith-based programs 33 percent were sponsored by a religious congregation or network of congregations, while 68 were sponsored

by separately incorporated nonprofit organizations. (The percentage totaled more than 100 percent because several programs indicated they were sponsored by more than one type of organization.) See Stephen V. Monsma, *Putting Faith in Partnerships: Welfare-to-Work in Four Cities* (Ann Arbor, MI: University of Michigan Press, 2004), 68.

77. Michael W. McConnell, "Equal Treatment and Religious Discrimination," in Stephen V. Monsma and J. Christopher Soper, eds., *Equal Treatment of Religion in a Pluralistic Society* (Grand Rapids, MI: Eerdmans, 1998), 33.

78. NAACP v. Alabama ex rel Patterson, 357 U.S. 449, at 460 (1958).

79. Roberts v. United States Jaycees, 468 U.S. 609, at 623 (1984).

80. Ibid., 626.

81. Boy Scouts of America v. Dale, 530 U.S. 640, at 648 (2000). The internal quotation is from the Court's earlier Roberts decision: Roberts v. United States Jaycees, 623.

82. Ibid., 654.

83. Ibid., 656.

84. Christian Legal Society v. Martinez, 561 U. S. ____ (2010) (No. 08-1371 slip opinion), 15.

85. Sensenbrenner, "Faith-Based Initiatives," 3.

86. Kent Greenawalt, "Freedom of Association and Religious Association," in Amy Gutman, ed., *Freedom of Association* (Princeton, NJ: Princeton University Press, 1998), 116.

87. See any standard encyclopedia, relevant textbook, or trustworthy website for more details on the passage of these acts and their more specific contents.

88. 42 U.S.C. §2000e-1(a).

89. Corporation of Presiding Bishop v. Amos, 483 U.S. 327, at 339 (1987).

90. See the website created by the U.S. Department of Justice specifically dedicated to the Americans with Disabilities Act and its provisions and enforcement: www.ada.gov.

CHAPTER 4. THE PARTISAN-POLITICAL LANDSCAPE TODAY

1. Here and elsewhere I use "the Left" and "liberals" interchangeably. When I intend to refer to classical or Enlightenment liberals who see governments and their programs as a threat to individual freedom, I will say so. Not all persons who would be considered liberals or on the political left subscribe to all of the patterns of thinking or the positions and conclusions I outline in this section. I am speaking of tendencies and "ideal types." Nevertheless, as illustrated by the quotations and examples cited, I am convinced what I say here is an accurate reflection of very real patterns.

2. For a critique of the liberal concept of the autonomous individual, see Michael J. Sandel, "Freedom of Conscience or Freedom of Choice?" in James Davison Hunter and Os Guinness, eds., *Articles of Faith, Articles of Peace: The Religious Liberty Clauses and the American Public Philosophy* (Washington, DC: Brookings, 1990), 74–92.

3. Lemon v. Kurtzman, 403 U.S. 602, at 622 (1971).

4. Zelman v. Simmons-Harris, 536 U.S. 639, at 725 (2002).

5. "The Next Billy Graham," *The Economist* (August 14, 2008). Available at www.economist.com/node/11920933 (accessed November 8, 2010).

6. John Nichols, "Lowery's Preaching, Not Warren's, Will Illuminate Inaugural Day," *The Nation* (January 17, 2009). Nichols did praise another preacher, the African-American Joseph E. Lowery, because of the liberal stance he has taken on racial questions and gay rights. Available at www.thenation.com/blog/lowerys-preaching-not-warrens-will-illumine-inaugral.day (accessed November 8, 2010).

7. Maureen Dowd, "Liberties," *New York Times* (December 10, 1999). Available at www.nytimes.com/1999/12/1/opinion/liberties.html?scp=5&sq=Bush%20Christ%20Political%20philosopher&st=cse (accessed January 20, 2011).

8. Ross Douthat, "Sex Ed in Washington," *New York Times* (February 1, 2010). Available at www.nytimes.com/2010/02/01/opinion/01douthat.html?scp=1&sq=Douthat%20February%201,%202010&st=cse.

9. On Wilberforce, see Eric Metaxas, *Amazing Grace: William Wilberforce and the Heroic Campaign to End Slavery* (New York, NY: HarperCollins, 2007); on Shafesbury, see J. L. Hammond, *Lord Shaftesbury* (New York, NY: Harcourt Brace, 1924); on the American abolitionist movement, see David O. Moberg, *The Great Reversal* (Philadelphia, PA: Lippencott, 1972); and on Bourcart, see Lee Shai Weissback, *Child Labor Reform in Nineteenth-Century France: Assuring the Future Harvest* (Baton Rouge, LA: Louisiana State University Press, 1989).

10. Tip O'Neill, *Man of the House* (New York, NY: Random House, 1987), 376.

11. "New and Not Improved," *New York Times* (July 4, 2008), A18.

12. "A Matter of Church and State, *New York Times* (February 20, 2002).

13. See www.whitehouse.gov/the-press-office/remarks-president-state-union-address.

14. John D. Podesta and Reece Rushing, "Doing What Works: Building a Government that Delivers Greater Value and Results to the American People" (Center for American Progress, February 2010). Available at www.americanprogress.org/issues/2010/02/pdf/dww_framing.pdf (accessed February 18, 2011).

15. Ibid., 2.

16. Ibid., 14.

17. Sometimes citing an exception is the best way to make one's point. An exception here is the 15th Annual Kuyper Lecture delivered by Clarke E. Cochran and sponsored by the Center for Public Justice, entitled "Seeking Justice: The Imperiled Promise of Healthcare Reform" (October 22, 2009). Available at www.cpjustice.org/files/KuyperLecture2009.pdf.

18. Bart Kasko, "The Problem with Faith-Based Funding is Faith Itself," *Los Angeles Times* (February 19, 2001), B7.

19. Ibid.

20. Susan Jacoby, "Keeping the Faith, Ignoring the History," *New York Times* (March 1, 2009), wk11.

21. American Civil Liberties Union, "Program on Freedom of Religion and Belief: Government-Funded Religion" (November 2, 2006). Available at http://www

.aclu.org/religion-belief/program-freedom-religion-and-belief-government-funded-religion.

22. See, for example, the testimony of Barry Lynn, executive director of Americans United for Separation of Church and State, submitted to the Subcommittee on Constitution, Civil Rights, and Civil Liberties of the House of Representatives Judiciary Committee, for its November 18, 2010, hearing on "Faith-Based Initiatives: Recommendations of the President's Advisory Council on Faith-Based and Community Partnerships and Other Current Issues." Available at http://judiciary.house.gov/hearings/pdf.Lynn101118.pdf (accessed February 17, 2011). Also see the recommendations of the President's Advisory Council on Faith-Based and Neighborhood Partnerships, "A New Era of Partnerships: Report of Recommendations to the President" (March 2010), 127–51. This advisory council, on instructions from the White House, did not deal with the hiring issue, and it was divided on the issue of religious art or icons being present in rooms where services were provided, with the more liberal members insisting that such should be removed.

23. See Coalition Against Religious Discrimination, "Letter to President Obama" (February 4, 2010). This letter was supported by such organizations as People for the American Way, American Civil Liberties Union, and the American Humanist Association. Available at http://www.interfaithalliance.org/news/349-coalition-against-religious-discrimination-letter-to-president-obama (accessed November 9, 2010).

24. ACLU Reproductive Freedom Project, "Religious Refusals and Reproductive Rights" New York, NY: American Civil Liberties Union, 2002). Available at www.aclu.org/FilesPDFs/ACF911.pdf (accessed January 29, 2011).

25. Barack Obama, "Remarks of Senator Barack Obama: Council of Faith-Based and Neighborhood Partnerships" (July 1, 2008). Available at www.barackobama.com/2008/07/01remarks_of_senator_barack_obama_86.php (accessed November 9, 2010).

26. Quoted in President's Advisory Council on Faith-Based and Neighborhood Partnerships, "A New Era of Partnerships: Report of Recommendations to the President," (March, 2010), ix.

27. As was the case with the Left, what I am about to describe does not apply equally to all persons who would be considered conservatives or on the political right. Again, I am speaking of tendencies and "ideal types."

28. This quotation can be found many places. See, for example, www.youtube.com/watch?v=x59wNGHe6iI.

29. "Tea Party Patriots Mission Statement and Core Values." Available at http://teapartypatriots.ning.com (accessed March 15, 2010).

30. Quoted in Kate Zernike, "Tea Party Avoids Divisive Social Issues," *New York Times* (March 12, 2010).

31. "How to Label Cato," available at http://www.cato.org.about (accessed February 19, 2011).

32. On the thinking and influence of Edmund Burke, see Iain Hampshire-Monk, *The Political Philosophy of Edmund Burke* (London, UK: Longman, 1987).

33. Edmund Burke, *Reflections on the Revolution in France*, edited by L. G. Mitchell (New York, NY: Oxford University Press, 1993), 87.

34. Russell Kirk, *The Conservative Mind: From Burke to Santayana*, 7th ed. (Chicago, IL: Regnery, 1986), 8.

35. From website of the Heritage Foundation: www.heritage.org/About (accessed January 14, 2010).

36. From an address at the Freedoms Foundation, Waldorf-Astoria, New York City, NY (December 22, 1952). Available at www.eisenhower.archives.gov/all_about_ike/Quotes/Quotes.html (accessed May 26, 2011).

37. From the dissenting opinion of Justice William Rehnquist in Wallace v. Jaffree, 472 U.S. 38, at 113–14 (1985).

38. Michael W. McConnell, "Equal Treatment and Religious Discrimination," in Stephen V. Monsma and J. Christopher Soper, eds., *Equal Treatment of Religion in a Pluralistic Society* (Grand Rapids, MI: Eerdmans, 1998), 33.

39. See Robert F. McDonnell, "The Republican Response to the State of the Union," *New York Times* (January 28, 2010). Available at www.nytimes.com/2010/01/28/us/politics/28mcdonnell.text.html?sq=Republicanresponse (accessed January 28, 2010).

40. See, for example, the small yet influential 1977 book by Peter L. Berger and Richard John Neuhaus, *To Empower People: The Role of Mediating Structures in Public Policy* (Washington, DC: American Enterprise Institute for Public Policy Research, 1977), and, more recently, a public policy paper by the Heritage Foundation that argued for greater reliance on faith-based and other private sector agencies to find adoptive homes for children in foster care: Thomas C. Atwood, "Foster Care: Safety Net or Trap Door?" Backgrounder No. 2535 (March 25, 2011), The Heritage Foundation. Available at http://report.heritage.org/bg2535.

41. Jim Towey, "Next Steps for the President's Faith-Based Initiative," a speech given as a part of the Heritage Foundation Lectures, No. 752 (July 10, 2002). Available at www.heritage.org/Research/Lecture/Next-Steps-for-the-Presidents-Faith-Based-Initiative (accessed May 24, 2011).

42. Michael D. Tanner, "Obama's Faith-Based Boondoggle," *Washington Times* (January 29, 2010). Available at the Cato website: www.cato.org/pub_display .php?pub_id=11180 (accessed November 10, 2010).

43. George W. Bush, "The Duty of Hope" (a speech given at Indianapolis, Indiana, on July 22, 1999). Available at www.cpjustice.org/stories/storyreader%24343.

44. Marvin Olasky, *Renewing American Compassion* (New York, NY: Free Press, 1996), 26.

45. Tanner, "Obama's Faith-Based Boondoggle."

46. For a good survey of existing studies, see Robert L. Fischer, "In God We Trust, All Others Bring Data: Assessing the State of Outcome Measurement for Faith-Based and Community-Based Programming," in Pamela Joshi, Stephanie Hawkins, and Jeffrey Novey, eds., *Innovations in Effective Compassion: Compendium of Research Papers Presented at the Faith-Based and Community Initiatives Conference on Research, Outcomes, and Evaluation* (Washington, DC: U.S. Department of Health and Human Services, Office of the Assistant Secretary for Planning and Evaluation,

Center for Faith-Based and Community Initiatives, 2008), 179–211. For another help-
ful discussion of the comparative effectiveness of faith-based and secular social
services, see Steven Rathgeb Smith, John P. Barkowski, and Susan Grettenberger,
Comparative Views on the Role and Effect of Faith in Social Services (Rockefeller
Institute of Government, Roundtable on Religion and Social Welfare Policy,
December, 2006). Also see Stephen V. Monsma and J. Christopher Soper, *Faith,
Hope and Jobs: Welfare-to-Work in Los Angeles* (Washington, DC: Georgetown
University Press, 2006).

47. Ryan Messmore and Thomas M. Messner, "Protecting and Strengthening
Religious Freedom: A Memo to President-elect Obama," (The Heritage Founda-
tion, No. 11, December 16, 2008), 1–2. Available at www.heritage.org/Research/
Reports/2008/12/Protecting-and-Strengthening-Religious-Freedom-A-Memo-to-
President-elect-Obama (accessed November 10, 2010). The internal quotation is from
Matthew Spalding, "The Meaning of Religious Liberty," Heritage Foundation Web/
Memo No. 1722 (December 11, 2008).

48. Ibid., 3.

49. Michael D. Tanner, "Corrupting Charity: Why Government Should Not fund
Faith-Based Charities" (Cato Institute Briefing Papers No. 62, March 22, 2001).

50. Tanner, "Obama's Faith-Based Boondoggle."

CHAPTER 5. STRUCTURAL PLURALISM IN CHRISTIAN DEMOCRATIC THOUGHT

1. Douglas Laycock, "Formal, Substantive, and Disaggregated Neutrality toward
Religion," *DePaul Law Review* 39 (1990), 1001. This article and the quotation
also appear in Douglas Laycock, ed., *Religious Liberty*, vol. 1 (Grand Rapids, MI:
Eerdmans, 2010), 13. The latter is a collection of previously published essays by
Laycock, one of America's foremost legal scholars. Also see his essay, "Substantive
Neutrality Revisited," in Laycock, ed., *Religious Liberty*, 225–67.

2. Laycock, "Formal, Substantive, and Disaggregated Neutrality toward Religion," 1001.

3. For more on terminology, see Laycock, "Substantive Neutrality Revisited,"
229–31. Here Laycock points out that substantive neutrality is about neutral incentives, that is, government policies are to create incentives that neither favor or disfa-
vor, advantage or disadvantage either religion or nonreligion. Elsewhere I have used
the term, "positive neutrality," to refer to the same idea of governmental neutrality
on matters of religion, arguing that if government is to be truly neutral on matters
of religion it will sometimes need to take certain positive steps to recognize, accommodate, or support religion. See Stephen V. Monsma, *Positive Neutrality* (Westport,
CT: Greenwood, 1993). Laycock's term, substantive neutrality, has gained more
currency than my term, positive neutrality, thus it is the term I use in this book.

4. Kenneth L. Grasso, "The Subsidiary State: Society, the State and the Principle
of Subsidiarity in Catholic Social Thought," in Jeanne Heffernan Schindler, ed.,

Christianity and Civil Society: Catholic and Neo-Calvinist Perspectives (Lanham, MD: Lexington Books, 2008), 31.

5. See R. E. M. Irving, *The Christian Democratic Parties of Western Europe* (London, UK: George Allen and Unwin, 1979), 31.

6. Ibid. Italics present in original.

7. Jacques Maritain, *The Person and the Common Good*, trans. John J. Fitzgerald (Notre Dame, IN: University of Notre Dame Press, 1966), 38.

8. Abraham Kuyper, *The Problem of Poverty*, ed. James Skillen (Grand Rapids, MI: Baker, 1991), 45.

9. Dirk Jellema, "Abraham Kuyper's Attack on Liberalism," *Review of Politics* 19 (1957), 481. Italics present in original.

10. *Gaudium et Spes*, Section 25.

11. Kees van Kersbergen, *Social Capitalism: A Study of Christian Democracy and the Welfare State* (London, UK: Routledge, 1995), 184.

12. David Hanley, "Introduction: Christian Democracy as a Political Phenomenon," in David Hanley, ed., *Christian Democracy in Europe: A Comparative Perspective* (London: Pinter Publishers, 1994), 4.

13. Some clarification of terms is in order here. I use the term "nation" to refer to a society that is bound together by informal, organic ties of shared history, tradition, and perhaps ethnicity, language, and religion. The state is a political term that refers to the formal structures and institutions that make and enforce legitimate, authoritative decisions of all persons living within a defined land area. I use it interchangeably with government.

14. Robert A. Nisbet, *The Quest for Community: A Study in the Ethics of Order and Freedom* (New York, NY: Oxford University Press, 1953), 246–47.

15. Ibid., 231. The quotation is from John Dewey, *Individualism Old and New* (New York, NY: Minton, Balch and Company, 1930), 81–82.

16. "The Communitarian Platform." The platform and its signers are available at www.gwu.edu/~ccps.rcplatform.html.

17. John N. Figgis, *Churches in the Modern State*, 2nd ed. (New York, NY: Russell and Russell, 1914), 47.

18. Nisbet, *The Quest for Community*, 235. As noted earlier Nisbet cannot, strictly speaking, be considered a structural pluralist thinker, but his emphasis upon the social nature of human beings and the indispensable nature of intermediate social structures and associations places him intellectually close to the structural pluralists.

19. Ibid, 238.

20. Ibid, 205–6.

21. Grasso, "The Subsidiary Sate," 31–32. Also see Paul Misner, "Christian Democratic Social Policy," in Thomas Kselman and Joseph A. Battigieg, eds., *European Christian Democracy* (Notre Dame, IN: University of Notre Dame Press, 2003), 68–92.

22. *Rerum Novarum*, 1891, para. 71.

23. *Quadragesimo Anno*, 1931, para. 79–80.

24. Jonathan Chaplin, "Subsidiarity as a Political Norm," in Jonathan Chaplin and Paul Marshall, eds., *Political Theory and Christian Vision: Essays in Memory of Bernard Zylstra* (Lanham, MD: University Press of America, 1994), 87.

25. Van Kersbergen, *Social Capitalism*, 188.

26. See Grasso, "The Subsidiary State," 48.

27. Ibid., 32.

28. Kees van Kersbergen and Bertjan Verbeek, "The Politics of Subsidiarity in the European Union," *Journal of Common Market Studies* 32 (June 1994), 222.

29. Ibid., 224.

30. Chaplin, "Subsidiarity as a Political Norm," 92.

31. Grasso, "The Subsidiary State," 54.

32. Quoted by Charles L. Glenn, Jr., *The Myth of the Common School* (Amherst: University of Massachusetts Press, 1987), 46.

33. On Kuyper and his thought and influence see John Bolt, *A Free Church, a Holy Nation: Abraham Kuyper's American Public Theology* (Grand Rapids, MI: Eerdmans, 2001), James Bratt, ed., *Abraham Kuyper: A Centennial Reader* (Grand Rapids, MI: Eerdmans, 1998); Luis E. Lugo, ed., *Religion, Pluralism, and Public Life: Abraham Kuyper's Legacy for the Twenty-First Century* (Grand Rapids, MI: Eerdmans, 2000); Richard Mouw, *Abraham Kuyper: A Short and Personal Introduction* (Grand Rapids, MI: Eerdmans, 2011). Johan D. van der Vyver, "Sphere Sovereignty of Religious Institutions: A Contemporary Calvinistic Theory of Church-State Relations," in Gerhard Robbers, ed., *Church Autonomy: A Comparative Survey* (Frankfurt am Main, DEU: Peter Land, 2001), 645–81; and Nicholas Wolterstorff, "Abraham Kuyper (1837–1920)," in John Witte, Jr., and Frank S. Alexander, eds., *The Teachings of Modern Christianity on Law, Politics, and Human Nature*, vol. 1 (New York, NY: Columbia University Press, 2006), 288–327.

34. Van der Vyver, "Sphere Sovereignty of Religious Institutions," 654–55.

35. Arie Oostlander, "Politics Based on Christian Consciousness," in European People's Party, *Efforts to Define a Christian Democratic "Doctrine,"* 29.

36. Abraham Kuyper, *Lectures on Calvinism* (Grand Rapids, MI: Eerdmans, 1931), 90–91. Kuyper's emphasis.

37. Ibid., 96–97. Kuyper's emphasis.

38. Kuyper, *The Problem of Poverty*, 71.

39. Lew Daly, *God's Economy: Faith-Based Initiatives and the Caring State* (Chicago, IL: University of Chicago Press, 2009), 160.

40. Jonathan Chaplin, "Civil Society and the State," in Schindler, ed., *Christianity and Civil Society*, 78. Chaplin's emphasis.

41. Bolt, *A Free Church, a Holy Nation*, 347. See Bolt's excellent section on Kuyper not being a theocrat (ibid., 308–50).

42. Quoted in ibid., 308.

43. See the European People's Party website for a chronology of its history and the earlier European Union of Christian Democrats and its current nature and vision. www.epp.eu.

44. Irving, *The Christian Democratic Parties of Western Europe*, 29.

45. Bolt, *A Free Church, a Holy Nation*, 252–53.

46. Kuyper, *The Problem of Poverty*, 84. Not to overstate the case, this quotation is from a footnote, not the main body of the speech.

47. Van der Vyver, "Sphere Sovereignty of Religious Institutions," 657.

48. Jeanne Heffernan Schindler, "Introduction," Schindler, ed., *Christianity and Civil Society*, 8.

49. Irving, *The Christian Democratic Parties of Western Europe*, 30.

50. Ibid., 31.

51. Grasso, "The Subsidiary State," 40.

52. *Pacem in Terris* (1963), para. 23 and 24.

53. H. Henry Meeter, *The Basic Idea of Calvinism*, 5th ed. (Grand Rapids, MI: Baker, 1956), 159.

54. See http://en.old.cda.nl/default.aspx (accessed December 16, 2010).

55. Misner, "Christian Democratic Social Policy," 88.

56. EPP Congress, "Basic Programme," paras. 141, 142, and 143, 7. Available at http://www.32462857769.net/EPP/e-PressRelease/PDF/athene-BASIC_PROGRAM001_.pdf (accessed February 21, 2010).

57. Van Kersbergen and Verbeek, "The Politics of Subsidiarity in the European Union," 215.

58. Ibid., 224.

59. Ibid., 223.

60. Helmut K. Anheier and Wolfgang Seibel, "Defining the Nonprofit Sector: Germany," *Working Papers of the Johns Hopkins Comparative Nonprofit Sector Project*, no. 6 (Baltimore, MD: Johns Hopkins Institute for Policy Studies, 1993), 7.

61. See Stephen V. Monsma and J. Christopher Soper, *The Challenge of Pluralism: Church and State in Five Democracies*, 2nd ed. (Lanham, MD: Rowman and Littlefield, 2009), 198.

62. Gerhard Robbers, "State and Church in Germany" in Gerhard Robbers, ed., *State and Church in the European Union*, 2nd ed. (Baden-Baden, DEU: Nomos Verlagsgesellschaft, 2005), 83.

63. This is not to say that all is well in Europe in regard to the autonomy rights of faith-based organizations. Most European countries—including those with strong historical roots in structural pluralism and Christian Democratic thought—are marked by strong administrative states, with governments possessing a heavy and often intrusive regulatory hand. What I am saying is that these countries have a heritage and a set of beliefs to which faith-based organizations can appeal in their on-going efforts to remain free from interference with their faith-based practices. The general weakening of the churches in most of these European countries has not helped in these efforts.

64. I have developed the perspectives developed in this section more fully elsewhere. See Monsma, *Positive Neutrality*, 113–29.

65. For an excellent series of essays on civil society, see Don E. Ebberly, ed., *The Essential Civil Society Reader* (Lanham, MD: Rowman and Littlefield, 2000).

66. See, for example, The Pew Forum on Religion and Public Life, "Importance of Religion." Available at http://pewforum.org/Topics/Beliefs-and-Practices/Importance-of-Religion (accessed June 8, 2011).

CHAPTER 6. FAITH-BASED ORGANIZATIONS IN A PLURALISTIC PUBLIC SQUARE: APPLICATIONS

1. Gerhard Robbers, "State and Church in Germany," in Gerhard Robbers, ed., *State and Church in the European Union*, 2nd ed. (Baden Baden, DEU: Nomos Verlagsgesellschaft, 2005), 86.

2. See Stephen V. Monsma and J. Christopher Soper, *The Challenge of Pluralism: Church and State in Five Democracies*, 2nd ed. (Lanham, MD: Rowman and Littlefield, 2009), 176.

3. Many German Constitutional Court decisions can be found in translation in Donald P. Kommers, *The Constitutional Jurisprudence of the Federal Republic of Germany*, 2nd ed. (Durham, NC: Duke University Press, 1997).

4. Corporation of the Presiding Bishop v. Amos, 483 U.S. 327, at 342 (1986).

5. Article 6. The Dutch Constitution is available on line at www.servat.unibe.ch/icl/nl00000_.html. Italics added.

6. Quoted, based on a personal interview, in Monsma and Soper, *The Challenge of Pluralism*, 110.

7. Gerhard Robbers, "Religious Freedom in Europe," paper available at http://home.lu.lv/~rbalodis/Baznicu%20Tiesibas/Raksti&Gramatas/Religious_Freedom_GR.pdf, 3.

8. Sophie C. van Bijsterveld, "Constitutional Status of Religion in the Kingdom of the Netherlands," *The Constitutional Status of Churches in the European Union Countries* (European Consortium for Church-State Research, proceedings of the 1994 meeting, University of Paris), 207 and 211.

9. A closely related question concerns the right of a faith-based organization to make hiring decisions on the grounds of religiously based behavioral standards, such as same-sex sexual relationships and heterosexual involvements outside of marriage. I will consider these more fully in a later section of this chapter when I consider nondiscrimination standards as they apply to hiring and membership standards of faith-based organizations.

10. Corporation of the Presiding Bishop v. Amos, at 342.

11. Douglas Laycock, "Testimony of Douglas Laycock," in "Faith-Based Initiatives: Recommendations of the President's Advisory Council on Faith-Based and Community Partnerships and other Current Issues" (Hearing before the Subcommittee on the Constitution, Civil Rights, and Civil Liberties, Committee on the Judiciary, House of Representatives, November 18, 2010), 35. Available at http://judiciary.house.gov/hearings/printers/111th/111-156_62343.PDF (accessed June 13, 2011).

12. Laycock, statement prepared for delivery before the House Subcommittee on the Constitution, Civil Rights and Civil Liberties, "Faith-Based Initiatives," 47.

13. Quoted in "Bush Pushes Faith-Based 'Miracles' in Speech at New Orleans Church," Americans United for Separation of Church and State Press Release (January 15, 2004). Available at www.au.org/media/press-releases/archives/2004/01/bush-pushes-fait.html (accessed January 25, 2011).

14. "A Flawed Faith-Based Fix," *New York Times* (November 22, 2010). Available at http://www.nytimes.com/2010/11/22/opinion/22mon3.html?_r=1&scp=1&sq=faith-based%20fix%20November%2022,%202010&st=cse (accessed November 30, 2010).

15. Representative Bobby Scott, in "Faith-Based Initiatives," 7.

16. The Coalition Against Religious Discrimination, Letter to the Honorable Edward Kennedy and the Honorable Michael B. Enzi, Senate Committee on Health, Education, Labor and Pensions" (January 24, 2008). Italics present in original. Available at www.religionandsocialpolicy.org/docs/legal/other/2008-01-24CARDLetter.pdf (accessed January 26, 2011).

17. Quoted in "Congress Should Reject Conservative Religious Groups' Call for Taxpayer-Funded Job Bias, Says Americans United," Americans United for the Separation of Church and State (August 25, 2010). Available at www.au.org/media/press-releases/archives/2010/08/congress-should-reject.html.

18. See Section 702(a) of Title VII or the Civil Rights Act of 1964 (Pub. L. 88-352).

19. The 1972 amendatory act was Public Law No. 92-261. The unanimous Supreme Court decision upholding the constitutionality of the religious exemption in hiring was Corporation of the Presiding Bishop v. Amos.

20. See Heidi Rolland Unruh and Ronald J. Sider, *Saving Souls, Serving Society: Understanding the Faith-Factor in Church-Based Social Ministry* (New York, NY: Oxford University Press, 2005), 109–14.

21. Quoted in Bobby Ross, Jr., "Orphans on Deck," *Christianity Today* (January 2010), 12.

22. See President's Advisory Council on Faith-Based and Neighborhood Partnerships, "A New Era of Partnerships: Report of Recommendations to the President" (March, 2010), 140–41.

23. A survey of recipients of welfare-to-work programs in Los Angeles suggests that such persons may not be all that common. This study found that of the participants in faith-based welfare-to-work programs, 72 percent reported that they enjoyed the religious aspects of the programs, 88 percent that they felt the religious aspects of the program had never been a waste of time, and 81 percent that the religious aspects of the program had never made them feel uncomfortable. See Stephen V. Monsma and J. Christopher Soper, *Faith, Hope and Jobs: Welfare-to-Work in Los Angeles* (Washington, DC: Georgetown University Press, 2006), 83.

24. This language has been used in a number of existing federal government regulations. See President's Advisory Council on Faith-Based and Neighborhood Partnerships, "A New Era of Partnerships," 129.

25. See White House, Office of the Press Secretary, "Executive Order—Fundamental Principles and Policymaking Criteria for Partnerships with Faith-Based and Other Neighborhood Organizations" (November 17, 2010). Available at http://www.whitehouse.gov/the-press-office/2010/11/17/executive-order-fundamental-principles-and-policymaking-criteria-partner (accessed December 1, 2010).

26. Stephen V. Monsma, *Putting Faith in Partnerships: Welfare-to-Work in Four Cities* (Ann Arbor, MI: University of Michigan Press, 2004), 62.

27. White House, Office of the Press Secratary, "Executive Order", Section 2(g).

28. Ibid.

29. See President's Advisory Council on Faith-Based and Neighborhood Partnerships, "A New Era of Partnerships," 131.

30. See Richard N. Ostling, "InterVarsity Christian Fellowship Battles with Administrators," Associated Press, January 17, 2003. Available at www.rickross.com/reference/fundamentalists/fund98.html. Also see Lillian Kwon, "InterVarsitiy Head Laments: 'Evangelical Groups Are Out,'" *Christian Post* (July 1, 2010). Available at www.christianpost.com/article/20100701/intervarsity-head (accessed February 9, 2011).

31. "Letter to Members of Congress from the United States Conference of Catholic Bishops on the Employment Nondiscrimination Act (ENDA)," May 19, 2010. Available at www.americamagazine.org/blog/entry.cfm?blog_id2923.

32. Ibid.

33. National Association of Evangelicals, "Homosexuality 2004." Available at www.nae.net/government-affairs/policy-resolutions/181-homosexuality-2004.

34. See "Letter to Members of Congress from the United States Conference of Catholic Bishops" and National Association of Evangelicals, "Homosexuality 2004."

35. See Christian Legal Society Chapter v. Martinez, 561 U.S. ___ (2010). (No. 08-1371 slip opinion).

36. Christian Legal Society v. Martinez, Justice Alito dissenting, 22.

37. Brief *Amici Curiae* of American Islamic Congress, Coalition of African-American Pastors, National Council of Young Israel, National Hispanic Christian Leadership Conference, Project Nur, Sikh American Legal Defense and Education Fund, and Sikh Coalition in Support of Petitioners, in Christian Legal Society Chapter of University of California, Hastings College of Law v. Leo P. Martinez (No. 08-1371), 3. Available at www.clsnet.org/sites/default/files/center/litigation/2010-02-04_Amicus_AmericanIslamicCongress%2Cetal.pdf (accessed February 2, 2011).

38. Christian Legal Society v. Martinez, at ___. Opinion of the Court, 31.

39. Ibid., 15.

40. Brief of Gays and Lesbians for Individual Liberty as *Amicus Curiae* in Support of Petitioner in Christian Legal Society Chapter of University of California, Hastings College of Law v. Leo P. Martinez (No. 08-1371), 6. Italics present. The internal quotations are from NAACP v. Alabama, 357 U.S. at 460 and Roberts v. United States Jaycees, 468 U. S. at 622. Available at www.clsnet.org/sites/default/files/center/litigation/2010-02-04_Amicus_AmericanIslamicCongress%2Cetal.pdf (accessed February 2, 2011).

41. Spencer v. World Vision, No. 08-35532, United States Court of Appeals for the Ninth Circuit (August 23, 2010), 12544–12545.

42. Ibid., 12573.

43. Ibid., 12599.

44. ACLU Reproductive Freedom Project, "Religious Refusals and Reproductive Rights" (2002), 11. Available at http://www.aclu.org/FilesPDFs/ACF911.pdf (accessed January 29, 2011).

45. See the words of Jesus Christ recorded in Matthew 25: 31–46.

46. Richael Faithful, "Religious Exemption or Exceptionalism? Exploring the Tension of First Amendment Religion Protections and Civil Rights Progress within the Employment Non-Discrimination Act," Social Science Research Network, Legislation and Policy Brief, Vol. 3, No. 1, pg. 24. Availble at http://ssrn.com/abstract=1727707.

47. Ibid.

48. Douglas Laycock, "Afterword," in Douglas Laycock, Anthony R. Picarello, Jr., and Robin Fretwell Wilson, eds., *Same-Sex Marriage and Religious Liberty: Emerging Conflicts* (Lanham, MD: Rowman and Littlefield, 2008), 190.

49. See, for example, "Attitudes towards Evangelical Christians by College and University Professors." Available at www.religioustolerance.org/evanintol.htm (accessed June 17, 2011).

50. For a reference to hate speech being used in other countries to limit criticism of the gay rights agenda, see Laycock, "Afterword," 193, and for an example regarding the revocation of nonprofit status see Nicholas A. Mirkay, "Losing our Religion: Reevaluating the §501(c)(3) Exemption of Religious Organizations that Discriminate," Widener Law School Legal Studies Research Paper Series no. 08-35, 715–62. Available at http://ssrn.com/abstract=1112776.

51. Kevin Seamus Hasson, *The Right to be Wrong: Ending the Culture War over Religion in America* (San Francisco, CA: Encounter Books, 2005), 15.

52. Amy Pyle, "A Collision of Medicine and Faith," *Los Angeles Times* (January 3, 2000), A1. Also see ACLU Reproductive Freedom Project, "Religious Refusals and Reproductive Rights."

53. On the San Francisco case, see William J. Levada, "The San Francisco Solution," *First Things* (August/September 1997), and on the Sacramento issue, see Catholic Charities of Sacramento v. Superior Court, No. S099822, Ct.App. 3 C037025. The former is available at www.firstthings.com/ariticle/2008/09/003-the-san-francisco-solution-15, and the latter is available at www.caselaw.lp.findlaw.com/data2/californiastatecases/s099822.pdf.

54. See Patricia Wen, "Catholic Charities Stuns State, Ends Adoptions," *Boston Globe* (March 11, 2006), and Michelle Boorstein, "Catholic Archdiocese End D.C. Foster-Care Program," *Washington Post* (February 17, 2010), B1.

55. Telephone interview with William Blacquiere, president and chief executive officer of Bethany Christian Services (August 20, 2010).

56. See Barbara Bradley Hagerty, "Gay Rights, Religious Liberties: A Three-Act Story," (June 16, 2008). Available at www.npr.org/templates/story/story.php?storyId=91486340 (accessed February 3, 2011).

57. On this complex controversy see www.indypressny.org/nycma/voices/31/news/news_2/.

58. Hagerty, "When Gay Rights and Religious Liberties Clash."

59. See Jody Feder, "The History and Effect of Abortion Conscience Clause Laws," Congressional Research Service, the Library of Congress (January 14, 2005). Available at www.law.umaryland.edu/marshall/crsreports/crsdocuments/RS2142801142005.pdf (accessed June 16, 2011). Also helpful is Robin Fretwell Wilson, "Matters of Conscience: Lessons for Same-Sex Marriage from the Healthcare Context," in Laycock, Picarello, and Wilson, *Same-Sex Marriage and Religious Liberty*, 77–102.

60. This leaves the controversial question of whether or not for-profit businesses should, on religious grounds, be able to refuse service to persons they believe are acting immorally, such as—in the eyes of some—persons in active LGBT relationships. This question has arisen when, for example, a wedding photographer refused to photograph a same-sex wedding. I do not take a position on this question here, but only on the question of the right of faith-based, nonprofit organizations to refuse certain services that violate their religiously based standards. The question of the right of individual businesspersons being able to refuse certain customers certain services on religious grounds involves questions of individual religious liberty rights, and while I personally tend to be sympathetic with their concerns, this is an area that raises somewhat different issues than does the area of organizations' religious autonomy, the topic with which this book deals.

61. Laycock, "Afterword," 198.

62. For a number of medical case studies that illustrate medical challenges persons may face when receiving services in a faith-based hospital that does not provide certain services, see "Religious Refusals and Reproductive Rights," 15–17. While the three case studies presented here are not necessary either typical or frequent, they do occur.

63. ACLU Reproductive Freedom Project, "Religious Refusals and Reproductive Rights," 11.

Afterword

The question of faith-based organizations and their religious freedom rights raised in the hardcover edition of this book has become more, not less urgent since its publication nearly two years ago. What once had been an issue largely discussed in academic circles and law review articles has become a matter of news media stories, debates on television news shows, and a flood of lawsuits—all accompanied by charges, counter charges, and bitter recriminations.

This has occurred largely due to two recent developments. First, as part of its implementation of the Affordable Care Act (Obamacare) the Obama administration in August, 2011, promulgated rules that mandated both for-profit and nonprofit organizations with over fifty employees must provide contraceptive coverage in their employees' health insurance plans. And contraceptives were defined broadly enough to include Plan B (the "morning after" pill) and ella (the "week after" pill), which many consider to work by causing very early abortions (that is, they are not truly contraceptives, but abortifacients). "Religious organizations" were exempted from the mandate, but this category was defined so narrowly that only religious congregations and their integrated affiliates were included. Religiously-based educational, health, and social service organizations that are the focus of this book were subject to the mandate.

The Roman Catholic tradition has, of course, long held that the use of artificial birth control to be a violation of its religious beliefs and practices, and the Evangelical Protestant tradition, while generally not having a problem with contraceptives, does have a problem with what it views as abortifacients. Thus the Obama administration contraceptive mandate ignited a firestorm of protests and the filing of some sixty-five lawsuits, most of which are still wending their way through the court system.[1] Newspapers such as the *New York Times* and the *Washington Post* and cable networks such as CNN carried news stories, opinion essays, and debates on the issue.[2]

In reaction, the Obama administration backtracked and worked to accommodate the concerns of faith-based organizations with religious concerns over paying for contraceptive and abortifacient coverage for their employees. In July, 2013, the Department of Health and Human Services announced its final rules that sought to accommodate faith-based organizations objecting to providing contraceptive or abortifacient coverage in the their insurance policies by requiring their health insurance providers, not the faith-based organizations themselves, to furnish such coverage. But many faith-based organizations still feel they are being forced to facilitate—even if indirectly—access to services that are in violation of their religious beliefs. The charges, accusations, and lawsuits continue.

A second factor that has added to the urgency of the issues raised in the hardcover edition of this book is the continued progress of the gay-rights movement, and especially the movement of the nation towards the acceptance and legal provision of same-sex marriage. A total of thirteen states and the District of Columbia now provide for same-sex marriages on the same basis as heterosexual marriages. In June, 2013, the Supreme Court held unconstitutional the section of the federal Defense of Marriage Act (DOMA) that denied federal government recognition and benefits to married same-sex couples.[3] And many believe the language the Supreme Court used in this decision presages a future decision finding a constitutional right to marriage by same-sex couples. This movement of the nation towards the legal acceptance of same-sex marriage raises new and pressing questions of concern to faith-based organizations whose religious traditions hold same-sex relationships to be in violation of their long-held religious views, which they believe are rooted in God's will and his intent for society and human relationships. Foremost among these are the Catholic, Evangelical Protestant, and Orthodox Jewish traditions.

As a result of this second development, controversies already discussed in the hardcover edition of this book are certain to become more numerous and urgent. I am thinking here of such controversies as the adoption of children by same-sex couples, the use of married student housing on faith-based campuses by same-sex couples, and the use of faith-based organizations' facilities for same-sex weddings. In these and other instances the calls to force or pressure persons and organizations to violate their religiously-based beliefs are likely to increase when legally married same-sex couples are involved. When faith-based organizations refuse to provide legally married same-sex couples with services they provide to other married couples, the same-sex couples will feel more strongly than before that their rights are being violated, that they are being made victims of discrimination. Conflict and bitterness on both sides are likely to escalate. In short, the issues and challenges the hardcover edition of this book raised have become more urgent and prominent in our nation's public debates.

In this Afterword I first apply the concepts and approaches of the structural pluralist approach I develop in chapter 5 to the two recent events just mentioned: the contraceptive mandate and the societal trend towards same-sex marriage. Next, I briefly consider a question I did not consider in the hardcover edition, namely, the extent to which a structural pluralism would grant the same religious-freedom protections to for-profit firms that it extends to nonprofit, faith-based organizations. Then in two concluding notes, I first respond to some of my critics who believe the structural pluralism I advocate in the book would add to a supposed privileged position they see Christianity already possessing in American society and I renew the call for tolerance and pluralism I make throughout the book.

The Contraceptive Mandate in a Structural Pluralist Framework

The current controversy over the Obama administration's contraceptive mandate is a clear instance of what in chapter 6 I discuss as the government "requiring faith-based organizations to provide services they find religiously objectionable." (pages 177–183) In light of the claims, counterclaims, and evolving policy position of the Obama administration on this issue, what does the structural pluralism I advance in this book have to say? In this section I first consider the mandate as originally proposed by the Department of Health and Human Services (HHS) and then the mandate as it has subsequently been modified.

The HHS mandate as first set out in August, 2011, clearly illustrates a certain mindset that I point out at various places in the book and is as common—especially on the political left—as it is mistaken. This mindset views "religion" as limited to what takes place in religious congregations and the celebrations and rituals of their faith. Accordingly, freedom of worship is in practice the same as freedom of worship. The original HHS mandate of 2011 clearly illustrates both the presence and the pernicious effects of this mindset.

This original mandate indeed did recognize that some religious traditions—most clearly the Catholic tradition—have long-standing, well-documented positions on the immorality of artificial birth control. In addition, many in the Evangelical tradition agree with the Catholic tradition in seeing Plan B and ella not as contraceptives but as abortifacients.[4] Thus, the mandate would require their financial support of very early abortions. HHS's original mandate tried to take these positions into account by providing a religious exemption from the mandate. Well and good. However, the religious exemption applied only to organizations that met all four of the following criteria:

1. Its purpose is the inculcation of religious values,
2. It primarily hires persons who share the organization's religious tenets,
3. It primarily serves person who share those tenets, and
4. It is defined in the Internal Revenue Code as a religious congregation or its direct auxiliaries, associations of religious congregations, or the exclusively religious activities of any religious order.[5]

This original exemption thereby applied only to religious congregations and their integral affiliates as they serve their own members.

The exemption left out religious congregations as they sought to follow the dictates of their faiths by offering help to those in need in their communities, whether or not they were members of their congregations. More telling, it also excluded the hundreds of thousands of faith-based health, educational, and social service organizations. As seen in Chapter 2 and elsewhere in this book, such organizations are numerous, supply vital public services, and are often deeply and profoundly religious in nature. HHS's original religious exemption thereby showed little understanding of the role religion plays in the public life of the nation and gave little or no respect to the large Catholic and Evangelical religious traditions and their faith-based organizations that contribute much to meeting health, education, and social needs. Faith-based educational, health, and social service providers were not seen as possessing an inherent, rightful autonomy and their religiously-based beliefs not worthy of recognition and protection. It thereby was disrespectful and damaging to the religious freedom of these traditions to an extreme degree. Religion is more than religious worship; freedom of religion must be more than freedom of worship. It is hard to find any basis on which to defend HHS's original religious exemption.

That the mindset underlying this very narrow exemption was not limited to rule-writers at HHS is demonstrated by the fact that the *New York Times* editorially called the mandate "one of the [Obama] administration's proud achievements" and criticized President Obama's "apparent wobbling" because he was considering "caving" to church leaders' "call for an expansive exemption that would cover employees of hospitals, universities, charitable organizations . . ."[6] Clearly, the editorial writers at the *New York Times* could not conceive of service-providing organizations that are deeply and profoundly religious in nature and thereby possessing religious freedom rights.

But what about the contraceptive mandate as now modified by HHS? Has the religious liberty issue been resolved, or is there a continuing violation of the religious liberty rights of faith-based organizations? Basically the final rules promulgated by HHS and released in July, 2013 provide that religious congregations and their affiliates continue to be exempt from the mandate, for-profit firms have no exemption or accommodation at all, and nonprofit faith-based organizations can claim an accommodation that allows them to exclude contraceptive coverage from their employees' health care plan, but when they do so their insurance company or, if self-insured, their agent must provide contraceptive coverage free of charge to their employees.[7] Most, but not all, faith-based organizations that objected to the original mandate continue to do so, since they are convinced they will still be indirectly contributing to contraceptives and that in various forms they will be cooperating with what they see as a moral evil. Among those who continue to object strongly to the mandate are the United States Conference of Catholic Bishops, the National Association of Evangelicals, the Becket Fund for Religious Liberty, Notre Dame University, Wheaton College (Illinois), and the large for-profit firm, Hobby Lobby. Meanwhile, the Obama administration and others supporting the contraceptive mandate are arguing that they have leaned over backwards to accommodate the concerns of faith-based organizations and that any support for contraceptives the regulations require is highly indirect and inconsequential.

A mindset shaped by structural pluralism begins with the basic commitment I articulated in the hardcover edition: "To tell a faith-based, religious organization that by its actions it must condone, support, or affirm behavior that it condemns in its theology and its words is to do violence to its autonomy and its right of the free exercise of its religious faith." (page 179) But this is a starting point; it does not constitute a self-evident answer. This continuing controversy demonstrates that this book and the structural pluralist position it advocates is not a cookie cutter recipe that leads to automatic answers to all public policy questions. It offers a perspective, a mindset for thinking through and reacting to questions of religious liberty and the religious autonomy of faith-based organizations, not neat, inevitable answers to all questions.

Seeking to think through and react to the now revised HHS contraceptive mandate, I will make four observations rooted in a structural pluralist mindset. First, it is first important to acknowledge that HHS has moved significantly from its original position of a very narrow religious exemption. It now recognizes that faith-based organizations are indeed religious organizations with legitimate religious freedom claims that public policy ought to recognize and accommodate. The financial trail from the coffers of a faith-based organization with religiously-based contraceptive and abortifacient objections to their coverage by their insurance companies is indirect and perhaps even distant.

My second observation is that even with the changes in the contraceptive mandate HHS is still holding to an overly narrow view of religion and thus is continuing to constrain religious freedom. Churches and their integral affiliates are given an exemption from the mandate but faith-based schools, health organizations, and social service-providing agencies are not. There is no compelling reason why religious congregations should be exempt from the mandate, while deeply religious educational, health, and social service organizations are not. The latter are "accommodated' by processes that University of Virginia law professor, Douglas Laycock, describes as having a "jury-rigged quality about them."[8] But having a two-tiered system, with some religious organizations (religious congregations and their integral affiliates) being exempt from the mandate and other religious organizations (educational, health, and social service organizations) being "accommodated" by a complicated process seems to rest on the assumption that faith-based, service-providing organizations are not truly or fully religious in nature, an assumption this book has consistently rejected. A better solution would be simply to exempt faith-based organizations from the mandate, just as religious congregations and their affiliates are now.

A third observation is that there is an alternative to the HHS mandate that would achieve its goals as fully or even more fully without raising religious freedom problems. Government itself could simply make contraceptives freely available to those who need and desire them. It seems that even those who advocate freely available contraceptives would find this a better solution than the current complicated "accommodation," since under the mandate as modified those without health insurance and those in organizations with fewer than fifty employees would not be covered by it. And those who have religious objection to the mandate would be satisfied, since they would not, even in an indirect way, be linked to the support of contraceptives.[9] Contraceptive coverage would thereby be treated in the same way we as a society treat other controversial services or programs. All of us support with our tax dollars government-provided programs and services we think unnecessary, unwise, or immoral. Taxes from pacifists help pay for nuclear armaments. Some states provide abortion coverage under their Medicaid plans, even though many object strongly to abortion. Capital punishment is supported by the tax dollars of persons who see it as unnecessary and immoral. Yet the same religious groups that are raising objections to the contraceptive mandate do not raise objections to other government programs or services to which they object. Why? Because they are *government* programs and services. In contrast, the HHS contraceptive mandate is compelling them and their organizations to take part in—even if indirectly—a program they find morally evil.

A fourth observation is to note that the left's ingrained suspicion of a role for religion in the public realm I documented in chapter 4 (pages 85–87) may be playing a role in the failure to adopt the sort of resolutions to this issue that I just suggested in my second and third observations. Some view religiously-based objections to requiring contraceptives and abortifacients as part of faith-based organizations' health insurance policies as a retrograde position and part of a "war on women." They see these objections as an attempt to force religious views onto all of society, an attempt that must be defeated at all costs and with no compromise if religionists are not to foist a theocratic society onto all of us.[10] Religion must be brought to heel if society is to move ahead. A respect for religion and religiously-based points of view and a genuine desire to protect religious freedom rights even while continuing to pursue one's public policy goal of more freely available contraceptives would open the way for resolving this issue. A firm commitment to a genuinely pluralistic society where public policies make room for a diversity of belief and practice would go a long ways to resolving this conflict.

Same-Sex Marriage

As I noted earlier in this Afterword, thirteen states and the District of Columbia now legally recognize same-sex marriages. One cannot predict the future and it is always risky to assume a current trend will continue into the future. Sometimes societal trends will stall or even reverse themselves, as has occurred in the abortion controversy.[11] Nevertheless, it is likely that same-sex marriage—by legislation or by court decision—will become more common in the future. This also means, as noted earlier, the freedom of faith-based organizations with religiously-based objections to homosexual behavior to act in keeping with their religious beliefs will become more controversial—and will be put in greater danger. Potential areas of conflict come readily to mind: the ability of faith-based adoption agencies not to place children with same-sex couples, membership in on-campus faith-based student organizations being limited to persons accepting their faith tradition's stance on same-sex relationships, faith-based organizations being able to refuse to hire persons in same-sex relationships, and faith-based organizations being able not to pay for insurance benefits for same-sex partners of employees. In all these areas, it is one thing to refuse adoption, membership, employment, or insurance benefits to persons who are in same-sex relationships and not legally married, but it will be more controversial to do so when persons are legally married. Those claiming invidious "discrimination" will have an easier time making their case. In addition, questions arise concerning the use of facilities owned by faith-based organizations that are regularly made available for heterosexual wedding ceremonies, but not for same-sex wedding ceremonies. There is a basis to suspect that in the future government grants or contracts—and perhaps even tax exempt status—may be withdrawn from faith-based organizations that fail to recognize same-sex marriages as being on par with traditional, male-female marriages. The licensing and accreditation of professionals and organizations that hold same-sex marriages are not true marriages may also be challenged.

The clashing views and the possibility of lawsuits in all these instances are all too clear. About one-half of the population belong to religious traditions—Catholic, Evangelical Protestant, and Orthodox Jewish—that hold same-sex couples, even when legally married under civil law, are not truly married in God's sight and therefore neither in their eyes. Their religiously-informed consciences dictate that they not put such marriages on par with traditional, male-female marriages. Same-sex couples may be married in the eyes of the law, but not in theirs. Meanwhile, same-sex marriage partners and their supporters see their marriages as complete and as legitimate as heterosexual marriages, and any attempt by persons or organizations not to grant them full recognition and acceptance as invidious discrimination. In their view it is wrong for any organization, religious or not, nonprofit or for-profit, to deny them the recognition and all the rights granted all other marriages. The conflict seems unresolvable. The only answer is one side or the other to use its political clout to force its will onto the other.

But society and public policy have been able to deal with other instances of sharp conflicts, rooted in religious beliefs. There are religious pacifists who believe it a grave moral sin to take up arms and kill other human beings, and in the days of a military draft policies usually provided for alternative forms of service for conscientious objectors to military service. Abortion under most circumstances has been legal since 1974, but many hospitals, doctors, and nurses have been able to refuse to take part in abortions—and have been legally protected in their doing so. A pluralist approach to the issue of same-sex marriage, with its full commitment to a society where we can live together with our deepest differences, suggests the way we have handled persons who object to serving in the military or to providing abortion services offers a pathway in the same-sex marriage controversy.

This pathway involves the religious among us not seeking to impose their understanding of marriage as encompassing only male-female partners onto those who accept the appropriateness of same-sex marriage. But it also means those who accept the appropriateness of same-sex marriage not seeking to impose their understanding of marriage onto those who hold true marriages only encompass male-female marriage.

This position is fully in keeping with the structural pluralism I espouse in this book. If religious liberty is to have meaning in life as well as in theory, not only churches and other religious congregations, but also faith-based organizations of a wide and delightful variety must have their religious liberty rights protected. In the case of same-sex marriage, this means they must not be required to violate in practice what they in their theology hold concerning the nature and meaning of marriage. If faith-based organizations are a vital part of the structure of society, if they possess a true autonomy that frees them to be what they believe God has called them to be, and if their religious freedom rights accordingly are to be respected and protected—all contentions this book supports—they must not be forced to acknowledge and accept same-sex marriages, which their religious faith leads them to believe not to be true marriages but an affront to God's intent and ordering of society. Freedom of this sort would be violated by laws or regulations that force faith-based organizations to provide recognition or services to same-sex couples and also by only marginally gentler means of pressure such as denying accreditation, barring government grants and contracts for which other similar organizations are eligible, or withholding advantages (such as on-campus privileges to student groups) other similar organizations possess.

When in 2013 the Supreme Court, in its *United States v. Windsor* decision, held a major section of the Defense of Marriage Act unconstitutional, President Obama released a statement that included this: "How religious institutions define and consecrate marriage has always been up to those institutions. Nothing about this decision— which applies only to civil marriages—changes that."[12] Well and good. But I suspect the "religious institutions" Obama had in mind were churches and other religious congregations, not faith-based organizations whose religious freedom rights are as important as those of religious congregations. We are back to a basic contention of structural pluralism—and of this book—that religious liberty and its protections must extend beyond religious congregations in their religious rituals and ceremonies to include faith-based organizations in their wide and varied activities in the public sphere. Otherwise the religious freedom we espouse in theory will be violated in practice.

Structural pluralism, however, also insists that religious persons and organizations must not seek to impose their view of right and wrong onto all of society, and this includes their understanding of marriage. It is not at all inconsistent for a faith-based organization whose religious tradition rejects same-sex marriage as contrary to God's will to urge their members and others not to take part in same-sex marriage and at the same time to support public policies that allow same-sex marriage for those who come from other religious and secular traditions that disagree with them. It is hard to make the case that same sex marriage results in immediate, direct harm to others or to society as a whole. In fact, both the legal scholar, Thomas Berg of the

St. Thomas School of Law, and the *New York Times* conservative columnist, David Brooks, have pointed out that same-sex marriages can have a positive societal impact, in that they encourage stable, permanent family structures.[13] Whether or not one agrees with Berg and Brooks, even persons with deep-seated religious objections to same sex marriage should properly see it as being similar to adultery, easy divorce, and soft-porn—that is, as being contrary to God's will and having negative results for those who take part in them—but not with immediate, direct negative consequences for others as do drunk driving, abortion (for the human life being ended), and fraudulent business practices. Thus same sex marriage should be legally tolerated in a diverse, pluralistic society.

As hard as it will be for both sides in the same-sex marriage debate, this is a prime instance where both sides need to respect and make allowance for those with whom they have deep disagreements. Laycock has expressed this position well:

> The first step for the religious side would be to focus on protecting its own liberty, and to give up on regulating other people's liberty. . . In practical terms, that would mean giving up the fight against same-sex marriage *now*, instead of waiting until the fight becomes hopeless. . . .

> On the other side, the advocates of sexual liberty and marriage equality would have to agree to the same basic proposition: that it is far more important to protect their own liberty than to restrict the liberty of religious conservatives. They would agree not to demand that religious individuals or institutions assist or facilitate practices they consider immoral . . .[14]

The supporters of gay marriage need to recognize and respect those persons and organizations whose religiously-informed consciences will not allow them to treat same-sex marriages on par with traditional, male-female marriages. They need to defend the religious liberty right of those with whom they have deep disagreements not to accept in their programs and activities the equivalence of same-sex and heterosexual marriages. Strong religious exemptions are essential. By the same token, those whose religiously-informed consciences lead them to reject same-sex marriage need to defend the right of their fellow gay and lesbian citizens to marry, as long as strong religious exemptions are written into law so that gay rights activists' views are not forced onto them in violation of their religiously-shaped consciences.

In this instance the autonomy, religious freedom rights, and tolerance for which this book calls are easier to defend in theory than for most of us to pursue in specific, concrete instances. It is easy to transform the positions to which one's underlying belief structures lead into universal principles that should be the legal norm for all of society. Their rightness can appear so clear and their opposites can appear so dangerous that it is hard to recognize the legitimacy of other positions in the public square. But pluralism demands in this instance the difficult is what must be followed.

What about For-Profit Firms with Religious Liberty Claims?

Hobby Lobby is a for-profit corporation with 514 arts and crafts stores in 41 states and 13,000 full-time employees. It is a family-owned corporation, owned by the Green family of Oklahoma City.[15] The Greens are Evangelical Protestants who seek, as reported by the *New York Times*, to run their "company on biblical principles, including closing on Sunday so employees can be with their families, paying nearly double the minimum wage and providing employees with comprehensive health insurance."[16] Hobby Lobby's mission statement makes clear its religious foundation:

In order to effectively serve our owners, employees, and customers the Board of Directors is committed to:

- Honoring the Lord in all we do by operating the company in a manner consistent with Biblical principles.
- Offering our customers an exceptional selection and value.
- Serving our employees and their families by establishing a work environment and company policies that build character, strengthen individuals, and nurture families.
- Providing a return on the owners' investment, sharing the Lord's blessings with our employees, and investing in our community.
- We believe that it is by God's grace and provision that Hobby Lobby has endured. He has been faithful in the past, we trust Him for our future.[17]

As Evangelicals the Green have no objection to the use of contraceptives and have long provided for them in their employees' health insurance. But as Evangelicals they also object to abortifacients (morning-after or week-after pills), which many insist do not operate to prevent conception. They filed a lawsuit asking for an injunction, asserting they "face an unconscionable choice: either violate the law, or violate their faith."[18] The U.S. District Court noted that the "government does not dispute the sincerity of the Greens' beliefs" yet held they did not deserve immediate relief.[19] They faced the prospect of 1.3 million dollars in penalties per day due to their living out their religious faith. Later the 10th Circuit Court of Appeals, holding that Hobby Lobby was likely to prevail in their case, lifted the threat of the daily fines, pending the final outcome of its case.

There are many other religious believers who own or work for for-profit businesses that have felt they are being forced or pressured to act in violation of their religious beliefs. These include pharmacists who are required to dispense contraceptives and abortifacients, businesses that fall under the HHS contraceptive mandate discussed earlier, and wedding planners and photographers who feel conscience-bound not to provide their services to same-sex weddings or commitment ceremonies.

In the hardcover edition of this book I carefully avoided considering for-profit businesses owned by deeply religious persons and their religious freedom rights under the structural pluralism the book advocates. In considering nonprofit, faith-based organizations and their religious freedom rights, I felt I was covering enough ground for one book without adding a consideration of for-profit businesses. They raise somewhat new and different issues. However, since the hardcover edition has come out the two new developments I highlight in this Afterword have drawn special attention to the for-profit business world. Over half of the sixty plus lawsuits filed challenging the contraceptive mandate have been filed on behalf of for-profit businesses.[20] Also, I have been asked numerous times how my concept of structural pluralism applies to for-profit businesses. Thus I here make a few preliminary comments.

My first comment is that for-profit businesses can in fact be religious in nature. Many branches of Christianity, as well as other religions, hold that their faith is not a matter of observing certain religious rituals on certain holy days or at certain other times, but hold that their faith should permeate all they do. This means many devote religious believers hold that their businesses must be run in keeping with their religious principles. As just seen, this is certainly the case with the Green family of Hobby Lobby. Therefore, if public policy forces businesspersons to act or to run their businesses in ways contrary to their religious beliefs, their religious freedom is being violated. This can even apply to corporations. Mark Rienzi of the Becket fund for Religious Liberty has made the key point and reached the proper conclusion:

> We regularly encounter businesses making decisions of conscience. Chipotle recently decided not to sponsor a Boy Scout event because the company disagreed with the Scouts' policy on openly gay scoutmasters. It was "the right thing to do," Chipotle said. Starbucks has ethical standards for the coffee beans it buys. . . . You can agree or disagree with the decisions of these businesses, but they are manifestly acts of conscience, both for the companies and the people who operate them. . . . For many their conscience is informed by religious views about activities they can or cannot participate in. . . . If religious freedom means anything, it means that these people—just like Chipotle, Starbucks and everyone

else in our society—are allowed to earn a living and run a business according to their values. In a tolerant society, we should just accept that our neighbors will have different beliefs, and that government-enforced conformity is rarely the best answer to this diversity.[21]

There are, however, additional factors to be considered. One is that businesses vary greatly. One can think of a continuum that runs from a small "mom and pop" business with single owners who run the business directly with very few employees. Near the center of the continuum would be a family owned and operated corporation, similar to the Green family and Hobby Lobby. At the end of the continuum there would be large corporations whose stock is traded on stock exchanges and is run by a professionalized board of directors and managers. As one moves from a large, publicly-traded corporation to a family-owned company to a "mom and pop" business it becomes more likely for strong, persuasive religious-freedom claims to exist. This is due to the greater likelihood of the direct involvement of specific individuals in the running of a business, individuals who may hold to religiously-based moral standards with which they seek to imbue the business.

My second comment is that any business claiming religious freedom rights must be very clear and upfront about their religious basis. It cannot be hidden or implied, nor can it be a vague tradition handed down from a past. The Hobby Lobby mission statement is an example of the clear, upfront commitment I have in mind. This is important because anyone contemplating working for it or using its services has fair warning concerning its religiously-based moral standards and practices. Also, being up front about its commitments prevents a business from suddenly "discovering" certain religiously-based standards that grants it exemptions from a particular legal requirement. Then one suspects these standards may be based in nothing more than a desire to escape a regulation it finds onerous.

A third comment is that any business claiming a religious exemption from certain regulations must demonstrate a consistency in the applications of its claimed religious principles. For a small wedding business, for example, to claim an exemption on religious grounds from servicing same-sex weddings, but is quite willing to provide its services to persons who are notorious for their deceptive business practices or other blatant, public immoralities would suggest that this business is merely acting on a prejudice against gays or lesbians, not on a consistent refusal to participate in acts it views as immoral. Here again Hobby Lobby is a positive example. The owners seek to live out their Evangelical faith in more ways than in refusing to provide abortifacients in their employees' health insurance. As noted earlier, they also close their stores on Sundays and pay their employees above the minimum wage.

In summary, the structural pluralism I advocate in this book—while I largely developed and thought it through as applied to nonprofit faith-based educational, health, and social service organizations—also has implications for for-profit businesses. Structural pluralism's application to for-profit businesses deserves more thought than I can give it here, but especially in the case of family owned and run businesses and ones that have clearly articulated and consistently followed religious principles, most of what this book says in regard to structural pluralism and the religious freedom rights to which it leads applies to them.

Concluding Note #1: Is Christianity in a Privileged Position that Threatens Others' Freedom?

I conclude this Afterword with two notes, or observations, that relate not to specific points I make in the book, but underlie the over-all approach that I take. I am led to add them at the end of this Afterword due to comments or reactions I have received to the hardcover edition. They are observations worth making.

My first concluding note seeks to put to rest the often-held assumption that Christianity is in a privileged position in American society and politics. Typical is the reference a professor of history at the University of North Carolina once made to "Christianity's preferential place in our culture and civil law."[22] Superficially, this assumption seems to be accurate. Our national motto is "In God We Trust" and it is assumed this is a Christian God, not the Muslim Allah, the multiple Gods of Hinduism, or the impersonal God of Buddhism. Throughout most of our history there have been, and in a few places there still are, laws that restrict business activities on Sunday—the Christian holy day—and not the Jewish Sabbath nor Friday noon prayers observed by Muslims. Christmas is a public holiday; neither Yom Kipper nor *Eid al-Fitr*—marking the end of Ramadan—are. Each spring stores are filled with Easter displays. Therefore, many fear that if religion is allowed into the public realm—as this book advocates—Christianity, based on its numbers and long history of cultural influence, will exert inordinate influence and repress contrary faiths and beliefs.

This attitude helps to explain a puzzle. Go to the website of almost any college of university and one finds public commitments to diversity, but they have a blind spot in the way they put this commitment to diversity into practice. The State University of New York at Buffalo has an Intercultural and Diversity Center that proclaims on its website: "The Center offers students various opportunities to engage in dialogue, celebrate differences and commonalities, and promote awareness about diversity and how it affects their beliefs, perceptions, and the global society."[23] San Diego State University has a separate tab labeled, "Diversity starts here."[24] On its website Vanderbilt University's Dean of Students states: "The Office of the Dean of Students creates opportunities to involve students, faculty, and staff in diverse learning communities . . ."[25]

All this is well and good. But it is instructive to note that in all three of the universities cited here, whose websites proudly proclaim their commitment to diversity, Christian student organizations have struggled to keep from being denied official recognition—and its accompanying campus privileges—that other student organizations enjoy. At Vanderbilt University and San Diego State University Christian student organizations have lost their official recognition and no longer have on-campus privileges and at SUNY Buffalo a Christian student organization was initially denied official recognition, which was only restored after an appeal process.

Why is this? How can a university proclaim its commitment to diversity on the one hand and deny official recognition to Christian student organizations on the other hand? Why are they committed to a pluralism that excludes Christian student organizations with distinctive beliefs and behavior standards? I believe the answer lays in the fact that many colleges and universities praise and commitment to "diversity" is set in a context where Christianity is assumed to be in a privileged position. Diversity is rarely specifically defined, but from the examples given, universities seem to have in mind groups that have traditionally been minority groups in society and often the objects of discrimination and disrespect, such as women, racial and ethnic minorities, and LGBT persons. Meanwhile, Christianity is viewed as the white majority faith against which diverse minorities need to be protected and find an identity.

But this thinking, if it was ever valid, is 40 to 50 years behind the times. We need to look below the surface. Traditional Christianity in the sense of a Christianity, whether Protestant or Catholic, that holds to the basic teachings of historic Christianity is anything but culturally dominant in the United States today. Ross Douthat chronicles in his 2012 book, *Bad Religion: How We Became a Nation of Heretics*, important twentieth century changes in the American religious scene.[26] He persuasively argues that up until the 1960s and 1970s Christianity, especially in its mainline Protestant and Catholic traditions, played a major role in American society. American statesmen listened to leading theologians such as Reinhold Niebuhr, the news media paid respectful attention to the pronouncements of the National Council of Churches and its major denominational members such as the Presbyterians and Methodists, and Hollywood treated the Catholic Church and its representatives with deference. In the post-World War II years of the 1950s the mainline Protestant and Catholic churches grew rapidly in numbers and in influence. In the 1960s African American churches, with the support of mainline Protestant churches, were a leading force in achieving legal protection of the civil rights of African Americans.

Douthat goes on to demonstrate how all this has radically changed since the 1960s. The mainline Protestant denominations are losing membership in astounding numbers and their political and social influence has evaporated. Catholics are also losing in numbers and the church's clergy are now more often seen in light of sexual abuse scandals than as inspiring models. Evangelical churches are growing in numbers, but are failing to keep pace with population growth, and remain fragmented and largely ignored as serious players on the national scene.

I have some quibbles with Douthat's analysis, but believe its general outline is accurate. Christianity today is in anything but a culturally dominant, favored position. If Christianity is favored at all, it is a broad generic Christianity. The God of "In God We Trust" is not the triune God of historic Christianity. Christmas as a public holiday is more of a commercialized winter festival and Easter a spring festival than Christian observances of the birth or resurrection of Jesus Christ. Presidents and other public figures make references to God and his favor or presence, but these usually are references to a generic God invoked on ceremonial occasions or at times of national crisis or mourning. Supreme Court Justice William Brennan once wrote, "I would suggest that such practices as the designation of 'In God We Trust' as our national motto, or the references to God contained in the Pledge of Allegiance to the flag can best be understood . . . as a form a 'ceremonial deism,' protected from Establishment Clause scrutiny chiefly because they have lost through rote repetition any significant religious content."[27] This is a harsh, but far from inaccurate, description of the religious references still found in our public life.

Surely such references to God or divine providence are far removed from the God of the two major Christian traditions that hold to traditional Christian teachings: Evangelical Protestantism and Catholicism. As noted earlier these religious traditions make up at least one-half the American population. They believe in a triune God, the virgin birth of Jesus Christ, the reality of a life after death, the existence of a literal heaven and hell, and commands to conform one's life to certain standards that, if willfully ignored, will place one's eternal soul in danger. Generic references to God or religion in our public life are also far distance from Orthodox Judaism, which holds to beliefs and standards of behavior rooted in a millennial-old tradition and around which every faithful Jew is required to orient his or her life.

Evangelicals, Catholics, and Orthodox Jews are in anything but a privileged position in American society or law, even while commanding a majority or near-majority of the population. Their political and cultural influence in society is marginal at best. An Evangelical pastor was scrubbed from giving the closing prayer at President Obama's second inauguration because of his sincerely held beliefs on same-sex relationships, the centuries-old Catholic position on the immorality of abortion is often portrayed as a retrograde position and identified as part of a war on women, Evangelicals who raise questions concerning naturalistic evolution as a full explanation for the emergence of humankind are ridiculed and drummed out of public schools. The Evangelical and Catholic position on homosexuality has been described by a *New York Times* columnist as "a last bastion and engine of bigotry."[28] Evangelical professors have been denied tenure at public universities because they were "too religious" or their refereed publications in scholarly journals reporting empirical findings that run counter to prevailing elite opinion on gay rights have led to condemnations and landed them in controversy where their scholarly standards have been attacked.[29]

This book is a plea for a pluralism that accepts and tolerates the beliefs and practices of all faiths—including those of Catholicism, Evangelical Protestantism, and Orthodox Judaism—as well as the beliefs and practices of other faiths and of those holding to no religious faith. It is not a plea for retaining Christian advantages, which in any case are things of the past.

Concluding Note #2:
A Renewed Call for Pluralism and Tolerance

As societal disagreements and differences deepen—as demonstrated by the contraceptive mandate and the trend towards same-sex marriage considered in this Afterword—it becomes increasingly important that all sides in these debates recommit themselves to a pluralistic society in which we learn to live together, even when we are marked by deep differences. The human tendency is to admire and advocate a pluralism of belief and action when one or one's group feels it is being oppressed or ignored, but to embrace the importance of enforcing society-wide standards in light of practices that run counter to one's personal standards and beliefs. "Pluralism for me but not for thee" is, of course, not pluralism at all. Harvard law professor Mary Ann Glendon has warned that we are in danger of losing the pluralism and diversity that is at the heart of religious freedom: "Rather than seeking to resolve tensions among religious beliefs, sexual conduct, and marital status in a way that respects diversity, dissent and difference, governmental functionaries seem all too ready to allow religious liberty to be trumped by a range of competing interests."[30]

The central contention of this book, and one I need to reemphasize at the close of this Afterword, is that both the religious and the nonreligious, the straight and the gay, the progressive and the conservative need to respect and make room in the public square for each other. And they need to accept that those with whom they disagree have as much right to enjoy legal protections for their organizations and sincerely-held beliefs as their own do. My vision in this book is for a nation based on full and complete religious freedom, pluralism, and tolerance. I chose those words carefully. *Religious freedom* means that persons of all religious faiths and of none are free to believe and to act on those beliefs—in their lives as private individuals *and* as citizens active in the public life of the nation. Too often we are willing to grant the right of others to speak and advocate for their views, but any legal protection for practices quickly brings charges of forcing either religious or secular beliefs onto others. A robust religious freedom will result in *religious pluralism,* that is, in a society where Catholics, Evangelicals, mainline Protestants, Orthodox Jews, Muslims, Hindus, nonbelievers, and others are free to worship or refrain from worship as their beliefs dictate. Almost all are willing to grant this. Where disagreements begin is when one insists, as I do in this book, that religious freedom also means both individuals and the organizations they create are free to live out their fundamental beliefs as citizens, health care providers, educators, businesspersons, service providers, and public officials. Religious pluralism requires *religious tolerance.* We must indeed be free to believe deeply and debate vigorously, yet we also need to learn anew to live with, respect, and make room in our public policies for our fellow citizens with whom we have deep differences. An imposed uniformity is the opposite of freedom, pluralism, and tolerance.

Achieving this goal is not easy. The Evangelical pastor, Skye Jethani, expressed well the underlying attitude advanced in this book when he wrote in the context of gay rights that "the sensible path is to recognize the presence of our LGBT neighbors and cooperate with them to draft laws that ensures their rights while simultaneously protecting religious liberty," instead of engaging in a "winner-take-all battle for social control."[31] My hope is that when it comes to contraceptive mandates, same-sex marriage, and the other contentious issues considered in this book, Jethani's approach to protecting the rights of all can be achieved. For this to occur both the left and the right, and both the religious and the nonreligious, as well as advocacy groups at all points on the political spectrum will need to put a commitment to a genuine pluralism and freedom ahead of any attempt to gain "winner-take-all" victories.

AFTERWORD

1. For an account of these court cases as of August, 2013, see www.becketfund. org/hhsinformationcentral.

2. See, for example, Ethan Bronner, "A Flood of Suits Fights Coverage of Birth Control," *New York Times* (January 26, 2013), available at http://www.nytimes.com/ 2013/01/27/health/religious-groups-and-employers-battle-contraception-mandate .html?pagewanted=allmandate.html?pagewanted=all; "The Contraception Battle" *New York Times* (July 1, 2013); available at www.nytimes.com/2013/07/02/opinion/ the-contraception-battle.html; Sarah Kliff, "Here's Obamacare's Most Controversial Regulation," *Washington Post* (March 25, 2013); available at http://www.washington post.com/blogs/wonkblog/wp/2013/03/25/heres-obamacares-most-controversial -provision/; CNN "Contraceptive Mandate Angers Catholic," (January 30, 2012); available at http://www.cnn.com/video/?/video/living/2012/01/30/catholics-and -contraceptives.wluk#/video/living/2012/01/30/catholics-and-contraceptives.wluk. All of the above were accessed August 14, 2013.

3. *United States v. Windsor*, 570 U.S. ____ (2013).

4. The manufacturer of ella acknowledges on its website that it "may also work" by preventing the attachment of a fertilized egg to the uterus. See http://www.ella-rx .com/. Accessed August 16, 2013.

5. These four conditions are listed in the complaint the University of Notre Dame filed against the Department of Health and Human Services in United States District Court. See *University of Notre Dame v. Kathleen Sebelius*, Case No. ____, pp. 2-3. Available at http://media.cmgdigital.com/shared/news/documents/2012/05/21/ notre_dame.pdf. Accessed August 14, 2013.

6. "Battling Over Birth Control," *New York Times* (November 24, 2011). Available at http://www.nytimes.com/2011/11/25/opinion/battling-over-birth-control.html. Accessed August 14, 2013.

7. For a good summary and discussion of the final rules as promulgated by HHS see Douglas Laycock, "Religious Liberty and the Culture Wars," Public Law and Legal Theory Research Paper Series No. 2013-23, pp. 16-25.. Available at http:// papers.ssrn.com/sol3/papers.cfm?abstract_id=2304427. (Accessed August 8, 2013.)

8. Laycock, "Religious Liberty and the Culture Wars," p. 24.

9. The University of Notre Dame's lawsuit explicitly states: "This lawsuit . . . is not about whether people have a right to abortion-inducing drugs, sterilization, and contraception. Those services are, and will continue to be, freely available in the United States, and nothing prevents the Government itself from making them more widely available." *University of Notre Dame v. Kathleen Sebelius*, p. 1.

10. Less anyone think this statement is an exaggeration, read a web posting by the organization, Americans United for the Separation of Church and State, which stated: "Powerful sectarian forces continue their efforts to curb Americans' access to birth control. . . . [T]he all-male Catholic hierarchy and the male-dominated Religious Right . . . are intent on imposing their doctrines on others . . . But these aggressive

theocrats just demand more and more. They won't stop until they control as much of your private life as possible." See "Help AU Fight the Battle over Birth Control Coverage," at www.au.org/content/help-au-fight-the-battle-over-birth-control-coverage. Accessed August 15, 2013. The American Civil Liberties Union has made the same point in only slightly more temperate language. See www.aclu.org/american-civil-liberties-union-2013-workplan. Accessed August 16, 2013.

11. See Pew Research Religion and Public Life Project, "Public Opinion on Abortion." This study shows a drop in support for the legality of abortion in "all or most cases" from 60 percent in 1994 to 54 percent in 2013. Available at http://features.pewforum.org/abortion-slideshow/index.php. Accessed August 5, 2013.

12. "Supreme Court Strikes down the Defense of Marriage Act." Available at www.whitehouse.gov/blog/2013/06/26/supreme-court-strikes-down-defense-marriage-act. (Accessed August 9, 2013.)

13. Thomas C. Berg, "What Same-Sex-Marriage and Religious-Liberty Claims Have in Common," *Northwestern Journal of Law and Social Policy*, 5(2010) and David Brooks, "Freedom Loses One," *New York Times* (April 1, 2013). Available at http://www.nytimes.com/2013/04/02/opinion/brooks-freedom-loses-one.html?ref=davidbrooks. Accessed August 14, 2013.

14. Laycock, "Religious Liberty and the Culture Wars,"

15. The facts in this situation presented here are from *Hobby Lobby Stores v. Sebelius*, No. CIV-12-1000-HE, U.S. District Court, Western district of Oklahoma (November 19, 2012) [available at http://scholar.google.com/scholar_case?case=11193347871033276555&q=hobby+lobby+v.+sebelius&hl=en&as_sdt=2,23&as_vis=1]; The Becket Fund for Religious Liberty, "Hobby Lobby versus Sebelius" [available at www.becketfund.org/hobbylobby]; and Barbara Farfan, "Retail Industry April 12-18, 2009: Major Best Buy and Hobby Lobby Pay News," About.com Retail Industry [available at http://retailindustry.about.com/od/retailindustryweeklynews/a/retailnewsapril122009.htm]. All of these accessed January 10, 2013.

16. Ethan Bronner, "A Flood of Suits Fights Coverage of Birth Control," *New York Times* (January 27, 2013), 1 and 11.

17. The mission statement is available at http://retailindustry.about.com/od/retailbestpractices/ig/Company-Mission-Statements/Hobby-Lobby-Stores-Mission-Statement.htm. Accessed August 15, 2013.

18. *Hobby Lobby Stores v. Sebelius*, p. 2.

19. *Hobby Lobby Stores v. Sebelius*, p. 2.

20. See www.becketfund.org/hhsinformationcentral.

21. Mark Rienzi, "Don't Force Owners to Violate their Conscience," *USA Today* (August 11, 2013). Available at http://www.usatoday.com/story/opinion/2013/08/11/contraception-mandate-becket-fund-for-religious-liberty-editorials-debates/2641223/. Accessed August 15, 2013.

22. Molly Worthen, "One Nation Under God?" *New York Times* (December 22, 2012). Available at http://www.nytimes.com/2012/12/23/opinion/sunday/american-christianity-and-secularism-at-a-crossroads.html?pagewanted=all.k Accessed August 15, 2013.

23. http://www.student-affairs.buffalo.edu/idc/aboutus.php. Accessed January 25, 2013.

24. http://newscenter/sdsu.edu/lead/Default.aspx. Accessed January 25, 2013.

25. www.vanderbilt.edu/deanofstudents/mission-purposes. Accessed January 25, 2013.

26. Ross Douthat, *Bad Religion: How We Became a Nation of Heretics* (New York: Free Press, 2012).

27. *Lynch v. Donnelly*, 465 U.S. 668 (1984), at 716. [Underlying present in the original.]

28. Frank Bruni, "Reading God's Mind," *New York Times* (March 4, 2013). Available at http://www.nytimes.com/2013/03/05/opinion/bruni-reading-gods-mind.html. Accessed August 15, 2013.

29. See Byron Johnson, *More God, Less Crime* (Philadelphia, PA: Templeton Press, 2011), chap. 1 and Christian Smith, "An Academic Auto-da-Fe," *Chronicle of Higher Education* (July 23, 2012).

30. Mary Ann Glendon, Religious Freedom Is Not a 'Second Class Right,'" *Washington Post* (June 21, 2013). Available at http://www.washingtonpost.com/blogs/on-faith/wp/2013/06/21/religious-freedom-is-not-a-second-class-right/. Accessed August 13, 2013.

31. Skye Jethani, "Gay rights and Religious Liberties." 42-43. Available at www.qideas.eas.org/blog/gay-rights-and-religious-liberties.aspx. Accessed August 7, 2013.

Selected Bibliography

Atwood, Thomas C., Lee A. Allen, and Virginia C. Ravenel, eds. *Adoption Factbook IV*. Alexandria, VA: National Council for Adoptions, 2007.

Bailey, Maureen K. "Contraceptive Insurance Mandates and *Catholic Charities v. Superior Court of Sacramento:* Towards a New Understanding of Women's Health." *Texas Review of Law and Politics* 9 (2000): 367–88.

Bellah, Robert. *The Broken Covenant: American Civil Religion in Time of Trial*. New York, NY: Seabury, 1975.

Bellah, Robert, Richard Madsen, William M. Sullivan, Ann Swidler, and Steven M. Tipton. *Habits of the Heart: Individualism and Commitment in American Life*. New York, NY: Harper and Row, 1985.

Berger, Peter L., and Richard John Neuhaus. *To Empower People: The Role of Mediating Structures in Public Policy*. Washington, DC: American Enterprise Institute for Public Policy Research, 1977.

Black, Amy E., Douglas L. Koopman, and David K. Ryden. *Of Little Faith: The Politics of George W. Bush's Faith-Based Initiatives*. Washington, DC: Georgetown University Press, 2004.

Bolt, John. *A Free Church, a Holy Nation: Abraham Kuyper's American Public Theology*. Grand Rapids, MI: Eerdmans, 2001.

Bratt, James, ed. *Abraham Kuyper: A Centennial Reader*. Grand Rapids, MI: Eerdmans, 1998.

Brinton, Crane. *Ideas and Men: The Story of Western Thought*. New York, NY: Prentice Hall, 1950.

Burke, Edmund. *Reflections on the Revolution in France*. L. G. Mitchell, ed. New York, NY: Oxford University Press, 1993.

Chaplin, Jonathan, and Paul Marshall, eds. *Political Theory and Christian Vision: Essays in Memory of Bernard Zylstra*. Lanham, MD: University Press of America, 1994.

Clotfelter, Charles T., and Thomas Ehrlich, eds. *Philanthropy and the Nonprofit Sector in a Changing America*. Bloomington, IN: Indiana University Press, 1999.

Cnaan, Ram A., and Stephanie C. Boddie. "Philadelphia Census of Congregations and their Involvement in Social Service Delivery." *Social Service Review* 75 (2001): 559–80.

Cousins, Norman, ed. *In God We Trust: The Religious Beliefs and Ideas of the American Founding Fathers*. New York, NY: Harper and Brothers, 1958.

Daly, Lew. *God's Economy: Faith-Based Initiatives and the Caring State*. Chicago, IL: University of Chicago Press, 2009.

Ebberly, Don E., ed. *The Essential Civil Society Reader*. Lanham, MD: Rowman and Littlefield, 2000.

Faithful, Richael. "Religious Exemption or Exceptionalism? Exploring the Tension of First Amendment Religion Protections and Civil Rights Progress within the Employment non-Discrimination Act." Social Science Research Network, Legislation and Policy Brief, Vol. 3, No. 1: 1–31.

Figgis, John N. *Churches in the Modern State*, 2nd ed. New York, NY: Russell and Russell, 1914.

Frumkin, Peter. *On Being Nonprofit: A Conceptual and Policy Primer*. Cambridge, MA: Harvard University Press, 2002.

Gautier, Mary L., and Anna Campbell Buck. *Catholic Charities USA: 2009 Annual Survey*. Washington, DC: Center for Applied Research in the Apostolate, Georgetown University, 2010.

Glenn, Charles L., Jr. *The Myth of the Common School*. Amherst, MA: University of Massachusetts Press, 1987.

Gutman, Amy, ed. *Freedom of Association*. Princeton, NJ: Princeton University Press, 1998.

Hampshire-Monk, Iain. *The Political Philosophy of Edmund Burke*. London, UK: Longman, 1987.

Hanley, David, ed. *Christian Democracy in Europe: A Comparative Perspective*. London, UK: Pinter Publishers, 1994.

Hasson, Kevin Seamus. *The Right to be Wrong: Ending the Culture War over Religion in America*. San Francisco, CA: Encounter Books, 2005.

Hatch, Nathan O. *The Democratization of American Christianity*. New Haven, CT: Yale University Press, 1989.

Hernandez, Edwin I., and Neil Carlson. *Gatherings of Hope: How Religious Congregations Contribute to the Quality of Life in Kent County*. Grand Rapids, MI: Center for Social Research, Calvin College, 2008.

Hughes, Richard T., and C. Leonard Allen. *Illusions of Innocence: Primitivism in America, 1630–1875*. Chicago, IL: University of Chicago Press, 1988.

Hunter, James Davison. *Culture Wars: The Struggle to Define America*. New York, NY: Basic Books, 1991.

Hunter, James Davison, and Os Guinness, eds. *Articles of Faith, Articles of Peace: The Religious Liberty Clauses and the American Public Philosophy*. Washington, DC: Brookings, 1990.

Irving, R. E. M. *The Christian Democratic Parties of Western Europe*. London, UK: George Allen and Unwin, 1979.

Jelen, Ted G., and Clyde Wilcox. *Public Attitudes towards Church and State.* Armonk, NY: M. E. Sharpe, 1995.

Jellema, Dirk. "Abraham Kuyper's Attack on Liberalism." *Review of Politics* 19 (1957): 472–85.

Joshi, Pamela, Stephanie Hawkins, and Jeffrey Novey, eds. *Innovations in Effective Compassion: Compendium of Research Papers Presented at the Faith-Based and Community Initiatives Conference on Research, Outcomes, and Evaluation.* Washington, DC: U.S. Department of Health and Human Services, Office of the Assistant Secretary for Planning and Evaluation, Center for Faith-Based and Community Initiatives, 2008.

Kersbergen, Kees van. *Social Capitalism: A Study of Christian Democracy and the Welfare State.* London, UK: Routledge, 1995.

Kersbergen, Kees van, and Bertjan Verbeek. "The Politics of Subsidiarity in the European Union." *Journal of Common Market Studies* 32 (June 1994): 215–36.

Kirk, Russell. *The Conservative Mind: From Burke to Santayana*, 7th ed. Chicago: Regnery, 1986.

Kommers, Donald P., ed. *The Constitutional Jurisprudence of the Federal Republic of Germany*, 2nd ed. Durham, NC: Duke University Press, 1997.

Koppelman, Andrew. "You Can't Hurry Love: Why Antidiscrimination Protections for Gay People Should Have Religious Exemptions." *Brooklyn Law Review* 72 (2006): 125–46.

Kselman, Thomas, and Joseph A. Battigieg, eds. *European Christian Democracy.* Notre Dame, IN: University of Notre Dame Press, 2003.

Kuyper, Abraham. *Lectures on Calvinism.* Grand Rapids, MI: Eerdmans, 1931.

———. *The Problem of Poverty*, James Skillen, ed. Grand Rapids, MI: Baker, 1991.

Laycock, Douglas, Anthony R. Picarello, Jr., and Robin Fretwell Wilson, eds. *Same-Sex Marriage and Religious Liberty: Emerging Conflicts.* Lanham, MD: Rowman and Littlefield, 2008.

Laycock, Douglas. "Formal, Substantive, and Disaggregated Neutrality toward Religion." *DePaul Law Review* 39 (1990): 993–1018.

———. *Religious Liberty*, vol. 1. Grand Rapids, MI: Eerdmans, 2010.

Lugo, Luis E., ed. *Religion, Pluralism, and Public Life: Abraham Kuyper's Legacy for the Twenty-First Century.* Grand Rapids, MI: Eerdmans, 2000.

Maritain, Jacques. *The Person and the Common Good*, trans. John J. Fitzgerald. Notre Dame, IN: University of Notre Dame Press, 1966.

McCleary, Rachel M. *Global Compassion: Private Voluntary Organizations and U.S. Foreign Policy since 1939.* New York, NY: Oxford University Press, 2009.

Meeter, H. Henry. *The Basic Idea of Calvinism*, 5th ed. Grand Rapids, MI: Baker, 1956.

Mirkay, Nicholas A. "Losing our Religion: Reevaluating the §501(c)(3) Exemption of Religious Organizations that Discriminate." *Widener Law School Legal Studies Research Paper Series* No. 08-35: 715–62.

Monsma, Stephen V. *Positive Neutrality.* Westport, CT: Greenwood, 1993.

————. *Putting Faith in Partnerships: Welfare-to-Work in Four Cities.* Ann Arbor, MI: University of Michigan Press, 2004.

Monsma, Stephen V., and J. Christopher Soper. *The Challenge of Pluralism: Church and State in Five Democracies,* 2nd ed. Lanham, MD: Rowman and Littlefield, 2009.

————, eds. *Equal Treatment of Religion in a Pluralistic Society.* Grand Rapids, MI: Eerdmans, 1998.

Nichols, J. Bruce. *The Uneasy Alliance: Religion, Refugee Work, and U.S. Foreign Policy.* New York, NY: Oxford University Press, 1988.

Nisbet, Robert A. *The Quest for Community: A Study in the Ethics of Order and Freedom.* New York, NY: Oxford University Press, 1953.

Noll, Mark A., ed. *Religion and American Politics.* New York, NY: Oxford University Press, 1990.

————. *The Scandal of the Evangelical Mind.* Grand Rapids, MI: Eerdmans, 1994.

Olasky, Marvin. *Renewing American Compassion.* New York, NY: Free Press, 1996.

O'Neill, Michael. *The Third America: The Emergence of the Nonprofit Sector in the United States.* San Francisco, CA: Jossey-Bass, 1989.

Peterson, Merrill D., and Robert C. Vaughn, eds. *The Virginia Statute for Religious Freedom.* Cambridge, MA: Cambridge University Press, 1988.

Robbers, Gerhard, ed. *Church Autonomy: A Comparative Survey.* Frankfurt am Main, DEU: Peter Lang, 2001.

————, ed. *State and Church in the European Union,* 2nd ed. Baden-Baden, DEU: Nomos Verlagsgesellschaft, 2005.

Salamon, Lester M. *America's Nonprofit Sector: A Primer,* 2nd ed. New York, NY: Foundation Center, 1999.

————. *The Resilient Sector: The State of Nonprofit America.* Washington, DC: Brookings, 2003.

————, ed., *The Tools of Government: A Guide to the New Governance.* New York, NY: Oxford University Press, 2002.

Schindler, Jeanne Heffernan, ed. *Christianity and Civil Society: Catholic and Neo-Calvinist Perspectives.* Lanham, MD: Lexington Books, 2008.

Shain, Barry Alan. *The Myth of American Individualism.* Princeton, NJ: Princeton University Press, 1994.

Simon, Scott. *Baby, We Were Meant for Each Other: In Praise of Adoption.* New York, NY: Random House, 2010.

Smidt, Corwin E., Kevin R. den Dulk, James M. Penning, Stephen V. Monsma, and Douglas L. Koopman. *Pews, Prayers and Participation.* Washington, DC: Georgetown University Press, 2008.

Smith, Steven Rathgeb, John P. Bartkowski, and Susan Grettenberger, eds. *Comparative Views on the Role and Effect of Faith in Social Services.* Albany, NY: Roundtable on Religion and Social Welfare Policy, Rockefeller Institute of Government, 2006.

Tocqueville, Alexis de. *Democracy in America*, vol. 2. New York, NY: Vintage Classics, Random House, 1990.

Unruh, Heidi Rolland, and Ronald J. Sider. *Saving Souls, Serving Society: Understanding the Faith Factor in Church-Based Social Ministry.* New York, NY: Oxford University Press, 2006.

Vandivere, Sharon, Karin Malm, and Laura Radel. *Adoption USA: A Chartbook Based on the 2007 National Survey of Adoptive Parents.* Washington, DC: U.S. Department of Health and Human Services, Office of the Assistant Secretary for Planning and Evaluation, 2009.

Willmer, Wesley K., and J. David Schmidt. *The Prospering Parachurch.* San Francisco, CA: Jossey-Bass, 1998.

Witte, John, Jr., and Frank S. Alexander, eds. *The Teachings of Modern Christianity on Law, Politics, and Human Nature*, vol. 1. New York, NY: Columbia University Press, 2006.

Witte, John, Jr., and Joel A. Nichols. *Religion and the American Constitutional Experiment*, 3rd ed. Boulder, CO: Westview, 2011.

Wright, David J. *Taking Stock: The Bush Faith-Based Initiative and What Lies Ahead.* Albany, NY: Roundtable on Religion and Social Welfare Policy, Nelson Rockefeller Institute of Government, 2009.

Yoon, Jamie, and Jessica Nickel. *Reentry Partnerships: A Guide for States and Faith-Based and Community Organizations.* New York, NY: Council of State Governments Justice Center, 2008.

Index

About the Author

Stephen V. Monsma is a senior research fellow at the Paul Henry Institute for the study of Christianity and Politics, Calvin College (Grand Rapids, MI) and a professor emeritus of political science at Pepperdine University (Malibu, CA). He is the author, editor, or co-author of 12 books dealing with faith-based organizations, church-state relations, or religion and politics.

CPSIA information can be obtained at www.ICGtesting.com
Printed in the USA
BVOW04s2323261113

337451BV00001B/4/P